Your TAROT TOOLKIT

About the Author

Ru-Lee Story is a non-binary and disabled author, tarot practitioner, and witch. They are a professional tarot reader and a certified spiritual coach through the Life Purpose Institute.

Your TAROT TOOLKIT

SIMPLE ACTIVITIES *for your* DAILY PRACTICE

RU-LEE STORY

LLEWELLYN PUBLICATIONS
WOODBURY, MINNESOTA

First Edition
First Printing, 2023

Book design by Samantha Peterson
Cover art by Kaari Selven
Cover design by Shira Atakpu
Editing by Marjorie Otto
Interior art by Llewellyn Art Department

Llewellyn is a registered trademark of Llewellyn Worldwide Ltd.

Library of Congress Cataloging-in-Publication Data (Pending)
ISBN: 978-0-7387-7411-4

Llewellyn Worldwide Ltd. does not participate in, endorse, or have any authority or responsibility concerning private business transactions between our authors and the public.

All mail addressed to the author is forwarded, but the publisher cannot, unless specifically instructed by the author, give out an address or phone number.

Any internet references contained in this work are current at publication time, but the publisher cannot guarantee that a specific location will continue to be maintained. Please refer to the publisher's website for links to authors' websites and other sources.

Llewellyn Publications
A Division of Llewellyn Worldwide Ltd.
2143 Wooddale Drive
Woodbury, MN 55125-2989
www.llewellyn.com

Printed in the United States of America

Dedicated to Ralph Jay Passman, the most incredible dad anyone could ask for.
Knowing you taught me to bring stories to life.
Losing you taught me to find life in stories.

CONTENTS

INTRODUCTION

So you've bought your first tarot deck. You've studied your guidebook or the wealth of online resources available to you. Maybe you're feeling a bit overwhelmed by the ins and outs of this card versus that card. Or maybe by now you have a basic understanding of each card's meaning. Maybe you've even gotten into the habit of drawing a card for yourself regularly, both to familiarize yourself with the seventy-eight cards in a traditional tarot deck and to start developing your style as a tarot reader.

But one morning when you faithfully sit down for your daily tarot practice, you may find yourself looking down at a card and saying, "I know what you mean on paper, sure, but what am I supposed to do with that?" If you drew the Lovers, should you expect to meet Mister, Miss, or Mixter Right as soon as you step outside? If you're looking at the Five of Cups, should you be braced for an abrupt onslaught of sorrow even though the day ahead promises to be relatively routine? If your morning card is the Ten of Pentacles and you're currently broke and living on a friend's couch, should you throw your tarot deck out the window and call the whole thing a wash?

If this sounds familiar, don't worry. It's exactly where I was, too. After a few months of practice with my first tarot deck, I felt comfortable with the symbols and messages in the cards, but I struggled with how to apply that information—especially when it came to my daily readings. I'd draw a card for myself in the morning and understand it in theory, but in practice, what did it mean? How could I take what I knew about my morning card and apply it to my daily life? I was quickly amassing a small library of tarot guidebooks but they all seemed to fall into two general categories. Either they were beginner books designed to help the tarot newbie to learn the basics of reading tarot cards, or they were books full of detailed spreads and layouts. I wanted a book that gave me the practical applications of each card, how to incorporate its message into the nitty gritty of each day.

Nearly three years later, this is that book.

On Tarot as a Practice

From movies and books and cultural osmosis, there's a general assumption that tarot is capital "w" Witchy. And listen: I'm not here to tell you that tarot can't (or shouldn't be) a tool for spirituality. It's certainly become that for me in many ways. But it didn't start out that way—I got my first deck with the idea that it would be a tool for my meditation/mindfulness practice. The spiritual aspect crept in over time. But you won't hear me talk too much about that aspect of my tarot practice in this book because I firmly believe that tarot is, at its core, a tool. Nothing more or less. If you're looking for a way to incorporate communication with ancestors or fortune telling into your regular practice, a tarot deck can absolutely act as a medium for that. But it can just as easily act as a tool for meditation, self-reflection, and discovery that has no mystical overlay to it. Each of the seventy-eight cards stands for a universal experience or emotion, from love to conflict, from innovation to destruction. When you draw cards, the way that you interpret them and apply them to your life is profoundly personal. Intimate, even. That self-reflection and consideration are what I'm interested in helping you cultivate. Whether or not you believe that there's an element of divine intervention at work in which cards you pull, the power is in the interpretation, the intersection between your mind and heart and the story in the card.

About Me

Hello! I'm a non-binary, disabled writer, tarot reader, and spiritual coach. My mission is to inspire more people to pick up a tarot deck and start slinging cards. I love the fact that tarot is edging closer and closer to the mainstream. I see it as a relative of mindfulness that speaks through storytelling and archetypes (which, of course, appeals to my bookwormish, writerly soul). But tarot is still subject to a lot of misunderstanding and stereotyping. I've heard of people asking tarot readers to predict how they'd die, for instance. Once a lady approached my table at an event where I was offering readings, and as soon as she saw the cards arrayed in front of me, she audibly gasped and speed-walked away from me as if I might infect her with my Satanic cartomancy. So, my highest hope for this book is that a few more folks see tarot as a tool, a lens of sorts, rather than writing it off as a plot hook for movies with witchy characters.

As you read, you'll notice a few things about my style as a tarot practitioner. First off, I have a very gentle hand when it comes to interpreting the cards. I believe that each card has an inherent encouragement and warning hidden in its imagery. Cards that seem entirely positive like the Nine of Cups still have a potential pitfall to watch out for, and cards that seem entirely negative, such as the Tower, have a silver lining. Which aspect of the card is most relevant now entirely depends on you, your current situation, and how you interpret the card yourself.

This leads into my approach to reversals, aka the altered meanings that some tarot readers apply to a card when it comes out upside down instead of right side up. I don't talk much about reversals in this book because I don't use them in my own practice. I tend to believe that a card's primary meaning and its "shadow" meaning are already inherent (especially when you're using a spread and multiple cards for a reading). But that doesn't mean that you shouldn't read reversals if they feel right to you! The activities and suggestions you'll find for each card apply no matter how you interpret the reading. The whole point of this book is to get you developing your tarot practice into something that works for *you*. If that includes reversals, more power to you!

I've written this book to be as inclusive as possible. I've kept the cards' traditional names in place (such as the Emperor or Queen of Swords) so we're on the same page about which card we're discussing. But because I'm a non-binary reader, I use they/them pronouns for all the characters and archetypes that appear in the deck. As with everything (you may already be noticing a trend here), if you prefer to read the cards in a more gendered way, that's entirely valid and up to you. But I wanted to leave the gender of each card open-ended. That way you're free to interpret in whatever way you see fit.

I also tried to keep in mind that each reader has a different level of ability—physically, mentally, and emotionally. This is particularly applicable to the "actions" section for each card. I've done my best to include a range of activities so that if one activity doesn't work for you (for example, an activity for the Chariot asks you to go for a walk, but maybe you experience chronic pain that prevents you from walking for any length of time) you can instead take on the other suggested activity (in the case of the Chariot, the second activity would be starting a pride journal). You may notice, too, that the activities include a disproportionate amount of writing. I am, unsurprisingly, a bit biased toward writing-related activities. This is partially because writing lends itself to varying levels of ability and/or effort; based on the same prompt, you could spend five minutes jotting things down, or you could write a fifty-page essay. I also believe that putting words on paper carries a great deal of power, and it dovetails nicely with the self-reflection and storytelling that make tarot reading so effective for personal development. But again, you're welcome to riff on any of the activities to make them work better for you. If you find writing to be tedious or you're not a verbal learner, you might choose to interpret a writing prompt as inspiration for a painting, for example. Everything in these pages is meant to be a jumping off point, not a list of ironclad instructions.

This is why I've framed the coming activities and reflections as a toolkit. I've been living with chronic pain and fatigue for nearly ten years now, and I've learned that no single medication, lifestyle change, or technique is a cure-all. (If only.) I have my daily items: meds and supplements, a consistent bedtime routine, etc. And then I have a big mental list of things that I can use when I wake up in an exceptional amount of pain, from heated blankets to special teas to YouTube playlists. None of them make the flare-up go away. But together, they form a toolkit that I can always fall back on. In the same way, it's unlikely that any one of the activities in this book will be life-changing. But sprinkling a variety of them through your days can provide a sense of alignment and self-awareness, building up your toolkit card by card.

How to Use this Book

Although you're welcome to read this book from cover to cover, its intended purpose is to be a companion—a reference guide to keep on hand for your regular tarot practice. Each day when you draw your card, you can flip to the entry for that card and find suggested affirmations, reflection questions, and activities to accompany that card's message. From there, you can choose to incorporate some, all, or none of these suggestions into your day. Or you can use the suggestions as inspiration to develop your own activities or reflections. And for that matter, if you are newer to tarot and still working on learning its intricacies, it might be useful to read through the intro/overview sections for each suit and card.

The time of day when you can squeeze in a quick tarot reading will differ from person to person. If you tend to pull your daily card first thing in the morning, the affirmations and reflection questions are quick ways to engage with your card before you launch into your next morning activity. You might jot one of the affirmations at the top of your daily planner so you're reminded of it every time you check your schedule. You might whisper one of the affirmations to yourself every time you wash your hands and see your reflection in the mirror. You might take ten minutes out of your morning to ruminate on one of the reflection questions, or you might keep it in mind throughout the day and take quick notes about any answers or insights that occur to you as you go. However you choose to apply the suggestions or riff on them, using this book with your daily card in the morning is an opportunity to set the tone for the rest of your day by engaging with your card first thing.

But maybe you're not a morning person and you're doing good to roll out of bed with enough time to make coffee and jam a bagel in your backpack before you're out the door. Midday might be a better time to do your daily reading. I sometimes draw a card if I've had an especially bad or especially good moment in my day, and often I'm comforted or inspired by whatever card I pull. If you find yourself in this scenario, it may be a perfect opportunity to try out one of the suggested activities for your card. Or if you're truly in the middle of everything and don't have more than a spare minute to draw a card and glance at the corresponding entry in this book, see if you can plan some time later in your day for one of the activities. You turned to your deck mid-activity, after all, so choosing a thematically appropriate activity to honor your card is only fitting.

And what about if you're a night owl and your best time for a daily tarot practice is at the end of your day? This is a great time to look back and reflect on how the card you draw fits the day you had—or didn't. If you're a journaling type, take a few minutes to write any thoughts that occur to you. Were there moments in your day that felt particularly suited to the card you drew? How could you have implemented more (or less) of your card's message today? Is there anyone you interacted with who seemed to carry a great deal of your card's energy or who could have used more of it? This might also be a good time to look at the reflection questions. See if any of them spark an insight or idea that seems worth exploring, either through journaling or just meditation/reflection.

No matter what time of day you find yourself reaching for your deck, there are a few more tips and tricks I'd like to share with you up front to help you make best use of your tarot practice and this book. First, whether you're a fastidious journaler or someone who only writes things down when it's absolutely necessary, I do recommend keeping some record of your daily card. Even if it's just a note in your phone where you keep a bullet-point list of each day's card, it'll help you notice if there are trends. An experience that seems to be nearly universal among tarot readers is the phenomenon of a card appearing in daily readings too frequently to be ignored. When a card keeps showing up and making its presence known, you want to pay attention. There's probably a message you're overlooking or a recurring theme in your current life that you need to be more mindful of. And if you haven't yet tried any of the activities or questions for your repetitive card, this may be the time. Cards that reappear over and over are demanding that you engage with them, and the suggested activities within these pages are a good way to start.

What if the situation isn't a card that keeps reappearing but that multiple cards have come up during the same reading? Sometimes you'll go to draw your daily card and another card will leap out alongside it. Or two. Or three. You can, of course, choose to focus on only the first card you drew, or the one that seems the most insistent or relevant. But if you do interpret this as multiple cards vying for your attention, I'd recommend reading both (or all) the cards' entries in this book and finding ways to incorporate bits of each entry into your day. Choose a reflection question from each entry to journal about, for example, or repeat the affirmations from both entries to yourself before you head off to work. You also might spend a few minutes reflecting or journaling about how the cards relate to each other. What themes do they share? Where do they differ? Do they seem completely incongruous, either to each other or to your current life situation? How might you synthesize the messages that they offer into a cohesive piece of guidance for your day?

Then there's the matter of court cards. Court cards are weird. There, I said it. They throw everybody off when they're first learning to read tarot cards. Many older/more traditional tarot guidebooks will tell you that court cards *always* represent specific people in your world. I've found that to be a limiting way of looking at them. To my way of thinking, the court cards are archetypes. Sure, they can speak to particular people you know—the King of Cups will always feel like my dad to me, no matter what context I draw it in—but they can also stand for personality traits and attributes that you may need to cultivate. Or personality traits that you have a bit too much of and could stand to temper. Because the courts can be a bit hard to navigate (especially at first), you'll notice that I've handled their entries a bit differently. They all share the same reflection questions: Who in my life reminds me of this court card? What aspects of this court card do I see in myself? What aspects of this court card would I like to cultivate in myself? But unlike the other cards, I've chosen a specific character from fiction to illustrate each court card's personality. My hope is that this will help you connect the dots between the general descriptions of a court card and the fleshed-out illustration of a known character. If I describe the Page of Pentacles as a methodical worker and loyal friend, you may still see them as a bit abstract and two-dimensional. When I tell you that Charlie Brown of *Peanuts* fame is the perfect representative for the Page of Pentacles, you immediately have a clearer sense of who this Page is and what they stand for.

Finally, what if the card just doesn't fit? All these activities and questions may be fine when your card seems to fit the day ahead, but what if you draw your card and it makes no sense to you? What if, for example, you draw the Nine of Swords at a time when your life actually feels relatively calm and centered? Well, first and foremost, it's worth reflecting on the card even if it doesn't *seem* to fit. You may find yourself making connections that weren't immediately apparent. For example, maybe you're dealing with a situation that, in the past, would have triggered your anxiety. But you've been doing a lot of mindfulness practice, and you've gotten through that previously-anxiety-inducing situation with minimal nerves. The Nine of Swords may still turn up as a reference to the anxiety that could have been. And the affirmations, reflections, and actions for the Nine of Swords might still be worth a look. But at the end of the day, your tarot practice is about self-reflection and engaging with the cards. If you spend some time thinking about your card of the day and you just can't figure out how it connects, there's no shame in letting it go and returning for a new card tomorrow—or even drawing a completely new card today! As many of my favorite spirituality books encourage, take only what works and leave the rest.

THE MAJOR ARCANA

The major arcana cards are so titled because they're the biggest and most intense cards in the deck. If the pips and courts speak in a conversational tone of voice, the major arcana shout for attention. If the pips and courts are comets and asteroids in your personal solar system, the major arcana are stars and planets. These cards represent broad events, themes, and players in your life. Thus, you may be a bit startled when you draw one of these Big Moment cards in your everyday drawing. Should you cancel all your plans and hide in your closet if you pull the Tower one morning? If the Fool strolls into your daily reading, should you be worried that you'll spontaneously catch that old wanderlust and blow all your savings on an impulsive package tour of Japan? Personally, I'd say no. (Although if you do the latter, I'd love to know what tarot deck you're using—it seems significantly more powerful than the decks I'm accustomed to!) When I draw a major arcana card in a daily reading, I don't (necessarily) see it as a sign that today is going to be much more intense than other days. Rather, I view it as a larger force checking in with me on this particular day. If I draw the Lovers in a daily reading, I know that connection and choice are major players in my life right now. I know to focus on the decisions that I'm making a bit more, and I know to lean into any new connections

I make. So, I'd encourage you to look at the major arcana as an invitation to zoom out a bit, to examine the trends and themes in your world now, and to invite the energies of your card into your day-to-day life a bit more consciously.

As you flip through the entries on the major arcana, you may notice references to "the Fool's journey." Just as each suit tells a miniature story starting at its Ace and ending with its Ten, the major arcana tell a story that begins with the Fool and ends with the World. It can be useful to examine whichever major arcana card you pull in this zoomed-out lens. For example, while the High Priestess and the Hermit both speak to solitude, the High Priestess appears early in the major arcana. That makes it more of a building block, a fundamental to incorporate as you navigate a situation. The Hermit, meanwhile, appears midway through the Fool's journey. This gives it a sense of retreating and reassessing in the middle of a process. Knowing where each card lives in the journey can enhance your relationship with them. But all of that said, each card can also stand on its own perfectly well, so if you're still learning the basics of reading tarot, don't stress too much about the Fool's journey and what it means for your practice.

The Fool

O The Fool always makes me think of the very first song in a Broadway musical, where the protagonist belts their heart out about their wildest dreams. It's Bilbo leaving behind everything he's ever known to follow a pack of dwarves to a dragon-guarded mountain of gold. I'll bet if you think back on your life so far, you can identify a moment or two where you yourself channeled this Fool energy. Think of your first day of school, or moving into your own place for the first time, or starting a new job that perhaps you didn't feel entirely ready for. The Fool is all about beginnings and more; it's about beginnings faced with an open mind and heart.

If you pull the Fool during a daily draw, it likely means that there is big new beginnings racing toward you (or perhaps already upon you)! Maybe the newness isn't something you asked for or expected; it might have come out of left field, or it might be looming over you like a storm cloud. And yes, this may make your stomach flip and your heart race. But the Fool asks you to be just as excited as you are scared. The unknown is vast, but it is filled with possibility, too. Put your trust in yourself and the world, race toward the cliff, and take the leap.

 ## Affirmations

I AM spontaneous.
I CAN take risks.
I WILL embrace new beginnings.

 ## Reflections

What would an adventure look like for me?
An adventure can be as big as taking a trip to someplace completely unfamiliar or as small as taking a different route to work than you usually do. What would an ideal

adventure look like for you? In what ways could you incorporate that spirit of adventure into your everyday life today?

How can I remain open to new opportunities?

Routine and structure are important parts of life, but the Fool challenges us not to cling to our routines so much that we let new opportunities pass us by. Whether your daily planner is your bible or you're allergic to schedules, we all have to be flexible from time to time. In what ways can you be more open to new possibilities today? Is there a specific routine or ritual that you can loosen your grip on (even just a little) to leave room for new developments?

How can I invite curiosity into my day?

The word *curiosity* always makes me think of someone clutching a magnifying glass, examining the smallest details of the world we take for granted. But you don't have to be a character from a children's book or Sherlock Holmes to be curious and inquisitive. It's so easy to let the world pass by as you go about your daily life. How can curiosity be part of your day? Perhaps it's as simple as people watching at the bus stop on your way to work or asking a coworker to tell you more about the family photo on their desk. In what ways might you cultivate that beginner's mind, that inquisitive approach to the world?

 **Actions**

Break Your Media Routines

Effort Level: Low ◉○○○○

In a world where we have instantaneous access to almost any type of media, we all have genres that we tend to stick to. (And with good reason—think how overwhelmed we'd get if we didn't have preferences to guide us!) But there could be new favorites waiting for us within genres that we've completely written off. So, for this activity, we'll challenge ourselves to venture into a genre that we rarely explore.

For the sake of this example, we're going to work with music. Load up whatever music service you use regularly (Spotify, iTunes, YouTube Music, etc.). Take a moment to identify the genres that you tend to comfortably live in. For instance, my go-tos tend to be instrumental soundtracks, musicals, and indie. Then, identify a genre that you would typically never venture into. I might choose punk or country, for example. With an open mind (as free and innocent as the Fool!) select an artist or playlist from one of these genres and listen to a couple of songs.

It's entirely possible that you'll hate the songs and will decide to never try this genre again—that's okay! The point of the exercise is to channel that Fool energy into something small but significant: taking a risk, exploring a frontier that is new and uncharted for you, and approaching it with an open mind. And who knows, maybe you'll find a song or an artist that you don't mind or (gasp!) even LIKE!

The beauty of this exercise is that it can work equally well for almost any form of media. If you're low on time, music, poetry, or artwork are perfect to explore. If you have a little more time to play with, choose a movie, TV show, or book that you'd typically never pick up. Figure out what works for you and your day and dive into something brand new with the Fool's joyful abandon.

Plan a Solo Adventure

Effort Level: Medium to high ●●●●○

First of all, identify someplace that you've never visited before that sounds interesting to you. This someplace can be as simple as a store or park in your hometown, or as elaborate as a city across the country that you've always wanted to travel to. Whatever works best for you and your resources (both in terms of time and finances). The key, though, is to choose a place that is brand new to you.

If you happen to have enough time to visit this place today, go for it! But more likely this will take a bit of planning and preparation, especially if you've chosen a location that requires significant travel. This may seem counterintuitive for the Fool, who thrives in spontaneity. But even adventurers who are heading into uncharted territory keep a compass in their pocket, and so you may imagine your plan as your compass.

Ideally, this is an adventure that you will undertake alone. But if, for whatever reason, you need to take a companion with you, try to choose someone who will let you take the lead. Because when you arrive at your chosen someplace, your challenge is to just…wander. Let go of any preconceived notions you may have had. Let your curiosity be your guide and explore with fresh new eyes, like a child full of wonder. Remember, for a child or a Fool, even someplace as mundane as a grocery store can be brand new! Catch your breath at the beauty of a blossoming tree or a colorful painting. Laugh with abandon at the antics of a street performer. Marvel at the tapestry of sounds and energies that surround you in a crowded place. Tune into the voice of your inner child and follow wherever they lead you.

The Magician

1 The Magician takes the discoveries that they made as the wide-eyed Fool and begins to study and craft them further. This is someone who is building their toolkit, gathering their resources, and tirelessly learning. If the Fool is a child who dives eagerly into new interests, the Magician is a college student developing their expertise in those areas of interest.

When the Magician appears in your daily draw, you are hard at work turning your goals and dreams into reality. You may be in a period of dedicated study, practicing your skills, or searching for opportunities to put your knowledge into action. The big takeaway is that your journey is well and truly underway. You're still at the beginning, but you're actively learning everything you need to make the trip ahead as successful and smooth as possible.

 ## Affirmations

I AM able.
I CAN manifest my dreams.
I WILL identify the tools I need.

 ## Reflections

What goals am I pursuing right now?

The Fool dove headfirst off the cliff without much of a direction beyond, "Go!" Now that you're in the Magician phase, it's important to clearly define what your goals are. You may have a map in hand, but without a specific destination in mind, that map doesn't do you much good. So what are you shooting for? What are your biggest dreams? Don't censor yourself as you answer this question—even though the Magician is more of a planner than the Fool, they still reach for the stars. Unfold that roadmap and put your finger on the exact place you'd like to end up, even if it's across the country or across an ocean.

What tools do I have access to?

Speaking of maps, an important aspect of the Magician is identifying what tools you have at your disposal. If you're trying to learn something new, what teachers or classes are available to you? Do you have books on the subject, or can you borrow some? Do you know someone else who'd be interested in learning alongside you? This is your opportunity to make a list of everything that you can use to achieve your goals. People who can help, places where you can work or study, literal tools that you already own, etc. To continue the metaphor of the journey, think of this as packing your bag and marking pit stop locations on your map.

What are my strengths?

It's too easy to focus on our weaknesses and character flaws, isn't it? When our anxiety talks us out of pursuing an opportunity or our outspokenness gets us into trouble with a coworker, that's all we can think about. But how often do we take the time to consider our strengths? In the question above, we identified the tools that are around us—what about the tools inside of us? Make a list and be specific. Are you a fast reader? Are you good at cheering up your loved ones when they're blue? Do you make a killer mac and cheese? For this question, don't worry too much about how your answers are applicable to your goals and dreams. Just list the qualities that you like about yourself, that make you feel powerful and capable. When things go wrong or don't pan out as you hoped, this is something to fall back on. Even if you're not yet fluent in Japanese as you wanted to be, at least you can make one heckuva mac and cheese.

 Actions

Make a Vision Board

Effort Level: Low to medium ●●○○○

The trouble with goals is that they tend to be big, far-off sorts of affairs, which make them easy to push aside in the rush of our everyday lives. "I want to run a marathon next fall" isn't quite as motivating when it's a February afternoon and you've already worked an eight-hour shift and the last thing you want to do is exercise. The Magician's appearance in a daily reading suggests that it's time to bring those far-off goals closer, make them a bigger part of your everyday. And what better way than to make yourself a visual reminder of those dreams of yours? Gather images and words that evoke your goal and put them together somewhere that you'll see regularly.

There's two main ways that you can accomplish this. The first is, of course, to make a real-life vision board. A bulletin board or magnet board can work perfectly for this, or you can get crafty and make a collage. This is one of those activities that can be as simple or as involved as you prefer. If you don't have the time or space for a real-life vision board, I also love using Pinterest to curate inspiration boards. Pinterest lets you gather as many images as you'd like from all over the internet and collect them all in one place, with little more than a click.

One caveat is that you should make sure you're choosing images that are inspiring for *you*, not for someone else. In our marathon example, I might cover my vision board with pictures of people running or long stretches of road. But maybe you'd be more inspired by images of running gear. I would also caution you not to include images that are more of a *negative* inspiration (for instance, using a photo of an empty wallet to remind yourself to save money). The whole point is to make this as personal and positive as possible so that you're truly motivated to chase those goals every single day.

Deck Out Your Workspace

Effort Level: Medium to high ⬤⬤⬤⬤○

When I first moved in with my spouse, we were living in a tiny, cluttered apartment that was much too small for two pack rats like us. I would end up sitting on the couch or in bed while I wrote, and it actively discouraged me from working on my writing projects. Once we moved into a larger apartment, I was actually able to put together a dedicated writing space with a desk and bookshelves. I can't even articulate how much it encourages and inspires me when I sit down at that desk. It may seem like a small thing but having your own workspace can be huge.

Maybe it isn't a desk for you. Maybe it's a space in the living room where you can keep your yoga mat, or a reading nook where you can study. Whatever your goals are, spend some time today dedicating a space in your home to that work. Tidy up your desk and put up a Post-it note to remind you of your ambitions. Rearrange your bookshelf. It can even be as simple as reorganizing your gym bag or sewing a patch on the front that makes you happy. The point here is to take your intention and direct it toward the space you'll use to pursue that intention. Make that space a little more comfortable, more inspirational, more you. You'll be surprised how much it motivates you.

The High Priestess

2 The High Priestess is the incarnation of your inner voice. They represent your intuition, your divine and highest self who whispers in your ear and tugs at your gut. While the Magician's energy and effort radiates outward, the High Priestess turns your focus inward. They encourage you to listen to yourself—not just to the words you speak, but to the echoes of thoughts and feelings in the most hidden corners of your mind.

When the High Priestess sweeps into your daily draws, look for profound stirrings deep in your subconscious. There are secrets that your mind has kept from everyone (including you) that it is ready to reveal—but only if you listen closely. Or perhaps you've already heard the whisperings, but you've let the cacophony of everyday life drown them out. Either way, now is the time to seek the kind of quiet that allows you to commune with yourself and yourself alone. You contain cathedrals full of glorious stained-glass windows…but you must be willing to go looking for them.

 Affirmations

I AM intuitive.
I CAN listen when I'm tempted to speak.
I WILL trust my inner voice.

 Reflections

What does my inner voice need to tell me?
This is one of those questions that will either be incredibly easy or impossibly challenging. There may be hidden truths that have been tugging on your shirt sleeve for a while now, and when you pose this question to yourself those truths may tumble out of your pen without a second thought. But if you initially draw a blank, I encourage you to sit with that uncertainty and pay attention to what comes out of it. Your inner voice may be

more eager for a platform than you think. Be patient with it, and don't censor yourself. Even if what comes up seems silly, or irrelevant, or surprising, or anything else. This is not the place to judge or second guess your inner voice's words. Just let it speak to you.

How can I listen better?

Talking is easy (especially talking about yourself) but listening is harder. The High Priestess asks us to listen more mindfully. When your loved ones speak, are you really paying attention to their meaning? Are you making sure to listen to yourself and stay attuned to your inner voice (as in the above question)? Are you uncomfortable with the idea of silence? How can you cultivate your skill in listening today?

What dreams have I had lately?

Whether you believe that dreams are divine messages from an outside source or just mental castoff as your brain sorts through the day's memories, they are worth paying attention to. Dreams can inform you of what events and situations are still sticking in your craw, so to speak. What recent dreams can you recall? Even if you can only remember bits and fragments, write those down anyway. If a dream unearths a subconscious memory or an idea, it's worth devoting some conscious thought to. Or if the dream seems utterly nonsensical, spend some time speculating about how those nonsensical fragments might be relevant to your day. No matter what you end up writing, this prompt will get you thinking about what your subconscious is trying to tell you. (Even if it's just that you're terrified of showing up to work naked.)

 *Actions*

Befriend the Silence

Effort Level: Low ●○○○○

How often do we sit in true silence? I almost always have music or a podcast playing in the background while I work. But silence can be enlightening. Think of the times when you crave solitude, when the company of other people is overwhelming. Seeking out silence is its own form of seeking out solitude; it's giving yourself an opportunity to sit with your own thoughts uninterrupted.

You can employ an aid like earplugs or noise-cancelling headphones for this exercise, or you can just find a space where it's comparatively quiet and you won't be disturbed. Find a comfortable position in this space. You don't have to close your eyes for this activity to be effective, but if you tend to get distracted by visual input, I would recommend it (at least at first). You also may wish to keep a notebook and writing utensil nearby.

Give yourself some time to notice and adjust to any background noise. Then start to pay attention to any cues that are coming not from without, but within. It might be something in your body, such as an ache, a tension, a tingling, etc. Or it might be something in your mind—thoughts, worries, emotions, etc. Whatever you notice, take some time to sit with it and trace its source. If you have tension in your shoulders, can you identify anything specific that might be making you tense at that moment? Can you breathe into the tension and slowly encourage it to dissipate? If you're stuck on a thought, what is it about that thought that's capturing your attention? Is there something deeper that you need to consider? Are there unresolved issues that you need to sort through?

If this seems like an especially freeform sort of exercise, that's purposeful. This is not unlike meditation, but instead of quieting your mind, the goal is for you to become better acquainted with those internal cues and dialogues. By minimizing any audio distractions in your environment, the voices of your mind and body will be easier to key into. This exercise is a good one to repeat from time to time. The more time you spend noticing how your body and mind speak to you in the silence, the easier it will be for you to hear them when you're in louder situations.

Start a Dream Log

Effort level: Medium to high ●●●●○

Numerous sources have suggested to me that I should keep a dream journal: family members, friends, books, even oracle cards. It always felt somewhat pointless because I so rarely remember my dreams. But as I've incorporated it into my spiritual practice, it's become apparent how meaningful this habit can be. Often the dreams I remember happen just before I wake in the morning, and the memories that remain are scattered images and (most importantly) overwhelming gut feelings about the meaning of the dream. Writing these down helps me hold onto them long after the images have grown fuzzy, and the feelings have faded into uncertainty.

To successfully keep a dream log of any kind, the key is to let go of any expectations or preconceived notions you may have about the practice. You don't have to have a gorgeous leatherbound journal filled with riveting narrative written in immaculate cursive. I don't even have a literal journal—at the moment, I just jot down any memories or impressions that linger in a note on my phone. That serves me just as well. You might only write in your dream log once or twice a month, or even less than that. Whatever works for you works. Full stop.

And what's the outcome? Well, for me, keeping a log of my dream fragments has made me feel more connected and attuned to my intuition. If you pursue any creative or artistic disciplines, keeping a log of your dreams may give you inspiration or spark new ideas. At a minimum, the practice will help you track your subconscious mind and its dialogue with your waking thoughts. Dreams are the byproduct of your subconscious sorting out thoughts, feelings, and memories. That seems noteworthy in and of itself, don't you think?

The Empress

3 The Empress is a cup of hot cocoa waiting on the table when you come inside from a cold, snowy day. They're the blanket wrapping you up in comfort and warmth when you're about to fall asleep. They're your favorite song playing in the car on your way to work in the morning. Everything about the Empress speaks of nurturing and support and the comforts of home. They encourage you to grow closer to your best self, and they promise all the hugs and high-fives you might need to get you there.

When the Empress settles into your daily tarot reading, it's a sure sign that someone needs some extra tender loving care. It may be you, or it may be someone you care about. The Empress reminds you that love doesn't only manifest in the grand gestures, but in the simple moments that fill up our daily lives. Add a little something to your morning getting-ready routine to make yourself feel good—have a second cup of tea or coffee, or put on a necklace or pair of earrings that you don't wear very often. Do something extra to make a loved one feel good, whether it's just a quick hug, a shared smile in the hallway, or making dinner for your significant other. These are the things that recharge our emotional batteries, and that's everything the Empress stands for.

 *Affirmations*

I AM caring.
I CAN nurture myself and others.
I WILL give freely.

 *Reflections*

What does "home" mean to me?
Home is more than a building where you keep your clothes and sleep at night. It's a feeling in the center of your chest when you're at your most open and comfortable. It's

that sense of warmth when you spend time with your closest loved ones. It's coziness. It's openness. It's simplicity. What feels like home to you? Is it snuggling into your bed at the end of a productive day? Is it sipping coffee at your favorite local cafe? Is it the pages of a book you've read too many times to count? Maybe home is a person, or several people. Maybe it's a place besides your current residence. Maybe it's a lot of these things, or something entirely different. But whatever it is, you know that feeling when you have it. What is that feeling for you?

What is one thing I can do to take better care of myself?

We ALL know the things we're supposed to do to feel better and live healthier. Whether it's eating five servings of fruits and veggies a day or turning off our phones an hour before bed, we're inundated with information about how to Live Better. This question is partly about that—but also partly not. You probably have a running list in your head of things you *should* be doing for your health (and I'm not only talking about physical health here—I'm talking about mental, emotional, and spiritual health, too). In answering this question, I'm only asking you to choose one of them. What is one thing that you can do right now to take better care of yourself? Can you start moisturizing your face before bed? Can you set up autopay on a bill that you always stress about paying on time? Can you switch out your daily soda with a lower-sugar alternative? Whatever it is, choose one thing that seems attainable right now, and write it down. Make a commitment to incorporate it into your life.

Who do I know that could use a little extra love today?

We all go through ebbs and flows with our mental health. If you're in a position of strength right now, who can you reach out to that might need extra help? It can be as simple as calling a relative to tell them you're thinking about them. Or it can be as involved as bringing a homemade meal to a coworker who's experienced a loss recently. Identify one person who could use the support and figure out what kind of support you're equipped to give right now (without overextending yourself).

 **Actions**

Clean Your Space

Effort Level: Low to medium ●●○○○

Most people I know hate cleaning. It's tedious, it can be physically demanding, and sometimes it's downright gross. But most people I know also feel *much* better working and living in a tidier, cleaner space—and I include myself in both categories. Now, of course everyone's level of comfort is different. Some people require everything to be put in its place and spotless before they can relax, while others are comfortable with a bit of clutter. But most of us let ourselves get past the point of comfort (far past) before they finally give in and tidy up.

Something else I'm very mindful of is level of physical ability. As someone with serious chronic pain, I'm not always capable of getting on my hands and knees to scrub the baseboards. So you may not have the time or energy for any kind of deep cleaning today, and that's perfectly fine. But there's probably one relatively simple thing you could do to improve the cleanliness of your home. For me, the one thing is often cleaning my toilet—I can clean my toilet in ten minutes or less, it doesn't require much physical exertion, and it immediately makes the bathroom feel cleaner and brighter. Another suggestion on this order might be quickly sorting through the clutter that's accumulated on your nightstand or kitchen counter.

Whether you just do that one thing or clean your entire house from top to bottom, the point of this exercise is to spend at least a few minutes cleaning and tending to your home. Not only does it make the space more livable and cheery, but it attunes you to your home base and renews your sense of, for lack of a better word, at-home-ness. This is where you work and relax, where you socialize and spend time alone, where you can be yourself most fearlessly. Taking a moment out of your day to clean it will probably feel good. Even if the cleaning itself is tedious, or physically demanding, or downright gross, you'll be proud of yourself afterwards.

Cook Something New

Effort level: Medium to high ●●●●○

There's not much in this world that's more comforting than a home-cooked meal, is there? Without even thinking too hard, I bet you can come up with a couple of favorite meals that loved ones have made for you over the years. I'm an extremely picky eater, for example, and my dad *loved* to cook and find special things to make for his family. So he made customized stir-fry for me that only included things I liked, such as shrimp and water chestnuts. And when I was in college and battling severe chronic illnesses, he would make it in huge batches, freeze individual servings, and bring them when he came to visit me. I'd heat them up and eat them when I was feeling especially awful, and it never failed to make me feel a bit better.

So why not take the time to try and cook something new? Again, this doesn't have to be hugely complicated—if you're running short on time, make a new kind of smoothie or oatmeal for yourself in the morning, or just do something new with your veggies at dinner. But if you have time and energy, it can be as involved as you'd like. Make a three-course dinner and dessert, if you're so inclined! This isn't just about the meal itself—it's about spending the time with yourself. About cooking for yourself (and your family, if you'd like). About taking care of yourself.

Of course, with any sort of experimentation, there's the possibility that your recipe won't come out the way you hoped. If that happens, try to embrace the failure as part of the learning process. Sure, it's a little disappointing—especially if you spend two hours cooking only to throw out the inedible fruits of your labor. But you've certainly learned what to do for next time. And if all else fails, there's always pizza delivery.

The Emperor

4 If the Empress holds you tightly and whispers encouragement in your ear as you dream of the stars, the Emperor designs and tests prototype rockets to get you there. They are the keeper of structure and order. In a theatrical production, the Emperor is the stage manager making sure every aspect of the show runs smoothly and efficiently. Without the Emperor, our gardens and orchards might never grow because we'd be so busy imagining fully-grown flowers that we'd forget to water and tend to our saplings.

The Emperor's appearance in a daily reading means that it's time to roll up your sleeves and get organized. Get your calendar updated and color-coded. Balance your checkbook. Make a to-do list. Reorganize your closet and donate the clothes you don't need anymore. You undoubtedly know what areas of your life are feeling scattered and disorganized at the moment. The Emperor tells you that it's time to face those areas head-on. Get to work.

Affirmations

I AM thorough.
I CAN create structures to sustain my success.
I WILL build a foundation beneath my dreams.

Reflections

What is my relationship with routine?

Everyone has a different level of routine that they're comfortable with. Some people schedule their days down to fifteen-minute increments; others fly by the seats of their pants from one activity to the next. Where do you fall on that spectrum? And is that your ideal relationship with routine, or would you like to adjust it? Perhaps you're feeling a bit too boxed in by your daily schedule and you'd like to loosen up a bit. Or perhaps it's just the opposite: you're a fly-by-the-seat-of-your-pants type of person and you're looking for a little bit *more* structure. If that's the case, do you have specific ideas for how you can fine-tune your routine (or lack thereof) so it's more comfortable?

Would I feel comfortable in a position of authority?

I don't necessarily believe that everyone falls neatly into the categories of leader or follower—I think it very much depends on the context for most of us. But if you were put in the position of leading a group of people, how would it make you feel? If you are the type of person who falls into leadership positions more naturally, how can you ensure that your leadership is balanced and mindful? If you think back over your life so far, are there times that you've been stuck leading when you didn't want to be? If you aren't usually comfortable in a leadership position, what would you need to feel more at ease?

Who in my life feels protective? Who might need protecting?

The character who always comes to mind when I think of the Emperor is Théoden from the Lord of the Rings. At different points in the trilogy, he is both someone who needs protection and someone who protects. Who do you know that looks after you and protects you when you need it? And likewise, who might need you to protect them? Are there other fictional characters who come to mind that feel protective or in need of protection?

 *Actions*

Schedule the Perfect Ordinary Day

Effort Level: Low to medium ⬤⬤◯◯◯

This is a thought experiment that requires both imagination and organization. Sit down with a notebook and pen or pencil, and start jotting down the activities and obligations that make up your typical days. You can be as detailed or as general as you'd like to start with—just make sure you've got a few activities to work with for now.

Now take one of these activities and start brainstorming ways you could make it go as smoothly and seamlessly as possible. For example, let's imagine your morning commute to work. If this is often a stressful drive for you, how can you make it less so?

Can you download a particular soundtrack or podcast to your phone to listen to as you drive? Can you leave fifteen minutes earlier and avoid the worst of rush hour? Can you take a different route that brings you past some prettier scenery? Whatever you come up with, write it all down. Draw up a specific plan.

Repeat this process with as many activities as you'd like. You can think of it like troubleshooting your daily routine. What's causing hang-ups or undue anxiety, and how might you smooth it out? Make sure that your fixes are attainable and specific: plans that can be implemented quickly, efficiently, and effectively. The Emperor does not deal in pie-in-the-sky prospects. They naturally locate the areas where structure is lacking, and they know how to fill in those gaps. Take that energy and apply it to your daily life.

Make a Budget

Effort Level: Medium to high ⬤⬤⬤⬤◯

If you're anything like me, the word "budget" automatically makes your stomach flip. Money and finances are stressful in the best of times, and unless you have the good fortune of being terrifically well-off, financial rough patches are likely to come up from time to time. Which is a very good argument for having (and attempting to stick to) a budget…but that's challenging for most of us. Fortunately, this is the Emperor's wheelhouse, so if you've drawn them in your daily reading, it's probably a good time to sit down with your bank statements and draw up some plans.

Maybe you already have a rough budget mapped out. If so, good on you! Take this as an invitation to revisit it and make any adjustments that may be necessary. Otherwise, start by simply writing all of your regular expenses in one place. How much do you spend on rent or mortgage payments a month? On gasoline or subway passes? On groceries and takeout? On Netflix or Hulu? If you're struggling to make ends meet, are there regular expenses that could be reduced or dispensed with? If you have a surplus even after you pay all your necessary expenses, can you be putting some into a savings account?

Be thorough and honest as you're working on this activity, but also be patient with yourself. It can be anxiety-inducing and overwhelming to be this transparent with yourself when it comes to matters of money. If you need to take breaks or even put the budget away for a while, that's perfectly okay. The purpose here is to make a start. As long as you've begun sifting through the lists of expenses and bottom lines, the Emperor is on board.

The Hierophant

5 The Hierophant has acquired a negative association in many traditional tarot circles. They're often seen as stodgy at best and restrictively conservative at worst. I personally don't tend to see them that way. For me, the Hierophant is the champion of spirituality. They invite you to check in with your own spiritual practice, to question what traditions are meaningful to you and which can be discarded. Certainly they can be an advocate for reaching into the past for current spiritual inspiration, but that doesn't mean that they are *only* interested in the spirituality of the past.

When the Hierophant appears in your daily cards, I encourage you to see them as a mentor rather than as an authority. Let them draw you into a space of introspection and wonder. They will remind you that prayer can be exchanged for words of affirmation whispered to your reflection in the mirror; that a church can be a cathedral of ancient trees or an ancestor's picture on your nightstand; and that you can be your own priest, rabbi, and oracle.

 Affirmations

I AM my own guide.
I CAN define my own spirituality.
I WILL keep the traditions that are meaningful and leave the rest behind.

 Reflections

What is one tradition that matters to me?
Whether you grew up in a deeply religious household or not, you undoubtedly have traditions that you've kept throughout the years. They can be complicated and grandiose (like cooking and eating Thanksgiving dinner with your extended family) or simple (like giving your younger sibling a stuffed animal on their first day of school every

year). Which of these traditions mean the most to you? Why? Has the tradition evolved or adapted over the years that you've practiced it? In what ways might it change in the future? Alternatively, is there a tradition that's become more of a chore? Is it possible to adjust it so that it recharges your spiritual batteries again? Or might it be time to say goodbye to this particular tradition altogether?

How do I define my spirituality?

At first glance, this may seem to be an impossibly broad question. There likely isn't a simple, one-word definition. But that's exactly why it's a worthwhile subject of meditation. Maybe you have (or had at one point in your life) a particular religious tradition you identify (or identified) with. If that's the case, what does that religious background mean to you? How, if at all, does it inform your daily life? How has it shaped you as a person? If you don't have a specific word or religious tradition to start with, consider beginning with adjectives and descriptive words. Is your spirituality reflective? Generous? Firm? Does it encourage you, inspire you, recharge you? Or if you've just started exploring your spirituality, what do you hope it will be like? How would you like it to grow? Don't worry about making this a comprehensive definition. Just allow it to be a beginning.

Who was one teacher who made an impact on me?

Every single person I know can point to at least one teacher who profoundly shaped their growth. Maybe it was a beloved elementary school teacher who helped you unlock the magic of reading. Maybe it was a college theater professor who encouraged you to speak with more confidence. Maybe it was a basketball coach who mentored you through your awkward clumsy stage in high school. Whoever this person is for you, spend some time recalling what they taught you. Does it continue to inspire you today? Can you trace those teachings as they inform your daily life in any way? What would you say to thank this teacher if you met them on the street tomorrow?

 *Actions*

Find a Spiritual Moment in Your Day

Effort Level: Low to medium ● ● ○ ○ ○

As someone who was not raised religiously, I remember being bemused but intrigued by my family and friends who prayed regularly. Even though I didn't identify with the religious thought behind it, the ritual itself felt Important—a way of weaving moments of spiritual reflection into mundane daily activities like meals and bedtime. Even though the Hierophant stands for big cosmic energies, they also invite this sort of regular, mundane spiritual recharging into your day. How might you accept their invitation? It could be as simple as finding a moment to be by yourself to speak your current worries and hopes aloud. Whether you believe that divine beings are listening or not, there's a power in voicing these dreams and dreads. Perhaps your spiritual moment could be a quick visualization exercise during your morning shower, imagining the water washing away your anxieties so you can face the day with a clean slate. Maybe you could take five minutes at lunch to slip on your headphones and lose yourself in a favorite piece of music. What activity you choose is, ultimately, not as important as the very act of considering what constitutes a spiritual moment for you personally. If you're feeling totally stuck, consider taking a whack at the question above (How do I define my spirituality?) if you haven't already. If you have even some general ideas of what spirituality means to you, you may find it easier to identify what activities could fit into that definition.

Compare and Contrast Your Spiritual Upbringing

Effort Level: Medium to high ● ● ● ● ○

Let's say you were raised in an orthodox Jewish household. You went to temple and Hebrew school, had a bat or bar mitzvah, and celebrated all the high holidays. Spend a few minutes journaling about (or just reflecting on) how this upbringing has shaped you. What did your childhood religion teach you? Are there parts you've given up or left behind over the years?

Now consider a spiritual upbringing utterly different from your own—perhaps being raised outside any particular religion as I was. How might you be different if this was your background instead of a traditional Jewish raising? Are there things about this upbringing you wish you'd had? Are there parts of yours that you're grateful for? What similarities can you find between these two wildly different backgrounds?

This exercise can work no matter how you were raised. Was your family more on the atheistic side? Choose a strictly religious upbringing for your comparison. If your family ascribed to a particular faith, choose an entirely different religious tradition. The key is finding a stark contrast, and then probing it. You may be surprised at what you learn about yourself as you compare.

The Lovers

6 The very word "lover" summons to mind any number of assumptions and pre-conceived ideas. Goopy love songs, romantic comedies, perhaps even racy novels. And certainly, this sort of love is part of the Lovers' lesson—but it is just that: a part of it. Not the whole. For me, the Lovers bear two overall messages: connections and choices. While romantic connections can be some of the most significant and formative ones in our lives, connections with family, friends, and even coworkers or neighbors can be equally impactful. The Lovers encourage us to chase those connections when they feel Right and Important. Pursue new friendships or reignite old ones. Get to know that coworker you always pass in the hallway. Call an uncle you haven't spoken with in months.

This leads into the Lovers' second meaning: the power of choice. While you can't always choose the company you keep, you call the shots about who you open up to, and when and how that occurs. Your inner circle may be very tight, or it may be broad and constantly expanding. It may consist of mostly relatives, or your blood family may be completely shut out of it. You may share everything with the majority of your loved ones, or there may be parts of your inner world that are reserved for you alone. The bottom line is that you are in control in ways that you may not know yet. Don't be afraid to make decisions that bring you more joy and comfort through the connections that you nourish (and those that you don't).

 *Affirmations*

I AM open to meaningful connections.
I CAN choose to open up to the right people.
I WILL develop my relationships.

 *Reflections*

Are there new relationships in my life that need care and attention?

The Lovers sometimes herald the first flush of a new relationship—and again, not necessarily a romantic one. A new friend, colleague, or perhaps even a new family member can step into our lives at any moment. Is there anybody newly arrived in your orbit who might need your attention? What steps might you take to nurture a positive relationship with this person? When might you carve out a few minutes to spend with them? How would you like to see the relationship grow and evolve?

Who can I open up to most easily?

We've all had those people in our lives whose companionship comes as naturally as breathing. People with whom you can share gut-busting laughter as easily as profound, life-changing conversations. People who you feel as if you've known your whole life. Who are these people for you? I encourage you to take a true moment of reflection before answering, because there's often more than meets the eye. We're expected to have this kind of relationship with close relatives, but for any number of reasons this may not be the case for you. At the same time, you may have a friend who you see very rarely, but when you do get together, it's as if no time passed. There may be a neighbor who you feel an inexplicable affinity for. Your list may even include a beloved pet who you pour your heart out to. Who can you unfold your deepest thoughts and feelings for, unafraid of judgment or pushback?

What choices can I make to invite more love into my life?

The Lovers is a very people-focused card—and certainly this question can include the love of other people. Maybe you need to consciously ask a partner for more hugs when you need them, or you need to set up a time for a regular coffee meeting with a friend. But beyond that, how can you bring more self-love into your everyday life? Can you make time to reread a favorite book every so often? Can you take the plunge and sign up for that sewing class you've been eyeing for months? Can you simply pack a tea bag in your lunchbox for an afternoon moment of warmth and tranquility at work? In a way,

I'm using "love" and "joy" interchangeably—but for me, there's a great deal of overlap between these two words. Perhaps not everything we love brings us joy, but it's safe to say that when something makes us joyful, that's a form of love.

 ## Actions

Let Someone Know You're Thinking About Them

Effort Level: Low to medium ●●○○○

Whether it's your closest sibling who you speak or text with regularly or a distant friend you only occasionally catch up with, you have a network of loved ones whose kinship means something to you. Why not take the Lovers' appearance as an invitation to pay that kinship forward? Choose someone who feels particularly important today and reach out to them. Like many of the activities I suggest in this book, you can make this as elaborate or as simple as you like. Send a quick text message to your best friend to remind them that you love and appreciate them. Call up your grandparent to ask how their week is going and to let them know what you've been up to. Or take the time to hand write a letter to a friend you miss and drop it in the mail. I don't know a single person who doesn't enjoy getting mail, and a handwritten hello is a fantastic way to brighten up someone's day. It's truly incredible how these simple acts can make the distance between you seem to fold inward, creating a warm and welcoming middle space for you to share. Much like giving a gift, you're likely to get as much joy out of this act as your recipient will.

Plan a Date

Effort level: Medium to high ●●●●○

Naturally the word "date" has deeply romantic connotations. And if you have a partner or partners, certainly the Lovers can encourage you to spend some quality time with them! But you may also wish to plan a get-together with a friend or family member—or even a date with yourself alone. All of these options can be equally valid and rejuvenating. Check out that new corner restaurant you've been driving past lately or go on a hike through your favorite local park or go to a baseball game and splurge on hot dogs and soda.

One of the keys here lies in the planning and anticipation of it. Spur-of-the-moment adventures are wonderful in their own right, but there is something special about choosing an activity and a companion, selecting a date, and then having time to look forward to it. Even if your perfect date turns out to be a movie marathon and microwave popcorn, make an occasion out of it. You, and whoever you may choose to share the experience with, are worth it.

The Chariot

Few cards make me grin the way the Chariot does when I turn it up in my daily draws. The Chariot thunders into the major arcana like reinforcements arriving on the field of battle. They stand for unbridled willpower, endurance, and stamina. Your inner Chariot is that stick-to-itiveness that urges you to keep going. To never give up or back down. To put one foot in front of the other, even if your steps are shaky or uncertain. Perhaps on occasion they charge ahead with too much stubbornness and trample anything (and anyone) in their path, in which case they need to be reined in just a bit. But most of the time they're the wind beneath our wings as we chase our ambitions.

When the Chariot turns up in a daily reading, it's a reminder that you've got this. Whatever challenges you're facing within and without, the Chariot recalls the footprints (hoofprints?) you've already left as you scaled mountains and won battles in the past. They guard the triumphs in your personal history, and when your present feels overwhelming, they help the strength of those memories pull you toward the future. They've seen you overcome insurmountable odds already, after all. What's one more challenge?

Affirmations

I AM dedicated.
I CAN triumph over any challenges the universe throws at me.
I WILL keep going.

Reflections

What makes me feel empowered?
"Empowered" is a big word to bandy about, especially when we're going through darker periods in our lives. So when considering this question, remember that empowerment can be as cosmic or as precise as you make it. And there's likely a myriad of answers that

range between those two extremes for you! For instance, I feel highly powerful when I complete a large, involved writing project. But I'm learning to also feel empowered when I decide to consciously take a rest day for the sake of my chronic pain condition.

If you'd like, turn your answer into a stream-of-consciousness list of what makes you feel empowered, what makes you feel that you're truly exercising your agency, reason, and free will. When do you get that proud, capable swelling in your chest? What lends you confidence? What inspires you to keep going, to be your best self?

What does success look like?

In Western culture, we have a very narrow and particular definition of success. Climbing a promotional ladder at work, marrying and settling down with a partner, owning a house, and so on. For the purposes of this question, try to clear that definition from your thoughts. This isn't about society's definition of success, but yours. If you were in your golden years looking back at your life, what would make you feel proudest and most fulfilled to remember? What would bring you the most joy and satisfaction to accomplish? What would you tell your descendants you'd achieved?

What progress have I already made?

It's very easy, as we navigate life's twists and turns, to only focus on what's coming next. When we do look back, it's often for the express purpose of criticizing ourselves and fixating on past mistakes. But what about past triumphs? What about acknowledging the survivor in you who has lived through those mistakes and emerged with new wisdom? It's just as important to learn from our successes as it is to learn from our setbacks. And when you look back, even though the path behind you may be fraught with ups and downs, the fact remains that you got through them. You kept moving forward, even if it felt impossible at the time. You are enduring and capable, whether you feel that way all the time or not (and precious few of us do). So, taking a moment or two to reflect on how far you've come is an important exercise—a way of remembering how hard you've worked and what strides you've made.

 *Actions*

Go For a Walk

Effort level: Low to medium ●●○○○

The Chariot is one of the most active and dynamic cards in the tarot. It's almost impossible for me to draw the Chariot without imagining movement of some sort to accompany it. So for this activity, we'll be leaning into the Chariot's inherent kinesthetic nature. This works particularly well if you have a dilemma you're mulling over, or a creative block you're trying to navigate.

The walk you take can be as short or as long as you like. If you're able to walk outside, that's the most ideal scenario; barring that, try to find someplace like a mall that you can walk through. It's not that walking on a treadmill can't be effective—half of this exercise is the physical activity itself, and that is effective whether you're on a treadmill or hiking through the woods. But the other half of this activity is the act of traveling, using your own body to get from Point A to Point B. The mile tracker on a treadmill is more abstract than literally watching the scenery go by. There's also a whole collection of walking programs on YouTube that allow you to "walk" almost anywhere in the world!

No matter where your walk takes you, focus your attention on the physical sensations as you move. The rhythmic feeling of your feet hitting the ground, one after the other. The swing of your arms at your sides. Your lungs expanding and contracting. Don't choose anything too distracting, but if listening to music helps you focus as you move, absolutely employ it here.

Oftentimes, taking a movement break seems to help loosen up my thinking. After a walk like this, it isn't uncommon for me to generate a new idea or discover a potential solution to a problem I've been stuck on. If you're so inclined, take five or ten minutes when you get back from walking to stream-of-consciousness free write whatever may come to mind. Too often we forget our bodies when we try to focus our mind and spirit—this exercise helps integrate your body into the process.

Start a Pride Journal

Effort level: Medium to high ●●●●○

The practice of keeping a gratitude journal is becoming increasingly mainstream. And no wonder—it's a great way to keep life's ups and downs in perspective. But in my experience, something we all struggle with is keeping our accomplishments in perspective. We might wholeheartedly congratulate a loved one for something that we ourselves have done, too, but in our own case we're more likely to pick it apart and only notice the flaws.

After having major surgery at 24, I struggled to remain patient with my recovery process. I wanted to leap back into my activities and goals all at once, but this was physically impossible. To alleviate how discouraged I was, I started writing down everything I'd done each day that I was proud of. Some days brought obvious milestones, like walking for an extended period of time or achieving a work goal. But other entries were much subtler—going a full day without using pain meds, for instance, or drinking a full 64 ounces of water.

Your list need not be as exhaustive as mine was, but I encourage you to get into the habit of writing down at least one thing you're proud of every day. Don't diminish seemingly small things—and take into account what's hard for you. If you have a hard time getting up on time every morning, write it down when you're able to rise with your alarm clock. If healthy eating is a challenge, write down the day you eat your packed salad instead of going to lunch with your coworkers. You can (and should!) even write down when you survive an especially bad flare-up of anxiety or depression. Whatever your entries end up looking like, they will catalog your triumphs of all shapes and sizes. You'll be able to look back on your pride journal and see true proof of the progress you've made and the resilience you possess.

Strength

While the Chariot pushes us forward, Strength stands at our back and whispers in our ear. It reminds us that we do not have to be stalwart and tireless—that our moments of vulnerability are as much a sign of our power as our moments of triumph. Strength has a lot in common with its sibling, courage. Courage is not the absence of fear, but the determination to be brave anyway. Likewise, Strength is not a lack of "weakness" (more on that in a second). It coexists with uncertainty, with anxiety, with crippling sorrow—and it buoys your determination to continue, even when it feels like these things make you incapable.

Now, a word about weakness. In our culture, any departure from stoic persistence tends to be written off as weakness. Breaking down in tears, having panic attacks, needing to bail on an obligation—the list could take up this entire book. The Strength card tells us to reexamine these moments with a compassionate eye. One of the strongest things you can do is admit when you're struggling, whether by asking for some time alone to process or by reaching out to a loved one for help. In the moment it may feel like a resignation or a defeat, but Strength doesn't see it that way. And if this card appears in your daily readings, it's inviting you to look at your vulnerable moments in a new light.

 *Affirmations*

I AM courageous.
I CAN find strength in vulnerability.
I WILL draw power from my heart.

 *Reflections*

Who is the strongest person I know?
Cast your mind across your circle of family, friends, and acquaintances. Who stands out as an extraordinarily strong person? Describe what exactly strikes you about them.

What makes them strong? What have they accomplished? What qualities do they display that you would like to cultivate in yourself? Have you seen this person go through a hard time? How do their behaviors and qualities shift during these bad spells? What do you admire about them in crisis mode? Do their problem-managing skills give you ideas to try yourself?

What's a form of strength that I embody?

Strength can take as many forms as there are people in the world. It can manifest as endurance and grit as you do your daily workout. But it can just as easily appear as vulnerability as you allow your partner to witness your usually-hidden anxiety. It can be a grand display of courage or it can be a mundane daily routine or habit you've built over the years. What forms of strength do you rely on to navigate your life? Are you steadfastly patient with a challenging loved one? Are you firm and powerful when confronting a toxic coworker? Are you honest when opening up to a therapist, even when it's truly terrifying? What does your strength look like? It's tempting to take it for granted, especially if it's a quiet form of strength that you've leaned on for most of your life. Now is your chance to name it and acknowledge it for the gift that it is.

When do I feel most vulnerable?

Let's be honest: vulnerability is petrifying. It means exposure of the most raw, jagged parts of yourself. For me, vulnerability means admitting that I'm overwhelmed with anxiety or sadness. It means crying so hard that I struggle to put sentences together. I used to be hideously embarrassed whenever someone saw this side of me—even my closest loved ones. Truth be told, I still fight with this instinctive feeling—as if my vulnerability is an imposition on the people who love me. When do you feel vulnerable like this? Are you acquainted enough with this part of yourself that it doesn't feel utterly alien to you? Who do you feel (at least somewhat) comfortable sharing this part of yourself with? If you aren't comfortable with it at all, can you put your finger on why? What are you afraid of?

 *Actions*

Create a Superhero

Effort level: Low to medium ●●○○○

For this activity, I ask you to access your playful, imaginative inner child. We are going to create an original superhero character. Use whatever medium you'd like—write a bullet point list of attributes, draw stick figures, create a vision board, or whatever feels most natural. The easiest place to start is with a superpower. What supernatural ability is the most intriguing to you? Or is your superhero an "ordinary" human who's buoyed by incredible gadgets? Don't limit yourself here—you're not writing a comic book, you're just creating a character for yourself. They can be as powerful as you'd like them to be. From there, you can fill out details about their persona. What's their name? What does their costume look like? What is their origin story—how did they come into their powers, if they have any?

What does this have to do with real-world strength, you might ask? Well, for starters, this superhero came directly from your mind. If you're capable of summoning this character into existence with just a thought, you can surely summon your own strength in difficult situations. As silly as it might seem, you can even use this character as a mental totem of sorts, imagining them at your back when you need to be brave. It's like a secret identity, but in reverse: instead of the superhero hiding their civilian identity for the safety of their loved ones, it is you who is hiding your inner superhero who helps you access your strength and fortitude.

Discuss One of Your Shortcomings With a Trusted Loved One

Effort level: Medium to high ●●●●○

It's hard to admit when we're struggling. It can be even harder to admit the flaws and failings in our personality. Beyond the vulnerability inherent in such an admission, there's something deeply humbling about saying aloud, "This is something I don't like about myself." But having an ally can be a huge advantage as you work to improve yourself and keep growing—and telling the truth about your inner demons can be step number one.

For one thing, your trusted loved ones likely know your flaws already—they're around you enough to notice patterns and behaviors that even you, a captive audience in your own skin, may not pick up on. And for another, your loved ones can help hold you accountable if you fall back into your old habits. So choose someone you trust, someone easy to talk to and who listens well. Sit them down and have an open conversation about a character flaw you'd like to work on. This is perhaps one of the strongest things you could do—not only asking for help but asking for help in the name of self-development and growth.

The Hermit

9 The Hermit is one of those cards that can prompt an immediate negative reaction when it pops up in a reading. The mental image we carry usually involves an antisocial, curmudgeonly elder who's retreated from society and lives alone in a hut on a mountaintop. But in the tarot, the Hermit stands for so much more than that. Whenever I pull the Hermit, the phrase that comes to mind is, "You are your own home." The Hermit's solitary nature is not born of a distaste for the company of others; rather, the Hermit's solitude provides a quiet place for introspection. They choose to spend time alone so that they can learn from themself, so that they can get more comfortable in their own skin.

When you pull the Hermit in a daily reading, it's often a reminder to take some alone time. They ask that you check in with yourself first and foremost, that you become fluent in your own internal language to better care for yourself. (As a side note, few cards remind me to keep up my meditation practice more insistently than the Hermit!) You have as much to learn about yourself as you have to learn about the rest of the world, and the Hermit's wisdom says that you are your own best teacher.

 ## Affirmations

I AM independent.
I CAN be my own best friend.
I WILL befriend solitude.

 *Reflections*

How comfortable am I by myself?

I know people who could spend a week in complete isolation and not only survive, but thrive. I'm the opposite—I can really only be alone for a few hours before I start to get antsy. Neither of these extremes are right or wrong, of course, but it's useful to know where you fall on the spectrum. I have a family member who learned to literally schedule time for herself to be alone regularly, and once she did so it always improved her mood. Could you benefit from a more consistent schedule for your solitary time? Or is it the opposite—are you alone more frequently than you'd like to be?

What does my inner voice sound like?

In one way or another, we are all engaged in an ongoing dialogue with our inner voice. Our minds are constantly accessing memories, sorting data, and planning ahead. When you're lost in thought, what exactly are you experiencing? For me, it's an ever-present narrative. My inner voice sounds like a whispered, older version of my own voice listing what I need to do next, how I should do it, and what I might be forgetting. Sometimes that voice is interrupted by music (I often joke that I have a DJ in my brain) or snatches of dialogues from movies or videos I've seen recently. My inner voice is all made up of sounds and words, but I know people whose minds find it easier to communicate in pictures instead. What does that internal conversation look like for you? Is it loud and bright, or is it quiet and gentle? Does it fluctuate and change shape, or is it consistent in how it speaks to you? Is it directive when it tells you what to do next, or is it softer in how it suggests your next move?

What does wisdom look like?

There is a difference between wisdom and intelligence; that's why they're separate stats in tabletop games. The Hermit is not merely a learned individual—they are someone who is willing to wait and watch before they act. So what does wisdom look like in your world? Is it deliberate and patient, or is it active and forceful? Does it require thoughtfulness, thoroughness, assertiveness? Who do you know that seems especially wise? Do you feel that you are a wise person? Why or why not?

 *Actions*

Visualize the Inside of Your Mind

Effort level: Low to medium ●●○○○

This isn't unlike the question from before about what your inner voice sounds like, but for this activity we're going a little deeper. It's one of my favorite things to ask people because I've never gotten the same answer twice. And as surprised as folks sometimes are when I ask them, their answer usually doesn't take long to formulate. Even if it's something they've never really thought about before, they can come up with their response without much consideration. It's always been there, in a way.

Although my mind deals more in words than in visuals, I've always pictured the inside of my mind as a cross between a museum and a library. I imagine a long hallway filled with doors. Each door leads to an exhibit or a wing dedicated to specific thoughts—memories, fears, dreams, and so on. And hanging along the hallway are beautiful paintings and photographs of my loved ones.

Begin exploring that internal space you inhabit and see what you find. Maybe it's an indoor space like mine, or maybe it's outdoors like a park or a forest. Maybe it's grandiose like a cathedral or a warehouse, or maybe it's humble like a cottage or a treehouse. Maybe it's too abstract to describe using man-made structures or ideas—an open, blank canvas upon which you scrawl your life story. The only thing that it unquestionably is? Unique. It is your space, the home that you reside in.

Now, there are certainly parts of this space that you don't like or don't identify with. There's that closet you stuff all the bad memories in, or the storm just off the coast that carries your depression or anxiety. We all have those places, and for some of us they can overshadow the calmer parts of our internal world completely. If that's the case for you, this exercise may be heavy or painful. I urge you to only undertake it if you feel safe and prepared to do so. It can be useful, of course, to draw up a map of that inner world when it seems hostile and unforgiving. But if it's too much right now, be respectful of yourself and wait for a better time. The Hermit is fundamentally patient; they will wait for you to be ready.

Spend a Day Alone

Effort level: Medium to high ●●●●○

Unless you live someplace very remote, you likely won't be able to spend a day without encountering any other human beings. That isn't exactly the goal here. If spending the day alone means going to your local library and reading a good book in solitude, that certainly fits the criteria even if you say good morning to the librarian. The heart of this activity isn't avoiding human contact altogether—it's taking a day to be your own companion, rather than accompanying a partner, friend, family member, coworker, etc. This can mean asking your spouse to take the kids on a day trip so you can play your favorite music at full blast as you tidy up around the house, or it can mean going on a hike through the woods with a picnic for one.

Whatever you choose to do with this time, it is your time. You get to be in the company of your own thoughts for a while. Even if journaling isn't typically your jam, I highly recommend keeping a notebook handy so you can jot things down if the mood strikes you. When I'm by myself, I find ideas come to me more suddenly and are more apt to get swept away quickly if I don't record them in the moment.

The Wheel of Fortune

10 The Wheel of Fortune is the spokesperson (spokesobject?) for change. It reminds us that nothing lasts forever; for good or for ill, this too shall pass. It carries with it that liminal, shifting energy of the changing of the seasons—the awareness that as one season is coming to an end, another is always just beginning. Like a pendulum swinging, the worst of winters will always be followed by spring, and the most plentiful of summers will fade into autumn. And so, it has always been, and so it will always be.

When you draw the Wheel of Fortune in a daily reading, you are receiving a gentle reminder of the ever-shifting nature of the world. Change is everywhere—not necessarily the abrupt, shattering change associated with the Tower, but a slower and steadier change that inhabits every second and every century at once. Know that if you are in a good place, you should not take it for granted. And at the same time, if you're going through a hard time, it will not last forever. This too shall pass.

 *Affirmations*

I AM adaptable.
I CAN weather life's ups and downs.
I WILL find steady ground to stand on.

 *Reflections*

What cycles do I tend to repeat?
Humans are pattern-seekers by nature. No matter how allergic you are to schedules and organization, there are habits and cycles of behavior that you inevitably fall into. Some of these cycles can be positive—naturally waking up around the same time every morning, for example, or reaching out to that same reliable friend when you need advice. But we all have bad habits and unhealthy patterns that we're guilty of, too. Can you iden-

tify a few of yours, positive and negative? How can you make sure you stick with your healthy routines going forward? And can you brainstorm ways you might interrupt and break the cycle of your more negative patterns?

How can I best navigate change?

My original draft of this question asked how you could embrace change. But I adjusted the wording on second thought because it felt too much like an empty platitude. I don't believe that all change should be welcomed with tireless joy and patience. Some change is just hard and painful, no two ways about it. I don't think we do ourselves any favors by trying to quash our natural reaction to it. But for good or ill, change is inevitable, and taking care of yourself in the face of change doesn't require a steadfast smile. Blowing off steam by writing angsty poetry or venting to a willing loved one is perfectly valid.

I do not believe that everything happens for a reason in a cosmic, predetermined sense. Rather, I believe that you can find wisdom in everything that happens to you. So no, you don't have to be thankful when change throws you for a loop. But how can you make sure you're learning from your experiences with change? And how can you tend to your wounds when that change is especially damaging?

What good moments can I hold onto during hard times?

At one of the most high-anxiety periods in my life, my (incredible) therapist gave me a challenge. She asked me to describe someplace from my past where I'd felt the most comfortable and calm. I wound up describing the library from my college campus where I'd spent long hours studying theater history with my best friends. She asked me to imagine myself in that library when my anxiety felt overwhelming. And you know what? Despite the fact that I struggle to hold onto mental images, that exercise still helps me during anxiety attacks. It doesn't instantaneously banish my panic, but it gives me something to hold onto. If you were to employ this exercise in your own daily life, what moments might you conjure up from your past? Is there a particular place that made you feel perfectly at ease? Do you have a friend whose company grounds you? Is there an especially happy or proud memory that might lighten your heart, just a little, when you're struggling with the present?

 *Actions*

Identify a Dialectic In Your Life

Effort level: Low to medium ●●○○○

In the fields of philosophy and debate, dialectical thinking refers to examining an issue from multiple points of view. But I always think of dialectics in the context of one of my favorite classes from college, in which our professor assigned us the task of identifying one of our personal dialectics. By this, he meant for us to name a pair of seemingly opposing forces that we felt pushed and pulled between in our daily lives. Creativity versus conformity. Confidence versus anxiety. Honesty versus diplomacy. Another way of looking at this exercise is identifying the positive and negative aspects of one of your personality traits. If you are passionate, for example, you're liable to have a hot temper. If you're stubborn, you're also persistent.

We live our lives between these forces. Sometimes we occupy one extreme or the other, but more often we're someplace in the middle. Putting your finger on words to describe these two poles in your personality can help you better navigate the space between them. Or if you tend to live at one end of the spectrum, identifying that tendency can help you chart a course to bring you closer to the center. What is your dialectic? What are the two poles that you are magnetically suspended between? Would you like to move closer to one of these poles? How might you go about doing so?

Start a "Good Things" Jar

Effort level: Medium to high ●●●●○

If you log onto Pinterest, you can find tons of picturesque suggestions and examples for this exercise. The gist of it is simple: whenever something good happens in your everyday life, write it on a slip of paper and drop it in a jar. The typical recommendation is that you keep this up for a year. Then at the year's end you can dump out the jar and look back at the good things that you may have forgotten. Personally, I wouldn't put such an artificial time limit on it. I would dig into that jar whenever you're feeling worn down and you need a smile. We are ALL apt to forget the little things, good and bad—but especially the good. Not only does it help you commit something to memory when you write it down but having those reminders within arms' reach when you need them can be a powerful tool in weathering your tougher times.

You can do a higher-tech but lower-effort version of this by simply keeping a running list in your phone. When a moment makes you smile or warms your heart, jot down a line or two in your list to help you remember. It doesn't have the visual or tactile appeal of a jar of little notes, but it has the advantage that your list of good things will always be in your pocket.

Justice

11   The one-word cards in the major arcana always seem to pack an extra punch for me. Justice is a punctuation mark halfway through the majors, returning us to the stark reality that this journey is not ours alone. In the Lovers, we nurtured our personal connections, but Justice teaches us to expand our awareness farther than that. Justice speaks of community, of the knowledge that our choices affect others and we must be wary of the consequences. Justice demands an eye for equality. To undertake this journey without considering its impact on others is to act selfishly.

When Justice appears in your daily reading, consider it a reminder of your responsibility to care for the world around you. This is the ultimate "check your privilege" card—its message is one of communal awareness and constant self-check-ins. Melissa Cynova points out in *Kitchen Table Tarot*, "Justice is about action. That's why social justice groups are always marching around and making things happen. They'd be called social idea groups otherwise," (85). There is work to be done, both within and without, to make this world a better place. Justice extends a hand to lead you deeper into this work.

Affirmations

I AM committed to my morals.
I CAN define right and wrong for myself.
I WILL keep an open mind.

 *Reflections*

How do I define equality?

First and foremost, Justice asks us to treat others how we wish to be treated, to always keep equality and fairness in the forefront of our minds. But what exactly does this look like for you? For some, prioritizing equality might manifest as marching in protests and calling lawmakers. For others, it might be quieter, like engaging family members in serious conversations about the state of the world. Or it might be subtler still, like writing books that give equal voice to characters of every background. While "equality" might seem like a straightforward definition to pin down, the ways that we nurture and protect it may differ wildly in practice. Where does the hard work of fighting for equality fit into your life? Is there more you could be doing? Are there blind spots or areas of privilege that you need to work harder to unlearn?

How do I decide what's right and wrong?

This question is not asking exactly what you define as right and wrong; rather, it asks what process you use to determine the morality of a choice or an action. Do you take some time alone with your thoughts? Do you journal or write about the matter at hand? Do you research every angle so you can feel better informed? Do you sit down with a trusted friend and talk it out? As with all these questions, there is no "correct" answer. But consciously mapping out your decision-making process will help you better approach ethical quandaries and difficult decisions.

What is one thing I consider an absolute truth?

An absolute does not change or shift, no matter what angle you approach it from. So while an impulsive initial answer may spring to your mind ("Killing is always wrong!"), consider whether you would truly believe that answer in every possible circumstance ("But what if it's self-defense?"). Is there a value, a belief, or a principle that you could hold onto no matter what? In both the best-case scenario and the worst? There may not be—at least, not something that you can adequately put into words right away. And that's perfectly valid. We live in a world of relatives, and what seems an unshakable truth in one context can easily fall apart in another. But even so, the exploration of your beliefs can be informative and meaningful.

 *Actions*

Put Yourself In Someone Else's Shoes

Effort level: Low to medium ●●○○○

One of my mother's self-titled "mom mantras" when we were growing up was that we should "put ourselves in someone else's shoes." By this, she meant that we should imagine a situation from another person's perspective. If we were frustrated with a classmate, she'd encourage us to see the tension from the classmate's point of view. When we were studying history, she'd draw our attention to how events impacted every side of the issue. She'd even ask us to see things from *her* point of view when we were upset with her for laying down a law: "Why am I making sure you get to bed on time? Is it because I'm just punishing you for fun?" she'd prompt. And, begrudgingly, we'd reply, "Because you love us and don't want us to be tired tomorrow."

Justice asks us to put ourselves in someone else's shoes willingly and consciously, like an eager student who is ready to learn. Seek out an article, an interview, or a memoir written by an author with a different background than yours. You can also sit down with a friend who is willing to share their experiences, but if you go this route, I would caution you to first check in with the person and make sure they're comfortable and willing to have this conversation with you. The last thing you want to do is put them on the spot (ESPECIALLY if they are routinely expected to represent an entire minority group).

Ideally, you should regularly undergo this exercise of imagining and taking into account someone else's point of view as you navigate your interactions with others. But doing it consciously like this is good practice, and it gives you a chance to expose yourself to viewpoints you might not encounter in your everyday life. There are, after all, a lot of pairs of shoes to try on.

Volunteer

Effort level: Medium to high ●●●●○

Time is perhaps the most precious gift we can give because there is no way to earn it back. That's one reason I love giving handmade gifts to my loved ones—it shows that I am willing to give my time for them. And of course, this doesn't make it meaningless when you donate hard-earned money to a charity you believe in! But for this exercise in particular, Justice asks that you dig in and get your hands dirty. It asks you to spend a few of your precious hours in the service of something larger than yourself.

So choose a cause that means something to you and start researching how to get involved. I've donated my time to my local library reshelving books and printing educational materials. I've tabled for my community theater at art fairs. I've petted and socialized with tiny kittens to prep them for adoption day. As usual, this activity can be as simple or as complicated as you'd like, whether it's a one-off event that you volunteer with or a year-long commitment to regular volunteering. There are causes in need of man hours everywhere—you just need to look for them.

The Hanged Man

12 Justice leaves us with a painful but necessary lesson: some things are truly beyond our control. We can learn, practice, and volunteer all we'd like, but at the end of the day we are each just one human. And so we meet the Hanged Man, who is calm and at peace despite their uncomfortable (and even potentially fatal) circumstances. The Hanged Man teaches us to sacrifice the illusion of control, to find our center in the eye of the storm.

When the Hanged Man appears in a daily draw, it's time for us to take a breath and loosen our grip on the reins. You may be in the middle of truly overwhelming circumstances, and it may feel like it's all you can do to survive. The Hanged Man replies that survival is plenty. Invite radical acceptance into your day and let go of the need to control the chaos around you. If all you can do is get out of bed in the morning, that is enough. If all you can do is keep breathing, that is *still* enough.

Affirmations

I AM patient.
I CAN relinquish the illusion of control.
I WILL take a step back.

Reflections

What am I trying to control that I can loosen my grip on?
It took me a long time to recognize that being a laid-back, go-with-the-flow type did not preclude me from trying (desperately, at times) to control situations well beyond my ability. For me, it manifests as the thought, "How can I fix this?" I've had to learn to follow up this thought by asking, "Is it my responsibility to fix?" The desire to control every factor of life is universal to some extent. Even if you are not a controlling personality, I'll bet there are at least one or two situations where you're trying to hold onto the

reins as tightly as possible. What do you think would happen if you took a step back and excused yourself from directing traffic? When you envision this, do you picture a realistic outcome, or a worst-case scenario? Be honest and fair with yourself. I have no doubt that you're a highly capable person, but no one person can single-handedly positively impact everything in their world. Try to really sit with that truth. It may feel deeply uncomfortable at first, but in the long term it will be a huge relief.

What does sacrifice mean to me?

We have a lot of stories about what sacrifice should look like, from Jesus on the cross to O. Henry's "Gift of the Magi." It can be challenging to detangle the idea of sacrifice from these grand gesture sorts of stories—and certainly these sorts of sacrifices are one version. But sacrifice can be much more quiet and seemingly small, too. It can be setting your alarm five minutes early to take out the trash so your partner doesn't have to. It can be skipping your usual Starbucks run so you can buy a birthday card for a friend. Put simply, sacrifice means giving something up for the sake of something outside yourself—a cause, a loved one's happiness, and so on. Where does sacrifice appear in your daily life? How do you sacrifice for others, and how do you see them sacrificing for you?

What in my everyday life makes me uncomfortable?

Nobody knows discomfort like the Hanged Man. Suspended, often hung upside-down by a single limb, they have to reckon with a great deal of discomfort. And it isn't just physical discomfort—it's also the discomfort of being helpless to change their circumstances. They are well and truly stuck. I'll bet there are many aspects of your life that make you feel stuck—a draining day job, untenable financial difficulties, or navigating a troubled relationship with a loved one, just to name a few possibilities. What are yours? Denial is certainly not the Hanged Man's game, so give a name to the things that make you uncomfortable. See if you can put your finger on where that discomfort is coming from, too. The what and the why of it may help you determine whether there's any action you could take to address the situation—and if it doesn't, it may help you foster the calm, detached endurance of the Hanged Man.

 *Actions*

Hang Upside-Down/Stretch

Effort level: Low to medium ●●○○○

One of the Hanged Man's gifts is flexibility of perspective. They hang suspended in an awkward position, yet they're able to accept and even embrace this view of the world. Even as blood rushes to their head, they look out with curiosity and calmness, open to the shift in perspective even though it isn't voluntary. What might this shift in perspective do for you? If you're able to, hang yourself upside-down off the edge of a bed or couch for a couple of moments. Let yourself see the space with new eyes, taking in the familiar shapes from a brand new angle. Don't take this to the point of serious discomfort, of course—just give yourself a quick chance to see your world inverted.

Another way to approach this exercise is to do a few of your favorite stretches. As you contort your body into unusual shapes and positions, take note of the views you end up accessing. Perhaps as you stand rooted to the ground, reaching one arm up and across, your head will tilt sideways and give you the image a spider might enjoy as it scurries up a wall. Or as you sit with legs outstretched in front of you, leaning forward will let you see what your room looks like from floor-level. Remain open to whatever sensory notes may enter your awareness. No preconceived notions, no expectations—just new perspectives.

Go People-Watching

Effort level: Medium to high ●●●●○

As a writer, people-watching is one of my favorite activities. I first started consciously practicing people-watching in middle school during theater and acting classes, and since then it's become such a natural instinct that I do it without thinking. I love taking note of what people are wearing, how they carry themselves, how they interact with each other. Of course, my impulse is to start speculating and filling in the blanks with my own stories—"Oh, they're in the middle of a big argument that they don't want to continue in public. That's why they're talking so quietly." The challenge in this activity is to observe without storytelling. Sit in a park or in the lobby of a library and take note of people as they come and go. Observe their style, their mannerisms, their methods of engaging the world around them. But resist the temptation to invent a narrative about them. The Hanged Man has let go of any need to directly engage their surroundings, and creating an internal narrative is a form of engagement. The Hanged Man is an observer. No more, no less.

 Death

*13* This is one of those cards that runs the risk of scaring the uninitiated to… well, to death. It taps into that deeply embedded cultural fear of fortune-tellers predicting the exact date and time that you'll perish. If you've studied tarot decks or writings, you'll know that Death is a much more abstract harbinger. It usually speaks not of literal death, but of the kind of transformation that necessitates leaving something behind. As we grow and change over the course of our lives, we inevitably leave parts of ourselves behind. It may be a painful goodbye, or it may happen so gradually that you don't notice the absence until much later.

When Death slips into your daily reading, know that this is not the end of the book; rather, it is the end of one chapter, and the beginning of another. We received similar wisdom in the Wheel of Fortune, but Death tells us that we need not begin this new chapter without mourning what we're leaving behind. I've seen a few decks that represent Death with a cicada, which I absolutely love. It is time to say your goodbyes to the shell that has housed you for so long. But it is also time to emerge with wings and face the world anew.

Affirmations

I AM a work in progress.
I CAN mourn who I was and honor who I am becoming.
I WILL transform when I need to.

Reflections

What parts of myself have I left behind?
I used to feel ashamed when I lost interest in something or decided to focus my efforts elsewhere. It felt like I was quitting, perhaps, or being fickle and flakey. But of course, this is a natural process. We all explore pastimes and pursuits that we ultimately let go of. Our goals and even our personalities shift over time. What has been left behind in

your journey? As you've learned more about yourself and grown into an ever-improving version of you, what has naturally sloughed away? Is there anything you've consciously worked to give up or set aside?

What is one transformation I'm undergoing right now?

Maybe it's deeply intentional—working to break a bad habit or interrupt an unhealthy thought process, going to a therapist for the first time, etc. Or perhaps it's more subtle and unconscious—are you becoming a more patient person as you navigate a challenging relationship? Is your assertive side becoming stronger as your work pushes you to speak up? Consider what's changed for you in the last few months, whether it's a huge life-altering change or a tiny one. Is this a positive adjustment, in your opinion? If not, how might you course-correct to make it more of a positive progression?

How do I hope to grow? What will it cost?

When you shade your eyes with one hand and peer into the future like an intrepid explorer, who do you see standing at the helm of your life? How is that person different from you right now? As you work to become more like that person, what will the cost be? Every action has its equal opposite reaction, after all. In order to reach that future you, what are you willing to let go of? And how can you honor the growing pains that come with any transformation?

 *Actions*

Plant Visualization

Effort level: Low to medium ⬤⬤◯◯◯

Find someplace quiet and make yourself comfortable. Take a few deep breaths before closing your eyes. Imagine yourself in a lush, green space of some sort—a garden, a forest, an orchard, etc. Find an area among the foliage with some open space, and visualize yourself tenderly planting a seed. Now imagine the seasons shifting around you like a time-lapse video. As time passes, watch your seed begin to take root and poke its sleepy head out of the soil. What does it look like as it sprouts? Is it a young tree that will shoot up and eventually tower over you and protect you in its shade? Is it a stout berry bush that you'll be able to draw sustenance from when you need it? Is it a gloriously colorful collection of flowers that can refresh your spirit with its beauty?

Whatever your seed grows into, really watch it as the seasons turn. How does it change as the autumn chill touches its leaves? Is it barren and skeletal in the winter months, or does it remain full and evergreen? Do flowers, leaves, fruits, or branches fall away as it ages? What does it look like in the prime of spring and summer?

As a plant grows, it undergoes radical transformations, and certainly it leaves things behind in the process. If we could speak the language of flora, perhaps trees would speak wistfully of the time they spent safely cocooned in their seeds. Perhaps flower bushes could recall each individual bloom they lost over the years. But they are still fundamentally the same flower, tree, plant, etc., even as they have grown and changed. The transformations you've undergone may have shifted your perspective or personality, but they have not redefined your underlying soul. Return to that certainty when you feel untethered. You are growing, and you are still you.

Write to Your Inner Child

Effort level: Medium to High ●●●●○

As a child, did you view growing up with fear, eagerness, or some combination of the two? I'd imagine most of us longed for the independence and autonomy of adulthood, but also dreaded the seeming inevitability of drab, stressful adulthood we saw in movies and books. I remember my younger brother sobbing at the end of *Peter Pan* because the children grew up. What would you tell your younger self if you could speak to them? Sit down with pen and paper and address a letter to yourself in the past. How can you comfort and reassure your inner child's worries about the perils of growing up? What might you share with your younger self to help them look forward to your present-day life? Are there any major roadblocks or opportunities you'd like to warn the younger version of yourself about? Be gentle, but honest. Remember that children are stronger and smarter than we give them credit for.

Once you feel that the letter is complete, sign it off and put it someplace safe. You might wish to revisit it at times when you feel especially overwhelmed. In writing to your younger self, you are also writing to that inner voice that fears and craves change at the same time.

Temperance

14 Temperance is, quite simply, balance. It is not only learning to manage opposing forces, but learning to weave them together. It is occupying the space between water and fire and alchemizing them into something new and powerful. It is also plumbing the depths of your own psyche, confronting the dark corners of your mind, and inviting them into the light with you. In some ways this card is a return to the Hanged Man mentality, but while the Hanged Man tells us to accept what we cannot control, Temperance tells us to mindfully engage with what we *can* control.

When you meet Temperance in a daily reading, now is the time to consciously seek balance in your life. Approach your day with a holistic view and stay centered. You are up to the challenge of inhabiting the middle space between the ups and downs. It is not always easy, but that is the wisdom Temperance offers: the shades of gray between black and white are the hues you should seek to paint with.

Affirmations

I AM balanced.
I CAN alchemize all the pieces of myself.
I WILL balance my shadow self with my waking self.

Reflections

How can I seek balance today?

The word balance often makes me think of a monk deep in meditation. But this may seem too lofty a goal when we're facing the rough edges of everyday life. Instead, approach this question by calling to mind times when you feel off-balance in your everyday life. How might you reorient yourself during these moments? For me, it often amounts to something as simple as going for a quick walk around my office to burn off a bit of anxious energy. It's almost like planning your homeostasis—when life pulls you off-kilter, how will you pull back in the opposite direction to find center again? How will you know what that centered, balanced place feels like when you reach it?

What does my shadow self look like?

Your dark side. Your flaws, fractures, and feelings that you try not to acknowledge. These are the domain of your shadow self. They are not your evil twin; rather, they are the dust bunnies and castoffs you've swept into the corners of your mind. Temperance asks you to extend a hand to your shadow self. But first you must identify them. What do they look like? What parts of you do they represent and control? How do you feel about their company? Is there something about them that you're afraid of? Disgusted by? Ashamed of? Where does that reaction stem from?

What is one of my strongest personality traits, and how can I better temper it?

I'm a big believer in every trait having a positive and a negative side. If you are passionate, you are more likely to have a fiery temper. If you are harsh, you're also direct and assertive. As such, every trait could stand a measure of Temperance. Think of one of your most dominant and evident traits. The goal isn't to dull that piece of you; rather, the goal is to learn and incorporate lessons from the opposite personality type. Suppose you are an outgoing and friendly individual. What could you learn from someone introverted and shy? And how could you carry that wisdom back into your life?

 *Actions*

Meditation Tea

Effort level: Low to medium ●●○○○

Many depictions of Temperance include the element of water. It's a good calling card for Temperance—as tempestuous as water can become, it can also be still and calm. And there's something to be said for the calming effect of water's sounds, from gentle raindrops to the ebb and flow of waves on the beach. In my opinion, the process of making tea is like a microcosm of this water magic, and this exercise taps into that process to help you re-center and find your Temperance.

Make sure you're unlikely to be disturbed as you prepare your brew. The type of tea doesn't matter (though I suggest avoiding highly-caffeinated varieties), nor does the method you use to heat your water. But whether you're employing a stovetop kettle or a countertop water heater, pay close attention to the sights and sounds of the tea-making process. Soak in the melody of the water filling up your kettle and the hiss of steam as it heats up. Focus on your breathing as you wait for your tea to steep. Once everything is prepared, sit comfortably with your cup and really savor the warmth, scent, and taste as you drink. Think of this as a form of focused meditation, but rather than counting your breaths or scanning through your body, you're tuning into an everyday activity and the simplicity of enjoying a warm drink. Nothing better encapsulates Temperance than taking a few moments out of your day to relish the product of a synthesis between water and fire.

Elemental Writing

Effort level: Medium to high ●●●●○

I love the symbolism in the classic elements of water, earth, fire, and air. It's such a simple way of classifying the world around us, yet it is profoundly layered with meaning we've assigned to it. Is there a particular element you identify strongly with? Passionate fire, steadfast earth, rejuvenating water, or flexible air? If you're unsure, take a few minutes to research the four elements and their associated meanings and personality traits. Then grab something to write with and get comfy.

Write first about your chosen element. What is it about that element that you identify with? How do you see that element manifest in your personality? What strengths does it lend you? What drawbacks or flaws do you see in this element—and in yourself? This is an opportunity to write as simply or as ornately as you feel compelled to. Write a bullet-pointed list or write a flowery narrative. Then consider whatever element is opposite the one you just wrote about. (Fire and water are opposites, and earth and air are opposites.) Does this element feel like your opposite? How? What qualities of this element can you nevertheless find in yourself? What wisdom could you gather from this element?

Next examine the two elements you've missed and repeat the above process. Which of the pair do you identify with more strongly? Why? In what ways do you see that element in yourself? How can you learn from its opposing element?

As I'm sure you've gathered by now, everyone has all four elements in some combination within—and like any method of examining the squishy human personality, it is a limited system. The power lies in the reflective process as you probe your psyche and make your own connections to each element.

The Devil

15   This is the other card that causes a visceral negative reaction when it's drawn by (or for) someone unfamiliar with tarot. And certainly, this is one of the more challenging cards to face. But the tarot's Devil does not signify what you might traditionally associate with them—hellfire, eternal damnation, and so on. The Devil is the spokesperson for your flaws, vices, and temptations. They discourage you from growing and changing. They would prefer you to remain static, stagnating in old toxic patterns. They are not your adversary but rather a side of your own personality that must be looked after and negotiated with.

When you draw the Devil in a daily reading, it is both a warning and an invitation. The warning is to pay attention to your unhealthy habits and toxic modes of thinking. You may be falling back on behaviors that are holding you down and actively damaging you or your loved ones. The invitation is to spend some quality time with your shadow self. Figure out what they need, why they're tugging at you insistently right now. There are almost certainly underlying reasons why you're facing the Devil in your everyday behaviors and actions. This is your opportunity to search for those reasons.

 Affirmations

I AM imperfect.
I CAN confront my weaknesses.
I WILL forgive myself when I make a mistake.

 *Reflections*

What is one of my worst vices?

This is not a comfortable question to ask yourself, but the Devil is not a comfortable companion. You undoubtedly know what toxic character traits you carry, or what unhealthy temptations you're vulnerable to. At the same time, do not use this question as an opportunity to beat yourself up unmercifully. Do your best to choose one of your vices and describe it through a dispassionate lens. Be honest, but fair. Wallowing in guilt and self-deprecation does not address the vice any more than ignoring it altogether does. If it helps, imagine yourself as a doctor diagnosing yourself. Your diagnosis needs to be comprehensive, but it does not need to dwell on every gory detail.

What is my greatest fear?

The Devil has a gift for digging all the monsters out from beneath your bed and encouraging you to hide from them. But this is much less potent when you have already peeked under and introduced yourself to those monsters. So who's under there? Can you speak their name and describe what about them is so terrifying to you? The goal is not to stop fearing them, but simply to look them in the face and be honest about what you see. Fear is a method of protecting yourself and is not inherently damaging but looking that fear in the eye prevents it from hiding in your bones and dissuading you from developing courage.

How can I strengthen my willpower?

I cannot take credit for this mental image, but I truly love thinking of willpower as a muscle. The more you train it, the stronger it becomes. And in turn, the more challenges you allow to fall by the wayside unmet, the more your willpower languishes. Willpower is an indispensable weapon in your quest to grow into a better you. How can you ensure that your willpower is being strengthened? What challenges turn up in your daily life that you can use to flex that willpower muscle?

 *Actions*

Meet Your Shadow

Effect level: Low to medium ●●○○○

With Temperance, we began the work of acquainting ourselves with our shadow selves. This exercise goes one step farther. You are going to actively create a character to represent that self. You may use whatever medium you wish—draw them, describe them with words, make a collage, even create a playlist to encapsulate their flavor. But whatever medium you employ, really take your time imagining that shadowy part of you. What shape do they take? What does their voice sound like when they speak to you? What colors do you associate with them? What symbols? If they live someplace in your body, where do they reside? How do you physically feel their presence?

A reminder here that your shadow self is not your enemy, even if they carry pieces of you that are painful, uncomfortable, and difficult. One of my favorite tarot authors, Cedar McCloud, says in their *Numinous Tarot Guidebook*, "Your Shadow needs comfort and care—can you give that to it? In other words, to yourself?" (55). So bring a measure of compassion with you as you undertake this exercise. Your shadow self is just that: the shadow of you, yourself.

Make and Enact a Plan to Break a Bad Habit

Effort level: Medium to high ●●●●○

Bad habits can fulfill any number of mental and emotional needs. My hands get restless when I'm anxious, which often leads to me picking at my fingernails, lips, and chin to occupy myself. That may seem very innocuous, but I'm one infected scab away from more serious consequences. Some bad habits are more verbal—my dad had a tendency to crack jokes when he wanted to diffuse tension, for instance, which could come across as an attempt to deflect blame or accountability.

What's one bad habit you'd like to start breaking? Write it down, and then begin brainstorming ways you could address the habit when you catch yourself falling back on it. In my skin-picking example, I might list things like keeping a fidget toy on hand to fiddle with when I'm restless or putting on lip balm and lotion. In my dad's case, it could be as simple as counting to ten to read the room before cracking a joke.

This is all the easy part, of course. The hard part is actually putting this plan into action. Inevitably you'll catch yourself falling back into the bad habit. When this happens, don't beat yourself up. Take note, take a breath, and employ one of the tactics you brainstormed. If it keeps up, you may need to revisit your plan and troubleshoot, maybe even come up with some different tactics. Be patient and persistent. Breaking a bad habit requires a great deal of practice, time, and work.

The Tower

16 The Tower yanks the rug out from under us and sends us tumbling into chaos and upheaval. Everything we took for granted may be abruptly unavailable. Everything we built our foundation on has dissolved. The Tower signals the sort of sudden life-changing events that leave us disoriented and devastated, the sorts of events that we cannot possibly prepare for because they come careening out of left field. While the uninitiated might be concerned at the appearance of Death or the Devil, those of us familiar with tarot are considerably more worried when they turn up the Tower.

This isn't to say that you should be consumed with anxiety if you draw the Tower in a daily reading. You may be in the middle of an upheaval, or there may be one on the horizon. But as my best friend always says, if the Tower is crumbling, it may mean the structure was decaying and needed to come down anyway. The best thing you can do with the Tower's message is take care of yourself. Ensure that you have tools on hand to weather the storm. You are by nature a survivor, but make sure you're listening to yourself and taking steps to replenish yourself as needed.

Affirmations

I AM resilient.
I CAN survive upheavals.
I WILL pick myself up and dust myself off.

Reflections

What upheavals have I experienced?
An upheaval is not inherently negative—it can be anything that profoundly disrupts your daily life. A move, a huge job change (whether a promotion or a layoff), a death or a birth

in the family—all of these are significant upheavals that could bring on a myriad of emotions. Think back over your life and consider what upheavals you've been through. How recently have you weathered sudden changes like this? Are you currently experiencing the fallout or ripple effect from any of these changes? Are there any significant changes on the horizon that you're aware of? What do you imagine their effects will be?

How would I take care of myself if a catastrophe struck?

In the first few weeks after my dad died, I developed a daily ritual out of necessity. Every morning, I would drive to the nearest Starbucks and spend a few minutes drinking coffee in solitude, away from the house where we were all mourning. Being with my family was incredibly important to my healing process, but so were these little snatches of privacy when I could be alone with my thoughts. How would you treat yourself with compassion and patience during difficult times? What sorts of little self-care tools and tactics might you rely on during the aftermath of a crisis? What might grant you a sense of normalcy amid the chaos, however temporary? And how could you ensure that you prioritized these things? Of course, the things that seem comforting right now from stable ground may be impossible or unhelpful when you're in the middle of chaos. But it's easy to overlook self-care when huge, life-altering events come up, so brainstorming a little ahead of time can't hurt.

When have I experienced a necessary upheaval?

I bet most of us can think back to a romantic breakup that felt, at the time, like the end of the world. And I bet that the passage of time has caused most of us to see that our ex was absolutely not the right person for us. There are all kinds of life events like this that seem catastrophic in the moment but inevitable in hindsight. Now, this isn't to downplay or dismiss the very real anguish that we feel in the moment itself. But it can be reassuring to know that things may look different once we're out of that first period of raw, unadulterated pain. What examples of necessary upheavals come to mind from your life? How did you feel at the time? Compare that to how you feel now. What might you tell your past self, if you had the opportunity, about how differently you view that experience now?

 *Actions*

Worst-Case/Best-Case Scenarios

Effort level: Low to medium ●●○○○

Humans have a tendency to catastrophize—in other words, to envision the most awful, dreadful outcomes of the situations we find ourselves in. It's a survival technique, we tell ourselves—if we're mentally prepared for the worst-case scenario, it can't hurt us as badly. (That's never worked for me, incidentally. In the instances when the worst-case scenario *did* come to pass, I was just as shellshocked as if I'd gone in completely unprepared. But that sure hasn't stopped me.) Take a look at a current situation in your life that has you worried. For a moment, let's go ahead and indulge that inner catastrophizer. What's the worst-case scenario—the most absolutely unbearable outcome you can envision? If you're so inclined, write it down. Be as horrifically detailed as you'd like. Once you've played everything out, push your mind in the opposite direction. What's the absolute best-case scenario? If all the stars aligned and everything went according to plan, how would things unfold for you? Make sure to be as detailed here as you were with the worst-case scenario. Again, if the mood strikes you, write it down.

Now compare your two scenarios. Odds are that neither will come to pass in real life—reality is too messy and complicated for that. The truth will probably be somewhere between the worst- and best- case scenarios. But spend a little time and consider the two anyway. Is there any reason one is more likely than the other? What makes you instinctively give more weight to the worst-case scenario?

Make a Bad Day Care Package

Effort level: Medium to high ●●●●○

What are some of your foolproof methods of cheering yourself up or relaxing? These are the sorts of activities that often go out the window in the face of a major upheaval. When you're truly overwhelmed, it's difficult to think of anything that might help. Why not do the legwork ahead of time? This can be a literal box if you so choose, filled with bubble bath and favorite books and movies and so on. Or it can be a list in your phone of the activities and possessions that bring you solace. However you build your toolkit,

I recommend including a variety of things and activities just in case one doesn't work out (it might be impossible to go for a run if you're recovering from an injury, for instance). Think of this like creating a weather shelter with flashlights, bottled water, and non-perishable foodstuff—but the weather, in this case, is emotional turbulence. What will you pack in your survival kit for that sort of storm? How will you remind yourself to pull out this survival kit in the middle of a crisis?

The Star

17 The Star is the light at the end of the proverbial tunnel. That glimmer of possibility when all seems lost. That feeling you cling to recklessly and desperately in the darkest of circumstances. The Star, in other words, is hope. It is that snatch of music that makes you catch your breath and listen, even if you've been shrouded in silence. It's the northern lights guiding you to a better, brighter, and more colorful future. The Star also stands for beauty, because beauty is something we can hold onto when everything seems lost. Beauty can remind us that even when things are at their bleakest, flowers grow and constellations twinkle.

When you draw the Star in a daily reading, take comfort and take notice. You may be at a moment in your life that feels overwhelming, but the Star urges you to hold on for the good things to come. Think of yourself as a child looking up at the night sky and wishing with all your might. There is a beacon of light reaching its hand out to you. Open your mind to accept it and follow its guidance to a brighter day.

 ## Affirmations

I AM full of hope.
I CAN practice mindful optimism.
I WILL find things to hope for.

 ## Reflections

What makes me feel hopeful?
When you're feeling particularly run down and stressed, what gets you hoping again? Note that this is not a question of what distracts you, what makes you laugh, etc. That's good information to consider, too, but it has more to do with how you endure the darkness. This is a question of what reminds you of the light. What convinces you that a

better future is worth fighting for? What bolsters you to face an uncertain tomorrow? When you're in despair, what lifts your heart even the tiniest bit?

What in the future am I excited about?

Having things to look forward to is so important. It anchors something positive in the murky unknown sea of tomorrow and next week and next year. Personally, I find it more effective if I have specific dates nailed down that I can count down to ("Only eight days until I visit my family!") but having more abstract future events can be helpful, too ("Sometime in the spring I'll be getting a promotion!"). What do you have to look forward to? Roughly when will each of these events occur? Do you have exciting events coming up soon? Or are all of your events far away and unscheduled? If nothing comes to mind, it may be a good time to visit the actions below!

How can I bring beauty into my everyday life?

Have you ever suddenly become aware of something truly beautiful in your daily commute—a sunrise, a tangle of flowers, a group of kids chasing each other around a playground? Can you remember a moment when the mundane was transformed by a moment of brilliance? How can you invite more of those moments into your day-to-day? Maybe it's as simple as putting some new artwork around your desk at work, or listening to a favorite song as you get ready for bed at night. Even an aesthetically pleasing new background for your phone can be enough to make you smile. What small tidbits of beauty can you weave into the hours that make up your daily life?

 *Actions*

Find Some Good News

Effort level: Low to medium ●●○○○

It's so easy to hop onto the internet and find bad news. And to a certain extent, that's a powerful feature—the internet gives us the ability to share our suffering, to expose injustice, and to connect to others who are experiencing similar difficulties. But it can also be incredibly overwhelming, especially if you're already in a diminished emotional space. So instead, use the internet to consciously seek out some good news. What's going on in the world that's worth celebrating? There are specific pages and sites curated with positive stories and uplifting news articles—those could be a great and quick starting place. (In fact, if you're the type to read the news every morning, I might even recommend bookmarking one of these pages and making them a part of your morning routine.) You can create a dedicated folder for stories and videos that lift your spirits and restore your faith in humanity. Having a ready-made cache of good news can make a big difference when facing some particularly bad news.

Alternatively, look to your loved ones to find evidence of good things happening. Do you have a friend who's expecting a new baby? Visit their social media page and scroll through their ultrasound photos. Did your sibling recently start a dream job? Give them a call and invite them to tell you how it's been going. In today's hyper-connected world, it seems unlikely that you don't know anyone who's experiencing some good things. Make the effort to seek them out and let their joy fill your heart, too.

Plan Something to Look Forward To

Effort level: Medium to high ●●●●○

In the reflections above, we touched on the importance of having things to look forward to. But what if you don't have much coming up in the near future? This is a *great* time to plan something yourself. Especially if you have things scheduled that you're actively dreading, this can help offset that entirely negative vision of the future. You don't have to plan anything huge—it could be as simple as planning to get coffee and catch up with a friend you haven't seen in a while. Or if you really want to go for it, you could plan something huge and elaborate like a trip. But whatever you choose, pick a specific date for it and put it on your calendar. That way you have a concrete something in the future that feels exciting and hopeful, something that will make looking ahead more of a positive undertaking. Ideally, you'll always have a few events or activities planned ahead. And really do be careful to follow through unless something major prevents it! If you're looking forward to getting lunch at your favorite restaurant but talk yourself out of it on the day of, it can actively discourage you from planning anything else fun like this in the future. Hold yourself accountable for this moment of joy just as much as you'd hold yourself accountable for a more neutral responsibility such as paying your bills.

The Moon

18 The Moon can illuminate that which otherwise goes unseen. It introduces us to a terrifying, exhilarating new world that we can explore. This is not a world of shadows, which may be obscured but remains familiar enough to our eyes. This is an utterly new world that comes to life in the dark of night. We may be tempted to stay safely indoors, but the Moon draws out our curiosity, our thirst for the unknown. We may uncover secrets and encounter illusion, but we are also caught up in the thrill of mystery.

When the Moon rises over our daily drawing, it's time for some serious self-reflection and risk-taking. There are whole realms that remain unexplored. The Moon once again invokes the intuition we sparked with the High Priestess, reminding us that we can trust that little voice in our ear, even in brand new circumstances. Your intuition lights your way as the Moon lights the unknown. You have all the tools you need to venture into the darkness and emerge with new insight.

 ## Affirmations

I AM reflective.
I CAN embrace the unknown.
I WILL befriend the dark.

 ## Reflections

What feels magical in my life?
The Moon invites peculiar happenings and inexplicable occurrences in our lives. When something happens that feels impossible, when circumstances align in an unlikely way, that is the Moon working its magic. Has anything like this happened to you recently, for good or ill? Whether it's as small as making every green light on your commute home from work or as large as several life-altering events happening all at once and seem-

ingly out of nowhere, what has made you stop and take notice of its unlikelihood? Is it a welcome or unwelcome sort of magic? What secrets might the Moon be revealing to you amid the coincidences?

How can I acquaint myself with the unknown?

Humans love to understand things, especially things that have an effect on our lives. Which is beautiful, in its own way. But we will never explain away that uncertainty about what comes next. The unknown is omnipresent in everything we do and everything we are. How can you become more comfortable with what's unknown in your life? When we met the Hanged Man, we accepted that we cannot control everything. The Moon confronts us with the fact that we cannot *know* everything. How does that awareness strike you? Is it a relief, or does the notion feel too daunting? What might help it feel less overwhelming?

What does nighttime look like for me?

What time do you typically get to bed? What do you do to prepare? Do you have favorite sleepwear? Do you read or listen to music to help you unwind? If you can't sleep, what do you do? Read? Play on your phone? Get up and have some tea or a snack? What does your living space look like at night? If you were to go outside during these midnight hours, what do you think you might see? Do you enjoy the dark and quiet of nighttime, or no? Why or why not?

 ❗ *Actions*

Connect With the Moon

Effort level: Low to medium ●●○○○

I find that paying attention to the cycles of the moon is one of the simplest but most effective methods of tuning into nature. There's a wide variety of ways you can tune into the moon's energies, from rituals to meditations and everything in between. Here I will offer two specific options, but of course feel free to do whatever else you feel called to.

The first is quite simple: go outdoors when the moon is out and visible. Find some-place quiet and comfortable to sit, and just spend some time soaking in the light. If you're so inclined, this is a great opportunity to do some meditation or journaling, or even just some deep thinking. Allow whatever comes up to flow through you. You may be surprised by the unilluminated thoughts that the moon brings to light.

For a slightly more involved method of connecting with the moon, consider doing a tarot reading to align with the next new or full moon. There are plenty of options online, or you can even design your own if you're feeling inspired. I love doing readings for the moon cycles to check in with my intuition. The moon will shine wherever your attention (our courage) is lacking, but you must open your eyes to its uncanny light first.

Step Outside of Your Comfort Zone

Effort level: Medium to high ●●●●○

I bet that, without too much thought, you can come up with a subject or activity that feels completely alien to you. Possibly more than one. What is something you can try that is 100 percent outside of your wheelhouse? Be sure to choose something attainable—vis-iting a country whose language you don't speak would certainly satisfy the criteria of being outside your comfort zone, but unless you have a significant disposable income, it's probably not feasible right away. Instead, what about going to a restaurant that serves a cuisine you haven't tried? Or going to a sporting event that you might otherwise turn up your nose at? Even joining an online book club that reads a genre you're unfamiliar with?

Make sure that you remain open and receptive throughout this process. The unknown often has much to teach you, but you have to listen to learn. As an example, I took a class in college that required me to attend several Indy car races. I was initially very unenthused—I'm not much of a sports fan in general, and loud, smelly car races sounded even less appealing. But I did my best to remain open, and you know some-thing? I wound up genuinely enjoying myself. It would have been easy to coast through the class and zone out during the races, but that is not the Moon's way. The Moon urges you to not only brave the unknown, but to really, truly look when we're there. When we carry this openheartedness into new situations, the Moon greets us with an outpouring of insight.

The Sun

19 The Sun's warmth soaks into our bones after a cold night and fills our hearts with confidence and optimism. It is far more than the guiding glimmer of hope that the Star gave us—it is full illumination, the reassuring brightness of broad daylight. Without the Sun's presence we would be in the dark, of course, but we would also freeze to death. The light of knowing and the warmth of being go hand-in-hand, and the Sun offers both. With this assurance we can step into the world with a heart full of gratitude, knowing that abundance awaits us.

When you draw this card, you have cause to be confident and proud of how you've grown. You may need to carry some of that confidence into your daily life. Embrace any little joys or triumphs that arise throughout the day. Take a moment to offer thanks for the little things that bring you joy, and take note of the areas in your life that feel abundant. The Sun's light radiates through you and everything you do—let it fill you up even when you're engaged in something mundane.

 ## Affirmations

I AM confident.
I CAN believe in myself.
I WILL bask in my accomplishments.

 ## Reflections

What does joy feel like?

Think of a time in your past when you've experienced pure, glorious joy. What caused it? What did it feel like physically—was there a specific part of your body where you felt that joy the most strongly? How did it shape your thoughts and emotions in that moment? How do you know when you are joyful? How might the people around you describe you when you're feeling joyful? Is there something impacting or blocking your ability to feel that deep, meaningful joy right now? Are you consciously or unconsciously resisting joy when it appears in your life? How might you address these blocks or resistances?

How can I nurture my confidence?

Like willpower, confidence is often a matter of practice. The more often you utilize it, the stronger the muscle becomes. In the case of confidence, it's sometimes a question of "fake it till you make it." Or it's a question of reminding yourself of past successes before tackling an activity that requires self-confidence. How might you flex that confidence muscle? What changes could you make or what habits could you develop and improve? What elements of your life actively kneecap your confidence and make you feel bad about yourself? How might you adjust your relationship to these elements, or reduce them altogether?

Do I consider myself an optimist?

There is no right or wrong answer to this question—like all these questions, it's simply intended to get you thinking and reflecting. If you do identify as an optimist, what are some ways that manifests or comes through in your daily life? If you are not a self-proclaimed optimist, how would you identify yourself? Are you comfortable with your identification, or would you like to change anything about it? We see stereotypes at both ends of the spectrum in movies and books—the ignorant optimist who closes their eyes to all the world's wrongs, and the cynical pessimist who refuses to crack a smile. Have these stereotypes affected how people see you in any way?

 Actions

---

Bring in Fresh Flowers

Effort level: Low to medium

There's something about a vase of colorful fresh flowers that brings so much joy and warmth into the room. Whether it's a handful of scruffy daffodils your child picked for you or a meticulously arranged bouquet from a florist, flowers are like inviting a tiny piece of sunshine into your house and home. Do you have a favorite flower? If so, consider taking the time to find or buy this specific flower. That brings an extra level of care and appreciation into your display of fresh flowers. But if you don't have a favorite flower, just browse. Either go outdoors and search for something beautiful to pick and bring home, or peruse the floral section at a store, or even visit a standalone florist shop.

Whatever you choose, put your vase of flowers someplace where you'll see it frequently. Make it a point to actively notice your flowers every day. Notice how the colors contrast with everything around them, how they brighten up the room, how their fragrance fills your nostrils if you take the time to sniff them. If you're so inclined, take some time to create something in honor of your flowers—do a quick sketch, write something in your journal, even just snap a picture on your phone. Really *enjoy* the experience of having fresh flowers at home. As bright and powerful as the Sun is, it governs these seemingly small moments of joy, too.

Do Something that Makes You Happy Just for Fun

Effort level: Medium to high ⬤⬤⬤⬤◯

When was the last time you consciously decided to spend time doing something just for the genuine fun of it? I'm not talking about automatically turning on Netflix after work to unwind—I mean thinking to yourself, "It's been a while since I watched my favorite Disney movie. I'm going to sit down and watch it." Other activities in this book ask you to really plan out a leisure activity like this. In this case, though, spontaneity is encouraged. What would bring you a few minutes of fun and happiness today? Maybe there's a craft or hobby you've struggled to keep up with, or an album you'd like to listen to and relish in, a local store you'd like to browse through. Listen to what your inner voice is asking for.

Note that your typical self-care activities may not be what your subconscious craves in the moment, and I encourage you to follow your in-the-moment impulse. Maybe soaking in the bath with a glass of wine is a habitual source of joy for you, but in this particular moment you decide you'd be happier taking a walk in the park. The bottom line is that you are taking time to listen to your inner voice and do something fun for you and you alone. By doing so, you are inviting the sunlight into your day with intention.

Judgment

2 0 As we near the end of the major arcana, we realize how far our journey has taken us and how much we've learned. Perhaps we couldn't truly appreciate the growth we achieved when we were in the thick of it, but now we become starkly aware of how different we've become. I've seen multiple decks rename this card "The Awakening," which I almost prefer to Judgment. Like coming out of a long tunnel and blinking in the sunlight, we are approaching the end of this chapter as a wiser and better version of ourselves.

When you pull Judgment as your daily card, you are nearing the end of a process that has brought you profound clarity and new awareness. Think of this as a eureka moment of sorts—before you close the book on this stage of your journey, you are able to look back on the ways you've transformed since you leapt off the cliff as the Fool. It may be that you have one final decision to face, one last choice to determine what comes next. You can synthesize the strongest emotions you've felt and the deepest knowledge you've gathered to face the end of the story with equal parts intuition and intellect. In other words, you are Awakening.

 ## Affirmations

I AM perceptive.
I CAN see clearly.
I WILL weigh every aspect of my situation fairly.

 ## Reflections

What does forgiveness mean to me?
As you look back on your experiences, it may be tempting to judge yourself harshly for missteps you've made. But Judgment asks you to see not only the future with fairness, but also the past—even your past. What would it mean to forgive yourself for these mis-

takes? What does forgiveness look like? Are you more apt to forgive others than yourself, or is the opposite true? How might you cultivate forgiveness as you move forward? Note that forgiveness does not mean condoning something unacceptable. You can forgive someone for a toxic behavior while still holding them accountable. The same goes for yourself. Maybe there's something you did in the past that you're ashamed of now. You can commit to doing better in the present while still forgiving yourself in the past. (For more on that, visit the "Absolve yourself of a mistake" activity below.)

What in my past has changed me?
The obvious answer to this question is, well, everything. Everything changes us, from the most earth-shattering events to the tiniest and most untraceable decisions we make every day. Yet we don't give this question much real thought, and if we do, we usually focus on the objective and tangible outcomes ("Because I went to such-and-such college, I met this professor who helped me land my first job"). Take a few minutes and consider the more abstract emotional and mental changes that you've undergone. How exactly did that first job shape your preferences about working alone vs. working as part of a collaborative team? How did that professor change your understanding of your favorite subject? How did your college's population impact the friends you make and keep?

How has my mind opened recently?
One of the hardest and most powerful things we can do as human beings is to realize that our understanding of something was limited or just flat-out wrong. Being able to admit that we were holding onto outdated knowledge or opinions is honestly terrifying, even if we're only admitting it to ourselves. It feels profoundly vulnerable, and the instinct is to get defensive about what we once thought. How have you fought that instinct and allowed your mind to open recently? What new things have you learned, and how have you integrated that new knowledge into your opinions and ideas about the world around you? What helped you change your mind or evolve your views?

 *Actions*

Absolve Yourself of a Mistake

Effort level: Low to medium ◉◉◯◯◯

In the Reflections section, perhaps we've already done some preliminary work by considering forgiveness and what that might look like. Now you are invited to put that consideration into action. Think about a mistake or misstep you've made that still haunts you. Maybe you dropped the ball on a responsibility and you're still putting out the resulting fire. Maybe it's something you're still embarrassed about, or maybe you hurt a loved one's feelings and the guilt hasn't yet loosened its grip on your heart. Even if the real-world consequences are long past, we all tend to dwell on our mistakes.

First of all, think about how you addressed the mistake in the moment it occurred or the immediate aftermath. What steps did you take to address it? Did you do everything you could have to problem-solve, and did you apologize to anyone who was affected by the consequences? If the answer is no, what remains undone? Resolve to take those steps as soon as possible. Then consider the future: how can you ensure that you won't make this mistake again? Are there behaviors or thought processes you need to adjust? Is there a situation that's bringing out the worst in you that could be avoided?

Once you've made sure that you (to the best of your ability) fixed the effects of your mistake, and that you will (to the best of your ability) be avoiding the mistake in the future, tell yourself that you forgive yourself for the mistake. I'm not kidding when I advise you to say these words out loud to yourself—even look at your reflection in a mirror as you do so. It may feel silly or corny or overdramatic, but in the same way that speaking a daily affirmation can give you strength and confidence, verbally forgiving yourself can anchor it in your mind that this mistake is officially absolved.

Now, it's possible and even likely that the guilt or worry or embarrassment will resurface at one time or another. That's perfectly natural. When it does, take another moment to mentally run through everything you did to fix the problem and how you're ensuring the mistake remains unrepeated. Then say again to yourself, "I forgive you." It can become a mantra of sorts. You are forgiven, and you are moving forward.

Head and Heart Decision Making

Effort level: Medium to high ●●●●○

As mentioned above, Judgment often comes up when you're facing a big decision. But unlike other cards that herald upcoming choices, Judgment assures you that you have all the tools you need to make this decision wisely and fairly. Your best and strongest tools are your head and your heart, after all, and those have been strengthened and sharpened by the journey you've made. So, let's take that decision and apply both tools.

First, consider the emotional aspect of the decision you're making. Do you have a powerful gut instinct about this? What do you anticipate feeling when you make this decision? How will those feelings change depending on what choice you make? Are your emotions about this impacted by an experience, positive or negative, and should that play into your decision-making process?

Then try to let go of the emotional reaction. Take a few breaths to recenter, and then shift into looking at the decision from a purely intellectual lens. What are the advantages and disadvantages of each choice you might make? Does one choice require significantly fewer resources, for example? What do you stand to gain from the outcome of this decision? What advice would you give to a loved one if it were them making this decision instead of you?

Once you've considered both the emotional and the intellectual side of the situation, take a moment and weigh them against each other. Where do they overlap and where do they differ? When they're taken together, is there an obvious choice that they push you toward? Or is there a relatively even distribution of positives and negatives on all sides? Is there a middle ground?

The World

2 1 At last, we have reached the end of our journey. A great undertaking has been completed. A long process has reached its conclusion. We can (and should) take some time to acknowledge the work we've done to get ourselves here. It's been harrowing. We are different, inexorably changed by our trip through the major arcana. But we have well and truly arrived, and we should be proud of ourselves for making it to this point.

When you find the World in your daily reading, consider what you have recently achieved or what parts of your life are coming to a stopping place. What have you learned from the journey? What do you feel now that you've crossed the finish line? Is there anything about the work that you will miss? Are you relieved? Proud? Enlightened? And are you ready to come full circle and begin a brand-new journey as the Fool once again?

Affirmations

I AM whole.
I CAN achieve my goals.
I WILL acknowledge my successes.

Reflections

What goals have I achieved recently?

Goals can be stressful. Like New Year's resolutions, we often set huge, difficult-to-stick-to goals that quickly become a guilty feeling in the pits of our stomachs when we think of them. But (like most of these questions) I encourage you to think of goals big and small. What projects have you finished at work? What frequently-postponed task around the house have you completed lately? If nothing comes to mind, think of a goal you're currently working to—what tangible steps have you taken toward that goal? These smaller sub-goals are still goals. Even if you haven't fully completed your larger goal, those smaller goals within goals are worthy of acknowledging and even celebrating.

How can I carry my accomplishments with me into the future?

It's so easy to let accomplishments fade to the back of your mind as you look to the next project. What ways can you make sure that you keep your achievements as top of mind as the so-easily-remembered setbacks? What causes your achievements to disappear under the weight of tomorrow's tasks and deadlines? How can you remind yourself of your successes when you need a confidence boost? What successes from your past do you still cherish?

What does contentment look like?

When you settle down after a job well done, how do you relax in the glow of that achievement? What do you need to reach that content satisfaction of knowing you've done well? Are you more likely to celebrate with friends, or to bask in your accomplishments in solitude? Do you feel this way often? Why or why not?

Write Your Own Fairy Tale

Effort level: Low to medium ●●○○○

In one of the best acting classes I've ever taken, my instructor assigned us a simple yet complicated task: we were to tell our life stories using any medium we desired (EXCEPT for standing in front of our classmates and just reciting a laundry list of facts about ourselves). In the classes that followed, we were treated to stories told through interpretive dance, collages, and mixtapes—but true to form, I opted for a literary approach. When my turn came, I took the stage wearing a cheap, green, Peter Pan cap with a red feather, and I wove a fairy tale starring myself as the hero.

From a tarot perspective, this is an on-brand exercise—after all, the major arcana themselves tell a complete story from start to finish. If you examine your own journey through a Grimm-brothers-esque lens, the beginning when you leapt from a meta-phorical cliff as the Fool is quite the fairy tale beginning. The twists and turns that you encountered along the way would be familiar to the likes of Red Riding Hood or Sleeping Beauty. And now with the World, you've reached the ending—perhaps not as tidy as "happily ever after," but an ending nevertheless.

So let your inner Hans Christian Andersen come to life and write your story in language as flowery as you choose. That infuriating coworker can become a cunning enchanter who you competed with for an appointment in the royal court. The vacation destination you've been saving up for can become a glorious palace at the edge of an enchanted forest. Let your imagination run wild as you tell the story of You, the fearless and conquering hero.

Ask a Loved One Why They're Proud of You

Effort level: Medium to high ●●●●○

Our objectivity is completely compromised when it comes to judging ourselves—and for most people, the tendency is not to judge ourselves with excessive understanding, but with excessive harshness. Every tiny setback or misstep seems larger than life, and every success feels like just another step toward what's next. The beauty of asking a trusted loved one this question is that your loved ones are liable to be biased, too—but biased in the other direction. They're looking for reasons to celebrate you and everything you do. Sometimes you need that caring outside voice to balance the judgmental inner voice you live with every minute of every day, and the World—the end of a journey—is a great opportunity to reach out for one of those voices.

It can feel a little uncomfortable soliciting praise from someone, even someone you're very comfortable with. If it helps, be completely upfront about why you're asking: "I'm doing a journaling exercise and I'm supposed to ask someone I love why they're proud of me." As long as you've wisely chosen the person to ask, they'll almost certainly have answers—and answers that you may not expect. With the benefit of seeing you from the outside, your loved ones can notice little successes and achievements that may not have even registered for you at the time. The key is to ask someone who knows you well, who you're comfortable with, and who is willing to tell you how much you kick butt.

I would highly recommend writing down whatever they say, too—even if you just jot down a quick bullet-point list of "why Aunt Cathy is proud of me" in your journal, it will give you something tangible to return to when a different journey has you feeling down on yourself. Heck, ask several loved ones and make a huge list, if you feel up for it. It can never hurt to have a reminder not only of your successes, but of the ways that your loved ones value you and everything you do.

THE SUIT OF WANDS
Inspire and Activate

Strike a match and step into the suit of Wands, the realm of action, inspiration, and the element of fire. This is a suit of *doing*. There's a reason that ideas are often illustrated as sparks and lightbulbs—they ignite something deep in our bones and get us moving. If you've ever felt your heartbeat quicken at the beginning of a new project, you know what the suit of Wands feels like. And you don't have to be an artist to feel at home within the Wands—every moment of innovation or inspired leadership falls within their milieu. But remember that fire can quickly get out of hand if it isn't closely tended. Embrace the spark of inspiration, but be cautious not to burn yourself in the process.

Some words to describe the suit of Wands: *creativity, inspiration, action, impulse, passion, competition, movement, desire, determination, will, power, vision, celebration, choice, drive, courage, innovation, achievement, growth, vigor.*

When Wands appear again and again in your daily readings, you may be at the beginning or in the middle of a project that you care about deeply. Perhaps you're chasing after a new idea or starting a passion project. Or it could be just the opposite—you may be in a period that feels dull and monotonous, and you might be craving inspiration.

In either case, now is the time to poke at the embers in your heart and stir them into a steady, powerful flame. Identify the things that push you to action and steep yourself in them. Watch movies and read books that inspire your creativity. Participate in activities like sports or games that rev you up. And when that spark lights within you, make sure to tend it carefully. Don't let it grow so quickly that it burns itself out, or sputter into silence when a new idea presents itself elsewhere.

Ace of Wands

The aces are the purest, simplest encapsulation of what their respective suits stand for, and with the Wands this means the spark of inspiration! The Ace of Wands is that moment when you can hear your muse whispering in your ear as clear as day. It's the beginning of a new project that gets your creative juices flowing freely. It's your inner innovator. It's an "aha!" But now that you've got that spark, the Wands ask what you plan to do with it.

When you draw the Ace of Wands in a daily reading, there are creative forces stirring within you. New projects may be catching your eye, or a new angle for a current project may occur to you. The Ace invites you to chase those big ideas, to explore the possibilities your muse presents to you. Feeling blocked or stuck is so common when it comes to creative ventures. When the creative sparks are coming to you unbidden like this, the best thing you can do for yourself is to pursue them. Who knows? You might create something that touches many lives.

 Affirmations

I AM inspired.
I CAN let my imagination run wild.
I WILL chase my ideas.

 Reflections

What opportunities do I have right now?
The Ace of Wands is all about striking while the iron is hot. What roads are open and available to you right at the present moment? Examine and consider every aspect of your life. It's tempting to narrowly define opportunity as career-oriented, but you likely have opportunities in your home and social life, in your personal development, and in your spirituality, too. Where is there space for you to make a change or enact a plan in

any of these spheres? Which foundations of your world offer a steady springboard to launch you into something new?

What do I do when I'm inspired?

Inspiration is not solely the realm of artists. I believe inspiration is simply that buzz of excited alignment when considering a project or an undertaking. You can be inspired to tidy up your workspace, for instance, or to visit a friend you haven't seen in years. When you experience that buzz of inspiration, what do you do with it? I know someone who used to leap up and literally run up and down the length of her house when an idea had her particularly energized. I always feel the need to grab my pen and scribble down my thoughts before an external distraction knocks them out of my head. What does inspiration—well—inspire you to do?

If I could create anything, what would it be?

This is a chance for that creative spark to run freely. Don't think about what you're "good" at or how much money it might cost. Don't even think of the boundaries of reality if you'd rather dispense with them! What would you love to create? An invention to solve a worldwide dilemma? A gloriously huge sculpture that could be seen from space? A series of books that could sense the native language of whoever picked them up and automatically translate themselves into that language? Be as fantastical and outlandish as you'd like! It may seem like pie-in-the-sky dreaming at first, but stick with it for a few minutes. It might get your gears turning and generate a down-to-earth, actionable idea, too.

 *Actions*

Make a List of What Inspires You

Effort level: Low to medium ●●○○○

When I read a truly incredible book or see an outstanding play, I am almost unable to contain myself as I overflow with inspiration. There are even moments from inspiring stories that have stuck so firmly in my mind that I can still conjure them for myself—

and they still inspire my creative side, even now. This is quite useful—it helps me get my creative juices flowing on command. What comes to mind as lastingly inspirational for you? List any particular artists, authors, films, productions, places, songs, speakers—even people in your life who inspire you. The longer, broader, and more diverse this list becomes, the better.

Once you've got your list, keep it someplace accessible; someplace where you can pull it up at a moment's notice. That way if you're feeling stuck in a rut, you have a ready-made list of ways to troubleshoot your muse and get it going again. Maybe you need to rewatch that one movie that touches your soul, or read a book of poetry by an author who stirs something deep within you. Maybe you need to call that friend who reminds you of your dreams and goals. Whatever it is, you'll have it organized in that list and you won't get pre-stuck trying to think of ways to get yourself un-stuck!

Make Terrible Art

Effort level: Medium to high ◉◉◉◉◯

I can't tell you how many times I've heard people (myself included) say things such as, "Oh, I'm a terrible singer," or, "I can't draw at all." I think we're all too eager to compare ourselves to masters of the craft. Of course, most people aren't Beyoncé or Michelangelo! But who said we had to be that "good" to do something artistic, just for the enjoyment of it? Why do we feel the need to impose this artificial grading system on ourselves, even when we're just trying to have fun?

So in case you need to hear it: I am absolving you of the need to make anything "good" for this exercise. Pick something artistic you would enjoy doing—singing, drawing, writing poetry—and just do it! Do it badly! Sing off-rhythm! Draw stick figures! Write cliche, overdramatic poetry! Do it just for you, just because it feels good to do it. Not to make the next Big Important Work of Art. This is yours and no one else's. Just make something. That's the only requirement.

Two of Wands

With the Two of Wands, we begin to take that spark of inspiration and bring it to life. The Wands are not just the suit of creativity, after all—they are the suit of action and drive. Great ideas are made to be implemented! The Two pushes us to take steps toward realizing our lofty ambitions. And, too, it pushes us to bring others into our process. Whether by fully collaborating or simply by bouncing your thoughts off a trusted friend, the Two encourages us to take the idea we had in solitude and share it.

When you draw the Two of Wands in a daily reading, it is ushering you into that exhilarating and bewildering phase of the creative process when the abstract idea is translated into work, development, and creation. Consider what tools you need to bring this idea to life, and what loved ones might help you hone or improve the idea in this early stage. Think of this card as the major arcana Magician of the Wands, in a sense. The idea itself is already afoot. Now's the time to roll up your sleeves and get to work!

Affirmations

I AM guided by my vision.
I CAN share my passions with others.
I WILL collaborate to achieve.

Reflections

What is my "true north" —the ideal I'm working toward?
Think about the big projects you're throwing yourself into right now, and consider what purpose you see in these ventures. In writing your book, what message or lesson do you hope to impart to your readers? In taking this dance class, what do you hope to gain? Even for more seemingly mundane projects, such as working your day job, what do you

strive to get out of it? Maybe it's as simple as earning a paycheck to take care of yourself and your loved ones, or maybe it's as grandiose as making the world a better place. Where is that compass needle pointing for you?

What do I need to do to bring my ideas to life?

Think of this as sitting down and drawing up an action plan. If you've had an idea for an amazing new skirt design, what steps do you need to take to make that skirt? Perhaps you need to take sewing lessons. Maybe you need to sketch the design until it's tweaked and perfected. Certainly you'll need to go shopping for the fabric, thread, and any other trim you might want to add to it. And so on. Take a look at the idea you want to flesh out and assemble a step-by-step plan for how to make it happen. Be as specific and detailed as you can.

Who in my life am I eager to collaborate with?

Have you ever experienced that incredible feeling of generating ideas with someone you love? Your idea sparks an idea or a suggestion for them, and that gives you even more ideas, and on it goes. There's a special kind of magic when your creative pistons are firing at the same time as someone else's. At its best, it can feel like puzzle pieces clicking smoothly into place. Who have you experienced this with? Or alternatively, who do you think might give you this feeling?

Lay the Creative Groundwork

Effort level: Low to medium ●●○○○

If you worked with the above questions, this activity will be that much easier. Identify one of the first steps you need to take to make your idea a reality. Is there a class you need to take? Research you need to do? Supplies you need to purchase? These are the sorts of things that are easy to postpone indefinitely, and then you wind up with an idea (or many ideas) languishing in the corner of your mind for years. (I am very guilty of this, so I speak from experience.) Again, you can imagine the Two of Wands as the Magician of this suit. The Magician is all about gathering the tools and resources they need to progress. You might even consider reading some of the reflection questions and activity suggestions in the Magician section.

And don't mistake this as a passive fact-finding mission, either. Once you've figured out the steps you need to take in order to lay your groundwork, take action! Sign up for that class. Make a folder in your bookmarks and start compiling research. Swing by your local craft store to get supplies. Get these housekeeping sorts of tasks checked off to make space in your brain for the main event: creating.

Brainstorm With a Trusted Loved One

Effort level: Medium to high ●●●●○

When I'm overflowing with creative ideas, I love calling my brother to talk through them. He's a writer, too, but our focuses and talents are complementary—he is a consummate plot-doctor and worldbuilder, and I am a lover of characters and language. This makes him an ideal sounding board for me—when I'm floating in an abstract idea, he's fantastic at asking just the right questions to get me to clarify and tweak my thoughts. Who fills this role for you? When you have an amazing idea, who are you the most eager to share it with? Does sharing it and getting their feedback help you further develop your idea?

If you have someone like this in mind, set up a time to talk to that person. If possible, take a few moments ahead of your conversation to jot down a few specific questions to start with. Make sure, too, that you take notes while you talk. When you're in the grip of a truly inspiring conversation, you might assume that you'll remember all the pertinent details. I have definitely forgotten some gems by making this assumption. Learn from my mistakes. Bring a notebook, or heck, record the whole conversation if it's easier. You might be surprised by how motivational these conversations can be. Even if you don't end up solving a specific challenge or developing a specific aspect of your idea, talking it through will likely get your creative waterwheel turning in ways you didn't expect.

Three of Wands

The Three of Wands is a waypoint, a hill that you can stand atop to look both ahead and behind. Here you can see how far you've traveled from your starting point, and you can clearly see the destination you're moving toward. Although the Wands are the suit of action and movement, this card is a breath—an opportunity to pause and consider the progress you've made as well as what remains to be done.

The appearance of the Three of Wands in your daily reading means it's time to take stock. Be proud of the work you've done and prepare for the work to come. Are there any adjustments you need to make in order to stay on course? Can you see your goal in the distance, twinkling tantalizingly on the horizon? Can you feel the energy of fire and creative purpose thrumming in your heart center? Tune into that vibration and let it carry you onward.

Affirmations

I AM moving forward.
I CAN see the progress I'm making.
I WILL keep my eyes on the prize.

Reflections

How can I expand my worldview?

With so much going on all at once, we usually keep our worldviews pretty narrow. If we didn't, we'd constantly be overwhelmed and overstimulated. But in the midst of a creative process, opening your mind from time to time is very important. It keeps your work from growing stale and outdated. How can you broaden your awareness of the world? What might open your mind? If you need a couple of activities to accompany this question, visit the Break your Media Routines action in the Fool, or any of the reflection questions or activities in Justice.

Am I at a crossroads?

The Three of Wands can herald a crossroads, a decision to be made that will have a significant impact on your life and your work. Does this sound like anything in your life right now? If so, detail the decision and all the possible outcomes. How has the journey thus far informed your opinions about the decision? What choice do you think will best serve your project as it develops further? Are there any decisions that would likely hold you back?

What progress would I like to make?

When you consider the goals you've been working on recently, how would you like to see yourself progress in the near future? What would make you feel that you'd accomplished a great deal? Do you feel that you've already made strides toward achieving this goal? What remains to be done? What is the timeframe you'd like to meet this goal? Does that feel achievable, taking everything else in your life into consideration? How might you hold yourself accountable for making this progress?

 *Actions*

Write a Reverse Goal

Effort level: Low to medium ●●○○○

Usually goal-setting asks us to first look to the future and imagine what we'd like to make happen to shape that future. But we are all in a constant state of achieving goals big and small, incorporating the successes into our present moment, and determining how to move forward. So let's approach our goals from a different point of view: what have you achieved recently?

Think of an accomplishment, big or small, and take a moment to consider how it's changed your reality. What impacts (positive, negative, and neutral) has this success had on your present day? If you've recently secured a coveted promotion, how has it changed your responsibilities and stress level at work? If you've had a difficult but much-needed conversation with a loved one, how has the atmosphere at home evolved?

Now consider how you'd like to move forward by incorporating the effects of your accomplishment into your daily life. What actions, steps, or (dare I say it) new goals emerge? Returning to the examples above, what could you do to settle into your new workload more comfortably? How could you make a habit out of any changes in behavior that come out of talking to your loved one? In other words, by looking back at the challenges you've already met, how can you strategize and plan for the future?

I Failed!

Effort level: Medium to high ⬤⬤⬤⬤◯

When was the last time you straight up admitted to failing at something? This is an exercise my dad (a consummate storyteller and improv comedy guy) used to do with corporate executives and businesspeople. (He didn't make it up—it's one of those theater games he picked up from years of working with other improv teachers, and I have no idea which one he learned it from.) I think it's most effective if you do this with a partner, but in a pinch just stand in front of a mirror and use your own reflection as a partner.

Think of something that didn't go according to plan recently. A responsibility you dropped the ball on, a task that you executed poorly, an unnecessary argument you got into. Put a big smile on your face, look your partner (or reflection) in the eye, and proclaim proudly, "I failed at…!" And fill in the blank with your particular personal failure. The key is to own the failure in this goofy, lighthearted way. It's much harder to feel ashamed about something when you're declaring it bombastically like this. And after all, why shouldn't we be proud of our failures? They teach us and encourage us to do better next time. So get silly and get proud. We all fail! And it's fantastic!

Four of Wands

The Four of Wands is a celebration! It heralds a time to put down your work and revel in the progress you've made and the company you've kept. In very traditional tarot decks and interpretations, this card can point to joyous life events like weddings and births. I don't necessarily take it quite so literally. Whether you're setting aside a moment in the morning to honor the day ahead or you're planning a lavish revel, this is certainly a time for joy and pride.

When you draw the Four of Wands in a daily reading, take the time to honor and celebrate where you are right now. You don't need to wait for a capital-O Occasion to celebrate with loved ones. Something doesn't need to be planned six months ahead to count as a celebration, either. And you shouldn't be afraid to rejoice for yourself, either—even if it feels like you haven't done anything noteworthy lately! You are an incredible masterpiece in progress, and the Four of Wands proclaims your successes from the rooftops. With an explosion of confetti. And maybe some streamers.

 ## Affirmations

I AM successful.
I CAN celebrate the good times.
I WILL take the time to rejoice.

 ## Reflections

What does a celebration look like for me?
When you decide it's time to celebrate something big or small, what do you do? Do you plan an elaborate dinner party for all your family and friends? Do you splurge on takeout and curl up with your favorite movie? What feels more celebratory for you: champagne or chocolate chip cookie dough ice cream? Do your celebrations need to include

any of your loved ones to feel truly complete, or do you prefer to celebrate in solitude? What would an absolutely perfect celebration look like for you?

Who helps me celebrate my accomplishments?

Do you have a cheerleader friend who you can't wait to call whenever you get good news? Does someone in your office plan the best celebrations and surprises? Is there a family member who always points out your achievements, even when you yourself can't see them? How do these people figure into your personal celebrations? Do you usually invite them to take part? If not, when might you invite them to rejoice with you? Or maybe it's time for *you* to celebrate *them* and everything they bring to your life?

What is a traditional celebration I've experienced?

Some celebrations are cultural touchstones of sorts. Birthdays and bat mitzvahs, Christmases and Kwanzas. Choose one of these occasions and describe it in detail, whether you do so by journaling or simply visualizing the occasion in your mind's eye. What were the traditional components—not just the societal traditions, but traditions that your loved ones put into place? (As a simple example, my family has always given each other pajamas on Christmas Eve.) Are these traditions still meaningful to you now? What do they signify? How have they shaped your concept of celebration? If you no longer observe these rites, where do you see their influence in the events you celebrate now? Are there any ways you'd like to incorporate elements of those traditions back into your life?

 Actions

Look Over Photos of Good Times

Effort level: Low to medium ◉◉○○○

Cameras are more likely to come out during celebrations and gatherings than they are in everyday life. More often than not, I forget to take pictures on a day-to-day basis, but I still have plenty of pictures from family Christmases, birthday get-togethers, and of course, my wedding. Sometimes I sit down and look through these photos just for the pleasure of reliving the memories. I particularly love pictures of myself in the middle of hugging a loved one—when I revisit these photos later, I can almost call up the kinesthetic memory of how that person's arms feel around me.

With modern tools like smart phones and Instagram, it's much quicker and simpler to take a trip down memory lane. With the push of a button or the swipe of a touch screen, you can instantly visit a collection of photos from years ago. And is this not a tiny celebration of its own, meandering through your own museum of meaningful memories? Take your time and really enjoy the process of appreciating each image. Rejoice for who you were and the emotions that burble up with each memory. Allow space for any feelings that seem more heavy than others, too, such as the heartache of seeing a lost loved one captured forever in an image. If you have some extra time to spare, arrange these photos into an album in your smart phone, or create an online board you can revisit next time around.

Plan a Celebration

Effort level: Medium to high ●●●●○

There are some celebrations that are regular parts of our calendar—holiday gatherings, loved ones' weddings, those sorts of things. But it's somewhat rare that we plan a celebration "just because." Why not put together a dinner outing to commemorate an achievement at work, or throw a picnic for friends in honor of your years of kinship? There doesn't have to be some huge life event to warrant a celebration! And it doesn't have to be a reception with a 200-person guest list to be valid and meaningful. A family trip to a beloved restaurant can be just as celebratory.

Another way to approach this exercise is to invent a personal holiday. The anniversary of when you met a close friend. A milestone in your self-improvement or recovery. The birthday of a lost loved one whose memory you want to honor. Put this on your calendar and make a promise to keep this holiday every year. The beauty of this is that there are no preconceived traditions as there would be for a "regular" holiday. This celebration is all yours—you set the tone, the traditions, and the rules!

Five of Wands

With any sort of collaboration, it is inevitable that friction will arise. Each of us brings our own experiences and opinions to the table, and that's the beauty of working together to create something…but it's also bound to cause disagreements from time to time. This is what the Five of Wands speaks to. It's the difficult side of working with others, the side that necessitates negotiation and compromise.

When you draw the Five of Wands in a daily reading, you may be in a period of tension with someone close to you. Egos may be clashing, opinions may be at odds, and it may even seem impossible to find a path forward with the person in question. Perhaps even worse, you may be feeling this way about yourself—sometimes we have too many ideas or we're arguing with different sides of ourselves so furiously that we get ourselves stuck! This card reminds us that collaboration sometimes requires us to let go of the reins. We have to be willing to sacrifice ideas and give up sole control over a project. Even when you are your own collaborator, you'll have to let go of some ideas to create a polished final product. That's all part of the process…but that doesn't make it any easier.

Affirmations

I AM open to compromise.
I CAN navigate conflict.
I WILL seek a middle ground in a group.

Reflections

How might my expectations get in the way of collaboration?
This question asks you to truly plumb the depths of your more challenging side. Whether or not you're in an active collaborative project at the moment, consider what traits and quirks you carry that might be a liability. Do you struggle to back down from

a confrontation? Do you get too attached to your own ideas? Do you hesitate to voice any opinions of your own in a group? Be as honest as you can. Knowing your potential drawbacks as a creative partner will help you notice them and address them when they crop up in the moment.

What is my relationship with compromise?

I've heard it said that a good compromise leaves all parties dissatisfied. I don't entirely agree, but it's true that compromise can be frustrating and disappointing at times. It requires all parties to check their egos and willingly surrender sovereign control over the project or question at hand. How do you navigate compromise? Are you a natural-born diplomat, or do you tend to stick to your guns as much as possible? In a collaborative setting, do you find yourself conceding points and ideas more often, or do you fight for your ideas to the bitter end? Is there anything about your relationship with compromise that you'd like to adjust? How might you go about doing so?

Do I tend to lead or follow more readily?

This is not dissimilar to the question above about compromise, and it's something we touch on in the reflections for the Emperor, as well. But an important element of compromise is knowing when to lead the charge and when to fall to the back of the pack. We all tend to lean one way or the other by default, but when you're working in a group you have to inhabit both roles from time to time. Where on the spectrum do you usually fall? What would it look like if you took the opposite role? If that feels uncomfortable, can you pinpoint why?

 *Actions*

Examine Your Collaborative Relationships

Effort level: Low to medium ◓◓○○○

I've talked a great deal about projects and creative work in this section. But even if your work is very solitary, you do have collaborative relationships, like it or not. Your household is a constant collaboration with your family or roommates. If you're in any sort of committed relationship, that is a collaboration. So how do those (or any) collaborations go for you? Really dig into one or two of your most formative collaborations and identify what works and what is challenging. My spouse and I, for instance, make a good team because we are both deeply thoughtful and caring people who go out of our way to take care of each other's needs. A challenge that we've identified recently is that we express and diffuse our frustration in very different ways. My spouse tends to vent and get angry, while I usually shut down and process internally. This has been an invaluable piece of information because it helps us understand each other, address any conflicts that arise, and better collaborate as life partners. Can you identify any key similarities or differences that inform your collaborative relationships? And how could you use this knowledge to improve those relationships?

Write to Someone You're Carrying Bad Feelings Toward

Effort level: Medium to high ●●●●○

We've probably all gotten this advice at least once, right? If you never got closure from an ex, a toxic work environment, or an estranged family member, you should write a letter you'll never send and unload all those pent-up emotions. I avoided this technique for years—it felt too cliche and overdramatic, for some reason. Finally, my therapist convinced me to try it, and I was genuinely shocked at how much it released in me. Being able to give a voice to all the hurt I'd been carrying for years was surprisingly powerful. It wasn't closure, exactly—it was more like I was giving validation to the feelings I'd quashed for so long. Acknowledging that they were real.

So even if this exercise feels uncomfortable or unnecessary, I encourage you to give it a try. Choose someone who still calls up pain or anger for you, and allow yourself to write everything you'd like to tell them about how they've affected you. Don't worry about writing "well" or sounding too harsh or mean. Just be honest and say what you need to say. Release all those feelings onto paper freely and openly.

Six of Wands

If the Four of Wands stands for celebration, the Six of Wands is achievement. It's the triumphant blast of trumpets as you break through the finish line at the end of a marathon. A goal has been met with success. This card is almost the Chariot of its suit. You've done a thing, whether it's a giant project at work that you've completed or a small reorganization of your pantry at home. Congratulations are in order!

When you draw the Six of Wands in a daily reading, you may be in a period of accomplishment and achievement. Don't be shy about soaking in the success! You've worked hard to get here. Bask in the fruits of your labor. You don't need the Official Celebration of the Four of Wands to acknowledge the milestone you've achieved. There may be fanfare and confetti in the Four, but the Six is that quiet glow of pride in your chest. It's the knowledge that you succeeded. Be proud of yourself—you've earned it!

Affirmations

I AM proud of myself.
I CAN celebrate my accomplishments.
I WILL congratulate myself.

Reflections

How can I acknowledge my successes more?
What would it be like to become more aware of your day-to-day successes? If that feels uncomfortable to imagine, can you identify why? Would it feel uncomfortable to acknowledge a friend's successes like this? If not, why do you feel differently about yourself? What might you do to feel more comfortable with noticing your own achievements, large and small? And how might you remind yourself to notice those achieve-

ments in the first place? It's easy to overlook our own success, after all. (If you're stuck for ideas, consider visiting the pride journal exercise in the Chariot.)

What is the difference between confidence and hubris?

I've heard more than one person with low self-esteem say things such as, "I have to be hard on myself so I don't get arrogant." But I'm sure you know plenty of people who come across as confident while not seeming cocky or smug. How would you describe confidence versus arrogance? Is it possible to be sure of oneself without being boastful? Think of someone you've known who seems to radiate arrogance, and then compare them to someone who seems quietly sure of themself. What do they share, and what differs?

What is one specific achievement I'm aiming for?

Think of a major goal you're working toward right now. Something that, when you reach it, you'll feel unquestionably accomplished and proud of yourself. How, specifically, will you know when you've reached this goal? Is it something you'll be able to check off your to-do list? Or is it something more subtle and internal? Either way, what will it feel like when you arrive there? When you do reach your goal (not if, but when), what will you do to congratulate yourself?

 Actions

Put up a Reminder of Your Success

Effort level: Low to medium ● ● ○ ○ ○

I think part of the reason that we're quick to forget our achievements is because they're in our past, while our unmet goals always lie ahead of us. The past is easy to push to the back of our minds as we look to the future. So here's a relatively easy way to remind yourself. Choose something that stands for one of your accomplishments. It might be a trophy, a newspaper article, a diploma. In a pinch you can even sit down and make a quick list of the things you've done that you're proud of. Then find someplace to put this reminder—someplace with high-visibility where you'll see it regularly, such as your fridge or near your desk. Think of it like keeping a picture of your family at work, only you're keeping a reminder of your best self at home.

A quick word of additional advice here: it may be necessary to switch up where you keep your reminder from time to time. Once we get used to something in our environment, it becomes "part of the furniture," easy to unconsciously overlook. When that happens, try moving your reminder to a different location to keep it fresh, eye-catching, and top of mind again.

Reward Yourself

Effort level: Medium to high ◉◉◉◉○

You don't need a huge, life-altering accomplishment to deserve a treat from time to time—and you don't need to drop hundreds of dollars (or any at all, for that matter) to give yourself a little pick-me-up. We're often tempted to see treating ourselves as expensive splurges and nothing more—and certainly if it's within your means to buy yourself a pricey gift or go to a fancy restaurant, by all means! But an indulgence can be as simple as clearing an hour in your evening to read a book in the bath, or going on a walk with a significant other.

The hardest part of this exercise is feeling worthy of an indulgence in the first place. So often we think we must *earn* our moments of self-care like this. But with that mindset, it's easy to keep moving the goalposts of what we need to do to deserve it. Give yourself a break, and give yourself a gift—big or small, extravagant or simple. I'm here to tell you that you deserve it, whatever it is.

Seven of Wands

The Seven of Wands calls upon us to stand our ground and trust ourselves. When you burn brightly, the people around you might clamor to get a bit of your flame for themselves. Or, too, they might doubt your flame altogether and try to make you second-guess yourself. The Seven of Wands is a bold declaration. It says, "I am here and I know who I am." Full stop. No matter what anyone else says.

When you draw the Seven of Wands in a daily reading, your confidence may be tested. People around you may not support you or believe in what you're doing. This card whispers, "Hold fast." Your unique magic is not meant to be suppressed for the sake of a skeptic. The world needs that magic of yours. Keep it coming. Believe in it, and in yourself.

Affirmations

I AM steadfast.
I CAN stand up for what I believe in.
I WILL not be pressured to give way.

Reflections

How can I trust myself more readily?

If you're a chronic overthinker, trusting yourself can be an immense challenge. Even when we have a strong intuition or gut feeling, we pick it apart and question ourselves. What might help you quiet down that internal doubter? What do you need to better trust yourself? Are there any particular steps you might take to combat your inner critic? When have your gut feelings been proven true in the past? When have you followed your instincts, for better or for worse?

How does competition affect me?

Some of us thrive with competition and use it as a powerful motivator. I'm quite the opposite—competition makes me anxious. I'd much rather come last in a competition if it keeps the peace intact. Where do you fall on this spectrum? Does competition give you a rush or a rash? Do you do some of your best work under competitive circumstances, or does anxiety consume your thoughts when competition enters the equation? If you typically dislike competition, what might help you become a bit more comfortable in competitive situations? If you enjoy competition, how can you ensure that you're a good sport?

What advice do I need to unlearn?

When someone you love, trust, or admire gives you advice, it's hard to dismiss it, even if it isn't great advice. I had a boss who insisted that telling a customer "I don't know" was the absolute worst thing I could do. He told me that I should make something up rather than admit to not knowing something. I looked up to him, so I took his advice to heart. It's taken me *years* to flush it out of my system and stop bullshitting when all I need to do is say, "That's a good question. I'm not sure off the top of my head. Let me find out for you." What about you? Is there any not-so-sage wisdom you've received from someone close? How did you go about unlearning it? What did you gain from the experience? If you're still in the process of unlearning it, what new steps might you take to continue that process?

 **Actions**

Back up Your Beliefs

Effort level: Low to medium

Have you ever leapt into a debate about an issue that you feel strongly about, only to realize that you have little real fodder to debate with besides, "But I think it should be this way!"? This isn't to say you'd be sure to win every debate with better-informed opinions, of course. But taking the time to research the issues can only make you more aware and nuanced in your beliefs. Choose a topic that you have opinions about (but not a great deal of knowledge) and sit down to do some research. We live in an age when a wealth of information is always at our fingertips. You can, with relative ease, locate everything from scholarly analyses of the issue to personal think pieces written by authors on both sides of the opinion. I encourage you to seek out material written by folks whose opinions are different than yours. As challenging as it might be to read, it will give you opportunities for deeper learning and growth. If you have a strong negative reaction, can you pinpoint where it's coming from and why? Even this will provide more nuance and depth to your opinion. Do be mindful of your emotional reaction to this content, however. If you're not careful, you can fall into a self-triggering spiral of obsessively reading this stuff and getting angrier and angrier, or more and more upset. If this sounds like you, consider setting a time limit for yourself. You won't learn much of anything if you're spending hours fuming about that one article.

Write a Manifesto

Effort level: Medium to high ●●●●○

A manifesto is, in essence, a place to say who you are and what you stand for. It's almost like writing a bio for your beliefs and deeply-held values. If you had to explain to someone what your principles are, what you value and work for and reach for, what would you say? What feels like an absolute truth to you? What do you value and hold in highest regard? Love? Value? Creativity? Freedom? There's no wrong way to write a manifesto unless you're parroting someone else's beliefs instead of baring your own.

This is a great space for some true free writing. Get yourself a blank page and write a beginning prompt at the top, something like, "I believe in…" or, "I live my life in pursuit of…" and then start filling in. Don't worry about spelling or grammar; don't even worry too much about the contents. You can always go back and edit or tweak. For now, just open your heart onto the page. Whether you end up with a bullet point list or a lovely poetic series of verses, you will certainly end up with something honest and open…and perhaps with something that teaches you more about yourself.

Eight of Wands

In the Ace of Wands, we enjoyed that "aha" moment of an idea first taking form. With the Eight, we find everything falling into place as we surge toward the finish line. This is what happens when all the stars align, when we can barely work fast enough to keep up with our racing minds. It's that feeling in the center of your chest telling you how close you are—and more, how capable you are of reaching your goal. My dad was an improv performer, and he always talked about those moments onstage when you were so connected with the audience and your fellow performers that time itself seemed to slow. That's the Eight of Wands: inspiration, synergy, and action all at once.

When you draw the Eight of Wands in a daily reading, really listen to that pull in your mind and heart. Is there a project or an idea that you can't stop thinking about? When you sit down to work on something does your heartbeat seem to shift? If you pay close attention and follow this pull, you may be shocked at how swiftly and powerfully you'll make progress. The Eight is leading you to a period of prolific and productive action. Let yourself follow and you will not regret it.

 ## Affirmations

I AM driven.
I CAN follow through.
I WILL act swiftly and purposefully.

 # Reflections

In what aspect of my life am I making the most progress?

Each facet of your daily life goes through a natural ebb and flow. When you're putting extra effort into your career, your friendships may take a temporary backseat. When a new romance is blossoming, you may find yourself neglecting the upkeep of your home. Which aspect of your life is currently experiencing the most growth or progress? Where do you find yourself focusing a majority of your attention and time—not because you have to, but because you want to? Or if it *is* because you have to, do you see all that effort and dedication paying off down the road? If not, how might you refocus your energies?

How can I maintain my momentum?

At the beginning of a project, it's easier to throw lots of extra attention and effort into the work. It's new and interesting and exciting! But as the novelty wears off, that momentum sometimes wavers in tandem. How might you hold onto some of that initial enthusiasm and utilize it to keep up the work? For me, it often means using some of that early burst of creativity to draw up a comprehensive plan or outline for the project. That way when I lose some of my oomph later, I've still got a roadmap to keep me on track. What methods can you think of to help you stay on course with your project from start to finish? If your momentum slows, what might connect you back to your original spark of passion and inspiration?

What does the rhythm of my life look and sound like?

When I hit my creative stride, it feels as if I've tuned into my own heartbeat. But it isn't exclusive to creativity—think of a time you've gotten a ton of work done around the house, totally unaware of the passage of time. This is rhythm, your own personal brand of it! Get abstract for a minute and describe what form that rhythm takes for you. Is it percussive only, or does it include melody as well? What instruments or voices make up the sound of it? Does it have a color? A temperature? Is there a particular part of your body where you feel its presence? If it were a living being, what would it look like?

 *Actions*

Drum

Effort level: Low to medium ●●○○○

I truly believe that we are all creatures of rhythm to a certain extent. We tap our toes and fingers when we're nervous or anticipating something. We walk at our own personal pace with arms moving in time. You don't have to have a strong sense of rhythm to have a personal beat that's specific to you and your heartbeat. If you are musically inclined, you can put on some of your favorite upbeat music to drum to—but this exercise works just as well without a backdrop. All you really need is a hard surface to start tapping out a rhythm. You can employ tools if you're so inclined (turn pens or pencils into makeshift drumsticks, for example), but I personally prefer to use my bare hands. It feels more powerful, somehow, as if I myself am the conduit for this invisible current of music. Let whatever rhythm strikes you set the tempo and just let yourself go in the kinesthetic satisfaction of tapping out that rhythm. Don't dwell on the thought that this is silly, or that your rhythm is somehow wrong. Just follow it—if the meter or pace shifts, let it. If it remains steady and consistent, stay with it. It's like tuning into your mind's heartbeat—and isn't that the Eight of Wands, marching to the beat of your own creative drummer?

Curate a Badass Playlist

Effort level: Medium to high ●●●●○

Is there anything better than putting on the perfect soundtrack for whatever activity you've got ahead of you? Whether it's a driving, upbeat playlist for your morning workout or a gentle instrumental mix to accompany a study session, there's a perfect musical backdrop for just about any activity. For this exercise, you'll be building a playlist that's motivational. Something that gets your blood pumping and your gears turning. Something that makes you feel powerful, capable, and ready. If you happen to be deaf or hard of hearing, you might replace this with a list of YouTube videos with imagery that gets you pumped up.

An important caveat to remember as you approach this exercise: this is *your* motivational playlist. Maybe a lot of folks would include the "Eye of the Tiger" in their list of motivational tunes, but maybe it doesn't do much for you. Don't include it just because it feels necessary! Maybe it's the opening movement of Vivaldi's *Four Seasons* that gets you in the mood to create and work. Maybe it's a Justin Bieber song. Maybe it's "Defying Gravity" from Broadway's *Wicked*. Whatever music motivates *you*, that's the music that belongs in this playlist. And don't worry about getting the length "right," either. Whether it's five songs long or fifty, this is *your* soundtrack.

Nine of Wands

There is no journey, no project, no process that does not encounter some difficulty. A roadblock, an obstacle, a setback—likely many of them, in fact. With the Nine of Wands, the end of the journey is in sight but there are yet more hurdles to leap before we arrive. The Nine reminds us of everything we've already overcome so far. It whispers "keep going" in our ringing ears. It tells us that our weariness, our bruises, and our aching muscles will all be worth it when we reach our goals.

When you draw the Nine of Wands in a daily reading, it's a good sign that your hard work is paying off but the journey is taking its toll. If you're feeling worn down or discouraged, look back at how far you've come. Know that you have everything you need to accomplish your goals. Keep breathing, keep pacing yourself, and most of all keep going.

 ## Affirmations

I AM experienced.
I CAN draw strength from my past.
I WILL remember what I've already overcome.

 ## Reflections

What makes me determined?
Everyone is perseverant as far as I'm concerned. We're all doing what we need to do in order to survive. Even when it feels like we're at the end of our ropes, there's no disputing that we survive. We endure. What makes you a determined person? How do you access that fighter inside of you, even if the fight you're facing is just getting through one more day, or getting out of bed in the morning? What keeps you going? When have you

come face-to-face with your innermost core of strength, and what did the experience teach you?

What have I learned from my hardest experiences?

I don't believe that everything happens for a reason. I believe that we can learn and grow as a result of everything that happens. You will never hear me say that I'm glad I battled severe endometriosis for four years. What I will say is that I learned to stand up for myself and be honest about my needs because of my health challenges. Think back to some of the hardest times in your life. Can you identify how they shaped you, the lessons they carried with them? Did you learn that you're stronger than you thought? Perhaps you're a more patient person now, or you don't take as much for granted. I don't believe that you have to be grateful for the bad things you've endured, but I also believe that acknowledging the growth you experienced as a result will make you a more resilient and self-assured person.

How can I keep from getting defensive?

When we've been through tough times, we develop defenses. This is natural and, indeed, often necessary—our shields help us survive. But we're also liable to throw up those shields when we don't really need to. Call it a reflex, an impulse, or a learned behavior. Whatever it is, our defenses can get in our way at times when we're trying to consciously let our guard down, or when the danger is only perceived. How can you keep that shield at your side unless it's absolutely necessary? Can you identify the situations that tend to put you on the defensive? What can you do to keep yourself more open and at ease? What damage comes of your unchecked defensiveness?

 *Actions*

Identify Your Walking Stick

Effort level: Low to medium ⬤⬤◯◯◯

We are, as my mother likes to joke, "tool-using mammals." We find, modify, or create objects to make a task easier. This is true both in the literal sense and the metaphorical sense—when an emotional task is challenging, we find mental and emotional tools to help ourselves. For example, I have a playlist of videos that I put on when my anxiety is running high to help myself calm down and recenter.

When you've faced challenges in your life, what tools have you leaned on? Maybe there's a comfort food that you only cook when you've had a particularly bad day. Maybe there's a self-help book with highlighted passages and dog-eared pages that you reread when you need a confidence boost. Maybe it's a prayer or mantra you whisper to yourself after a crying spell. The tools themselves can be anything under the sun. What's important is making a conscious mental note of the tools you use and what they're good for, because that will make it easier and more natural to reach for them the next time you need to.

Revisit a Place Where You've Struggled

Effort level: Medium to high ⬤⬤⬤⬤◯

Battlegrounds. We all have them in our past. Places where we've gone through the hardest times in our lives. Mine have included many doctor's offices where I've been doubled over in pain begging physicians to help me feel better. I could describe these places in detail, from the faux-comforting, off-teal chairs in the waiting rooms to the peculiar flavor of dread that would flutter through my gut every time I stepped into an examination room. Profound anxiety, grief, triumph, and relief—all of them colored my visits to these offices. These were battlegrounds where I fought—and where I survived, scars and all.

If you can physically return to one of your own personal battlegrounds, it can be a powerful pilgrimage to make. (Although I caution you to make sure that it's physically AND emotionally/mentally safe for you to do so! Don't go anyplace that might trigger your anxiety, depression, etc. And certainly don't go anyplace where you might encounter an old abuser. If you're unsure, err on the side of caution—or bring a buddy to keep you grounded.) Making the trip through visualization, meditation, and/or journaling can be just as profound. Put yourself back in the location where you've been through so much. Experience it with as many of your senses as you can. What do you remember visually and audibly? Are there smells, tastes, or textures you associate with this place? What did you feel when you were here?

Now recall how you made it through these experiences. Take yourself through the process of leaving these places, carrying with you the scars and wounds that were inflicted but surviving nevertheless. You are a warrior, a survivor of so many battles in this place. How can your scars from the past help you build your armor for tomorrow? If you made it out of this dangerous and painful war, what can't you conquer in the future?

Ten of Wands

The Ten of Wands is a harbinger of overwhelming circumstances. We may be putting too much pressure on ourselves or failing to heed early warning signs of impending burnout. Perhaps we're shouldering the weight of responsibilities that aren't ours to bear. In any case, we're taking on too much too fast. Whatever burden we carry is so heavy that we're in danger of breaking our back if we go much farther.

If the Ten of Wands appears in your daily reading, it's critical that you take a step back and identify ways to relieve some of the pressure you're experiencing. You may need to delegate or reach out to loved ones for emotional support. You may need to take a hiatus from a project that's eating up too much of your energy. Above all, this card reminds you that you need not carry everything alone.

 ## Affirmations

I AM willing to share responsibility.
I CAN recognize when I'm overwhelmed.
I WILL ask for help when I need it.

 ## Reflections

What are my responsibilities?
Think of the jobs and tasks that you take on every day. Do they have anything in common? What is their common denominator? What do you gain by carrying out these daily obligations? Are there any of these responsibilities you wish you could put aside? What would happen if you did? Is there anyone who could share or even take over this responsibility?

What have I taken on that isn't my burden alone?

Maybe it's a literal task, like a household chore that everyone else ignores, or assuming a leadership role in a group project because no one else steps up. Or maybe it's more internal, like expecting yourself to always cheer up your significant other when they're down. Whatever the nature of it, you likely have a few responsibilities and expectations that aren't truly yours to bear—at least not alone. Can you identify one or more of them? Why do you think you put this unnecessary pressure on yourself? How might you share the load with someone?

What would it look like if my life were more balanced?

What would an ideal life balance look like for you? You probably put too much time and energy into one pursuit—work, relationships, hobbies—and simultaneously overlook another. What would it feel like if you could bring these aspects into a more comfortable balance? How might your life improve? Can you think of any ways that you might make this vision your reality (or at least come closer to it)? What steps would you need to take?

 **Actions**

Identify Your "Check Engine" Light

Effort level: Low to medium ●●○○○

What happens when you become particularly stressed? Where in your body do you feel it—tight shoulders, a knot in the stomach, etc.? Does it manifest in the ways you interact with your loved ones—do you lose your temper more easily or become withdrawn and shut down? Does it impact how you do your daily work? How so? Would you say you work well under pressure?

When we know how we behave and feel during periods of great stress, it allows us to catch the early warning signs. Stress sometimes creeps up on us so insidiously that we don't recognize it until we're already completely overwhelmed. But if we spend some time (during lower-stress periods) identifying those early tells, we can learn how to catch ourselves before we get in over our heads. Think of it as taking an aspirin as soon as the first sign of a headache pops up, instead of taking it after the pain has already gotten too intense to bear. The former is MUCH more effective, and the first step is training yourself to notice those first signs. (For further action on this, visit the Make a Burnout Plan activity in the Knight of Wands.)

Find an Exit Buddy

Effort level: Medium to high ●●●●○

Think about some of the most stressful, overwhelming periods in your life. Is there a person who stands out as someone you've consistently turned to? When you've been at your worst, completely weighed down, who have you reached out to? Have you fulfilled this role for them during their worst moments as well?

Think of this person as your "exit buddy." This is the person who you can rely on for a distraction when you need to take your brain off the hook. The person who knows exactly how to make you laugh, even when laughing feels impossible. The person who makes you feel absolutely capable of handling whatever has you so stressed out, but who is also equally willing to be with you as you take a break and decompress. If it helps, you can actually sit down with this person and put together an agreement: "If your coursework is eating your brain, come knock on my dorm room door and we'll walk to Baskin-Robbins together," or, "I can always take a 15-minute break at work if you need to call me and vent." Having these little emergency plans for quickly relieving pressure can make it much easier to implement them in the moment, and having a predetermined person to help you utilize them? So much the better.

THE COURT OF WANDS

Artists, activists, and visionaries populate the court of Wands. They're dynamic, intense humans who get fired up at the drop of a hat. You know them because they're the folks who can get your blood pumping and your heart racing just by talking about the things they care about. Even if you don't share their area of interest, their enthusiasm and passion is contagious. Sometimes they're better at generating ideas than they are at following through, and they are also vulnerable to burnout if they don't pace themselves carefully. But without their spark, the world might grind to a dull standstill.

Some words to describe the court of Wands: *passionate, intense, creative, determined, bold, energetic, confident, joyful, fiery, decisive, impulsive, brave, protective, proud, charismatic, dramatic, adventurous, decisive, optimistic, driven.*

If you want to visit someplace to invite the court of Wands' energy into your day, here are some ideas:

- If possible, a fireplace or a bonfire to invoke the element of fire. If not, someplace sunny will work, too.

- An art museum, gallery, or some sort of live performance to invoke creativity and inspiration.
- A march, protest, or any volunteer opportunity for a cause you care about, to invoke action and passion.
- A gym or fitness center, to invoke energy and movement.
- Anything out of your usual comfort zone, to invoke adventurousness and boldness.

Page of Wands

Passionate writer, fiercely loving sister, and classical lady of literature, Josephine March of *Little Women* is the perfect candidate to represent the Page of Wands. She's got an appropriately fiery temper, but this also allows her to stand up for herself and speak her mind. She's intense in everything she does, whether it's pursuing a writing career (in a time when female writers were far less encouraged) or looking out for her loved ones. It's no wonder that Jo March has inspired generation upon generation of women to grow up strong and determined. She's creative, expressive, and swift to act—all attributes that she shares with the Page of Wands. We watch her grow into a confident and productive woman over the course of the book, but especially at the beginning, she's full of grand ideas with little idea of how to execute them. "I want to do something splendid before I go into my castle—something heroic, or wonderful—that won't be forgotten after I'm dead. I don't know what, but I'm on the watch for it, and mean to astonish you all, some day."

If the Ace of Wands were a person, it would be this Page. They indeed seem to blaze with the fire of creativity, but they sometimes struggle to follow through—the next grand idea is more exciting than finishing their last project. The good news is that their energy is contagious. They adore these early stages of creating, and they may have so many ideas that you'll have a hard time keeping up. Just don't be surprised if their momentum seems to suddenly flag as a new idea catches their attention. If you need a dedicated creative partner who will stick with you from start to finish, this Page might not be your best choice. But if you're looking for a brainstorming buddy to help you generate a million and one ideas, look no farther. The Page of Wands is the person for the job, and a lively and enthusiastic one at that. As Jo sings in *Little Women the Musical*: "Sometimes when you yearn, you burn the air, and someone else feels the flame you always knew was there."

 ## Affirmations

I AM an artist.
I CAN let my ideas run away with me.
I WILL begin new projects with joy.

 ## Reflections

Who in my life reminds me of the Page of Wands?
What aspects of the Page of Wands do I see in myself?
What aspects of the Page of Wands would I like to cultivate in myself?

 ## Actions

Revisit an Old Project or Idea

Effort level: Low to medium ⬤⬤○○○

I cannot tell you how many times I'll go through my old documents and find myself inspired by a forgotten idea. I'm definitely guilty of some Page-of-Wands-failure-to-follow-through, so I have a number of half-finished outlines and random scribblings floating around in my folders. The upside is that sometimes I'll find the beginnings of an idea that I jotted down five years ago, and it will suddenly snowball into a new fully-fledged outline. Some of my best writing has grown out of these uncovered half-ideas.

Now, you may not be a weirdo like me who has dozens of documents with two or three paragraphs of scribblings apiece, but you don't need to be. I guarantee you have some projects or ideas in your past that you left unfinished or forgot about altogether. Maybe it's the beginnings of a craft project that you meant to complete as a gift for a family member. Maybe you intended to reorganize your closet but you've just never gotten past a shelf or two. I say it several times in this book (especially in the suit of Wands) but you don't have to be doing capital-A Artwork to be creative. And old projects don't have to be paintings or novels to inspire you to action.

It's entirely possible that you'll revisit this old idea and decide that it isn't the right time to pick it back up—or even that you're never going to pick it up again. That's perfectly valid, too! This activity isn't meant to force you to work on something that feels lackluster. The point is just to get you thinking about old ideas. If you find a hidden gem that you want to start polishing, fantastic! But if you don't, you've still stirred up your creativity and taken some time to commune with your ideas. That, in and of itself, is Page of Wands energy.

Find a Mentor

Effort level: Medium to high ⬤⬤⬤⬤◯

When the Page of Wands decides they want to start something, they're definitely not lacking in enthusiasm or gusto. But they are lacking experience. Remember that this is the Page of the suit. They're bright-eyed and fresh, but they're likely to charge into something without a plan. What this Page needs is a guide, someone who can provide insight and advice as the Page learns, but still leave them enough space to dive headfirst into their new passion.

A mentor can take many forms. A parent or a teacher are two obvious examples, but there's plenty of other possibilities. It could be someone who's been at your workplace for many years and might have some tips to share. It might be an experienced knitter or pianist who can guide you through the awkward early stages of trying to learn a new skill like knitting or playing piano. It might be a spiritual advisor at your place of worship, or a meditation teacher, or a hairdresser who shares meaningful anecdotes every time you visit them for a haircut. A mentor doesn't have to be someone who coaches you over a long and dedicated period of time—it might just be someone who gives you excellent advice that sticks with you. Odds are good that you already have someone like this in your life, or several someones. If that's the case, congrats—those people are worth their weight in gold. If not, consider reaching out! If you're trying to learn something new or improve an existing skill, you could probably benefit from some experienced input. And the good news is that the internet makes it incredibly easy to ask for guidance! No matter how obscure or niche you think you are, there are forums and groups and tons of websites dedicated to your thing. If you're running into any sort of hang-up or uncertainty, I guarantee that you can ask a question online and get answers back from folks experienced in whatever field you're in. So don't be shy. You might get a straightforward answer that helps you continue your work, and who knows? You might even make a more lasting connection with someone who can continue to provide support and guidance as you grow.

Knight of Wands

The knights of the tarot are the movement-makers, the ones who take the raw elements of their suits and put them to work. Since the Wands are themselves the suit of action, the Knight of Wands represents action squared. And nobody says action squared like Alexander Hamilton. Not so much the real historical figure—although yes, him too—but the titular character in Lin-Manuel Miranda's stunning Broadway musical. The man literally has a whole song titled "Non-Stop" where a recurring line demands of him, "Why do you write like you're running out of time?" Hamilton is relentless. Everything he does, he does 110 percent. When he wants to overhaul America's fledgling financial system, he attends the Constitutional Convention and pontificates for six hours straight. When he sits down to pen a handful of papers defending the Constitution, he ends up writing fifty-one essays. He leaps into war, duels, writing, and governing with equal ferocious energy. The flip side of this energy is that he sometimes impulsively throws himself into unhealthy pursuits—like cheating on his wife, for instance—with that same gusto. Hamilton cares so much about everything he does that he'll gladly self-destruct if it means reaching his goal: "If they tell my story, I am either gonna die on the battlefield in glory or rise up."

This is the Knight of Wands, who might be voted the most likely to succeed in their high school yearbook, but is equally likely to burn themselves out in the process. If this Knight charges into your daily reading, it's likely that you're in a period of serious action and energy. There may be a particular person in your world who's pushing you to achieve and accomplish, or who is inspiring you by themself achieving and accomplishing. Or you may be in the midst of this creative, active fervor yourself. Embrace it and ride that spike in energy, by all means! Only be careful to keep an eye on sustainability. If you write half a book in a manic three-day marathon and then spend the next six months too burnt out to finish the other half, it's hardly worth it. There's nothing wrong with dedicating extra time to a project when you're in the zone, but make sure to take occasional breaks and let yourself rest between creative bursts of work. You do not, after all, want to throw away your shot.

 ## Affirmations

I AM a self-starter.
I CAN pursue my goals passionately.
I WILL make progress toward my vision.

 ## Reflections

Who in my life reminds me of the Knight of Wands?
What aspects of the Knight of Wands do I see in myself?
What aspects of the Knight of Wands would I like to cultivate in myself?

 ## Actions

Make a Burnout Plan

Effort level: Low to medium ●●○○○

Whether you spend most of your day-to-day life flexing your creativity muscle or not, we're all prone to burnout from time to time. Projects at work consume us, or we have a sick kiddo who takes up all our energy as we nurse them back to health, and at the end of it all we find ourselves slumped on the couch with no mental or emotional bandwidth to do anything but play mindless games on our phone. When you're in the thick of it, this can be a frustrating feeling, especially if you're a goal-oriented person who likes to always be doing. You want to be working on your drawing, or redecorating your office, or planning your sister's bridal shower, but you can't seem to muster up the oomph. So, it can be helpful to plan for these moments in your life—that way, you don't have to spend mental power in the moment to figure out what to do while you're recovering.

This is going to look very different for each individual, of course. I know people who can recharge by deep cleaning their kitchen or going on a two-hour drive. Both of those activities would contribute to my burnout, not alleviate it. The key (which is easier said than done, I realize) is to identify activities that give you that sense of doing something but still recharge you rather than depleting you. For example, cross stitching does it for me—I feel as if I'm doing something creative and productive, but it doesn't use up my mental energy the way that writing does. So before you find yourself in the thick of burnout blues, spend some time brainstorming what activities might bolster you when the burnout strikes. (And if you need some extra insight into your early warning signs for burnout, visit the "check engine" light activity in the Ten of Wands.)

Schedule a Passion Day

Effort level: Medium to high ●●●●○

Have you ever intentionally scheduled a day to work on whatever projects make you happiest? Sure, sometimes those days will fall into your lap—all your roommates will be out of the house, and you'll be able to blast your favorite music while you spread all your painting supplies out on the living room floor to work. But how often do we make a date with ourselves for this purpose? We schedule days to spend time with our family or friends, we schedule dates with partners, but why not schedule a time for our passion, too?

If a full day feels unachievable, start smaller. Set aside at least an hour or two where you can be largely uninterrupted. You want enough time to get lost in your work, for new ideas to blossom or existing ideas to come into clearer focus. If it's possible, I recommend getting out of the house to work. Something about being at home makes it easier for distractions to pop up, even if you don't live with anyone who might interrupt you. And most importantly, no matter where you choose to hold your passion time or what you choose to do, choose a time and do everything in your power to stick to it. Some rainchecks are unavoidable, of course, but don't allow yourself to downplay the importance of this time. When we're making dates with ourselves, it's easy to say, "Oh, but my friend just texted to ask if I'm free, and I don't see him often enough—my reading marathon can wait." Ask yourself if you would reschedule a hangout with a loved one if someone else asked you to visit. This is no different. You've made a commitment to yourself and whatever your passion is. Flaking on yourself is just as bad as flaking on a friend, and the Knight of Wands won't stand for it.

Queen of Wands

Supercalifragilisticexpialidocious! I always think of the Queens as the member of each court who's best equipped to pass on the gifts of their suit. Mary Poppins, who injects magic into everything she does and who teaches Jane and Michael Banks so many invaluable life lessons, is a Queen of Wands incarnate. (A note here that I am largely thinking of the film version of her, who is a bit warmer and bubblier than her original literary form.) Barbara Moore describes the Queen of Wands in *The Steampunk Tarot* like so: "If you want to move, she'll get you up to speed in no time. If you want to make excuses and whine, she'll spare a moment to give you a killer withering glance before turning her back on you," (262). And does this not describe Mary Poppins? She has confidence for days—she is "practically perfect in every way," after all—and while she takes a no-nonsense approach when Jane or Michael don't behave in a manner befitting their ages, she's simultaneously full of whimsy and magic. As she says herself in the film adaptation, "In every job that must be done, there is an element of fun." Does this combination of whimsy and gravity seem contradictory? In someone else, it might be. But in Mary Poppins it just makes sense, somehow. And she has no time for people who expect her to be anything but herself.

While this Queen is still a member of the court of Wands and still loves action and achievement, they're able to see a broader picture than their corresponding Page and Knight. The Queen of Wands knows that huge undertakings require a community to succeed in a sustainable, long-lasting way. They aren't the ceaselessly encouraging and supportive Queen of Cups, but they aren't the sharp-tongued Queen of Swords, either. This Queen pushes you to be your best, but in a way that makes you want to work harder and practice more. I had a director in youth acting classes who was a quintessential Queen of Wands type. She was INTENSE and would frequently stop all the action in the middle of a scene, shout directions and adjustments to the actors, and then start everything over…only to do the same thing three seconds later. But none of her shouting was malicious or cruel. It was just because she was so fired up about the potential in the scene that she couldn't contain herself. And she was equally fired up when you got the scene right. When she leapt out of her seat to shout, "YES!" at the end of your performance, you'd feel like a gold medalist. Mary Poppins is identical. She can be brusque and sharp in her rebukes, but it's only because she wants Jane and Michael to become their best selves. And it's obvious how much she loves them, even when she quietly excuses herself from their lives so they can enjoy their parents' company. She's helped them grow, and presumably now she's on to the next family to do the same for them.

 *Affirmations*

I AM a visionary.
I CAN inspire others generously.
I WILL share my spark with others.

 *Reflections*

Who in my life reminds me of the Queen of Wands?
What aspects of the Queen of Wands do I see in myself?
What aspects of the Queen of Wands would I like to cultivate in myself?

 *Actions*

Co-Creativity Time

Effort level: Low to medium

When I was in college, I started hosting regular writing nights on Sundays in my apartment. A rotating cast of my friends would come over, we'd usually order pizza or Chinese food, and we'd all sit around working on our various writing projects. Some of us would have papers or projects for class that we'd focus on, while others would spend the time working on personal projects. Sometimes one of my roommates (an actress) would work on memorizing her lines or analyzing her script. Even though we were focusing on different projects, there was something about being in the same room while we all worked that kept us honest about getting things done. Alone, it's easy to get distracted and procrastinate.

No matter how your creativity manifests, I highly recommend this approach to getting creative work done. Being in the room with other creatives at work is inspiring. It's motivating. And if you encounter a roadblock or need to do some brainstorming, you have other brilliant, innovative people sitting across from you! I can't tell you how many writing blocks I overcame because I took five minutes to talk the issue through with my friends at a Sunday writing night. You can even use Skype or Zoom to do a long-distance creativity night with friends who aren't able to visit in-person. Whether you host this co-creativity time as a special occasion or institute it as a regular occurrence, it's sure to kickstart your muse and inspire your momentum.

Teach Someone Something

Effort level: Medium to high ●●●●○

In the activities for the Page of Wands, I encouraged you to find a mentor. Now you're on the flip side of this relationship. The appearance of the Queen of Wands in your daily readings signals that you're in a new stage of your growth (whether it be a skill you've improved, a project you've completed, etc.). Why not get in touch with your inner Queen of Wands and pass your newfound knowledge on? You don't need to hang out a shingle and start offering lessons to strangers to be a teacher (although by all means, if you want to and feel ready!). I've taught friends how to cross stitch, for example, just for fun and because they wanted to learn. My brother (who studies history and can somehow keep five thousand discrete facts in his brain at the same time) has explained complicated historical events to me. These are just a few examples of ways that you can share knowledge in a casual way.

If you can't think of anyone who might want to learn something that you're knowledgeable in, you could always just record a video of yourself and upload it to social media. You can make the settings as private or public as you feel comfortable with, and then anyone who has any interest in your topic or skill can venture across your video and learn from it. It isn't quite as direct as sitting down with someone to teach them, but it's still a method for you to share knowledge. And even if only one or two people watch it, you've still had the opportunity to pass on your wisdom about a subject that you've honed and developed.

King of Wands

Who better to rep the leader of creativity and imagination than Willy Wonka? He inspired plenty of us as children. The King of Wands is someone with the creative spark to conceive projects, the drive to set them in motion, and the experience to see them through to the end. They learn from each undertaking and carry that wisdom onward and upward. Willy Wonka certainly fits the bill. "Invention is 93 percent perspiration, 6 percent inspiration, 3 percent perspiration, and 2 percent butterscotch ripple," he tells the children in the film. His magical chocolate factory is an example of a creative project done right—and Wonka knows when it's time to step back and allow new leadership to take his place, too. He has the wisdom to look for someone with integrity and dedication, but retains enough whimsy to look for a bright-eyed child. Sure, his methods may be a bit, um, unorthodox. But at the end of the day, Willy Wonka knows exactly the kind of person he wants to inherit his one-of-a-kind chocolate factory, and he knows how to find that exact person. He doesn't see limitations, he sees possibilities: "If you want to view paradise, simply look around and view it. Anything you want to, do it. Want to change the world? There's nothing to it."

The King of Wands is charismatic, creative, and capable. They see big ideas and they know how to capture them and bring them to life. They're an inspirational leader who intuitively brings the best out of their team. On occasion they may come across as disingenuous because their enthusiasm might seem impossible to maintain, but make no mistake—this is a King who is truly incapable of faking their joie de vivre. If they're guilty of anything, they may sometimes leap from the end of one project into the next without stopping to reflect. This doesn't come from an unwillingness to learn from their mistakes…it's just hard for the King of Wands (or any of the court of Wands, really) to slow down, even for a minute or two. Pair this King up with a member of the court of Swords or Pentacles, and you'll have a truly unstoppable team.

 ## Affirmations

I AM a creator.
I CAN see projects through from start to finish.
I WILL lead with passion.

 ## Reflections

Who in my life reminds me of the King of Wands?
What aspects of the King of Wands do I see in myself?
What aspects of the King of Wands would I like to cultivate in myself?

 ## Actions

Take a Personality Test

Effort level: Low to medium ●●○○○

All right, I admit it: I love personality tests. Myers-Briggs Type Indicator? Sign me up. Enneagram? Absolutely. Which Star Wars character would be your best friend? Sure, I'm in. Do I think that any one personality test can accurately capture every nuance of your mind and soul? Definitely not. But I DO believe that there's value in quantifying aspects of the human experience—not as a be-all-end-all, but as a starting place for reflection and growth. Even sillier or more lighthearted quizzes (like the aforementioned Star Wars best friend test) get you thinking about your identity, your preferences, and how you engage with the world around you.

For the purposes of engaging with this activity in a King of Wands manner, I'd recommend choosing one personality test to start with. With some of the more "serious" tests like the Myers-Briggs Type Indicator (MBTI), you may encounter paywalls and tests that only let you get your results if you provide your email address first. But even in these cases, you can find free, no-signup-required versions if you do a bit of poking around. I also recommend having a journal or notebook handy so you can jot down insights as they occur to you. When you get your result, write it down. Read whatever information the test provides about your personality type. Take note of anything that deeply resonates and anything that feels very off. If you're so inclined, you can do further research on your result—for higher-profile personality inventories like the Enneagram and MBTI, you can find whole books and webpages dedicated to your type. But as you learn, remember that nobody knows the King of Wands as well as they know themself. This personality test is a tool for analyzing bits and pieces of you, and it should be a jumping off point for reflection. Nothing more nor less.

Imagine Leadership

Effort level: Medium to high ◓◓◓◓○

In one of the reflection questions for the Emperor, I asked if you would feel comfortable in a position of authority. This exercise takes that question one step farther. Rather than simply speculating about your level of comfort, take some time to actively visualize yourself in a position of leadership. What exactly that looks like is entirely up to you. Maybe you've started your own business and it's grown to a level where you have multiple full-time employees working for you. Maybe you're a parent and have to be a leader when your kiddos need guidance and support. Maybe you've worked your way up in your office and you've been promoted to some sort of project manager. Choose to imagine something that's within the realm of possibility—there aren't good odds, for example, that you'll become president and lead the entire country. But there are good odds that you'll be asked to lead something in your life, whether it's a church choir or a *Fortune* 500 company.

Journal about your visualization if you're so inclined, or keep it all contained in the safe space of your own thoughts. But really try to play out that possibility in your head. What would it feel like to be in charge of something? Would you relish the opportunity to take the helm of something, or would you feel overwhelmed by the responsibility? What aspects of leadership would stress you out? Which would energize and ignite you? How would you keep yourself accountable and honest with the people you'd be leading? And are there people whose leadership styles have shaped your opinions about what makes a good leader—for good or for ill?

THE SUIT OF CUPS
Feel and Heal

The suit of Cups is associated with the element of water. Can there be a more apt element to reflect the suit of emotion? Water can be still, deep, and profoundly peaceful, like a babbling brook or the unbroken surface of a pond on a quiet day. Or it can be intense, dangerous, and overpowering, like an ocean in a hurricane or the driving rain in a thunderstorm. In this suit you'll experience every high and low of the human experience, from true love to crushing grief, from bewildering illusion to enlightening clarity, and everything in between. This suit also governs the relationships among us—how they have the power to pierce or mend our hearts, and how we can act to nurture or dissolve them.

Here are some words to describe the suit of Cups: *emotions, relationships, connection, love, loss, memory, cycles, heart, intuition, spirituality, dreams, mystery, enlightenment, transformation, beauty, trust, wishes, health, intimacy, forgiveness.*

If Cups keep appearing in your daily readings, you're probably dealing with feelings that you haven't acknowledged or fully come to grips with yet. It's time for reflection. Swords might invite you to reflect in solitude and silence, but the Cups are a suit of sharing, so this might be a good time to sit down with a trusted loved one (or a good therapist) and talk things through. And speaking of loved ones, repeated Cups in your daily readings may also encourage you to examine your relationships. Are there people in your life who need extra care or attention? Are there people whose presence is actively draining you, who might need to be distanced or given firmer boundaries? Are you taking any of your dearest loved ones for granted?

Ace of Cups

Welcome to the suit of emotions and relationships. The Ace of Cups is the fountain of our deepest and most powerful feelings, and it's currently overflowing. We each of us carry a neverending well of love, fears, hopes, and memories. With the Ace, all of these are flowing freely and easily. Our cup runneth over with new feelings and ideas. Or perhaps we're revisiting the old and nostalgic to renew our convictions, our passions, and ourselves.

When the Ace of Cups comes into your daily reading, you are pouring your energy into your loved ones and the world around you. Don't hold back any emotions or thoughts that burble to the surface. And if you find yourself wearing thin, don't hesitate to take a time out to nourish yourself. No one can be receiving OR outputting such powerful emotions 100 percent of the time. Lean into the feelings of the moment, whatever they may be.

 ## Affirmations

I AM passionate.
I CAN let my emotions flow.
I WILL express myself freely.

 ## Reflections

What does renewal mean to me?
What activities or pursuits truly recharge your batteries? For me, it's putting on a podcast or some soothing music and working on a cross-stitch project. If I were a videogame character, this would refill my energy meter. I'm not just talking about physical

energy—I'm talking about mental, emotional, and spiritual energy, too. I'm sure you know that feeling of being so emotionally exhausted that all you want to do is stare at a blank wall and recalibrate. So what do you do in those situations? What makes you feel that your energy meter is refilling?

How can I connect with my intuition?

The element of water brings us back to that well of emotions and instincts deep within us. Our intuition is like the tide in us—it ebbs and flows, but it is always present. How can you become more acutely aware of this tide and what it's telling you? Do you tend to listen readily when you have an intuitive feeling come up, or do you tend to dismiss it? What might it feel like to listen more closely? Can you remember a time when your intuition was correct about a person or a situation? What did that feel like? How does that make you feel about listening to your future intuition?

What happens when I pour from an empty cup?

Think of a time when you were completely overloaded. Stress, obligations, challenges with loved ones—whatever may have been piling up, it left you running on mental and emotional empty. What were the effects of operating from that place of emotional lack? What were you forced to let fall by the wayside? How did it impact your relationships with your loved ones? Did you have to make any difficult decisions? And how did you get yourself out of that rut and find more of an equilibrium again?

 *Actions*

Hydrate

Effort level: Low to medium

Making sure you're getting enough water seems like a baseline self-care activity, but for many of us it's much harder than it first appears! I don't get thirsty very often on my own so it's easy for me to go all day without thinking to take a drink—and then I wonder why I feel so gross at the end of the day! Look up how much water we're ideally supposed to get every day and it might seem daunting. (Plus current research suggests that different people need different amounts, so pushing yourself to drink the "right" amount every day could actually be bad for your health instead of good.) So rather than approaching it that way, consider this question: how could I fit drinking a glass of water into my everyday routine?

Maybe it's filling up a glass first thing in the morning and drinking it while the coffee maker is running. Maybe it's keeping a bottle filled up right next to your desk at work. (I found a bottle with time goals marked on the sides to help me keep track of how much I should be drinking as the day goes by, and that's made a *huge* difference for me!) Maybe it's making sure to keep water nearby as you watch Netflix in the evening.

Whatever you choose, don't come at it from the perspective of "I should be drinking 64 ounces of water every day!!!" Instead, find one small, achievable way that you can get one glass of water into your day. If that goes well, you can always build from there. But start small and increase at your own pace. Any water you're adding to your daily routine is better than none. And better that you start by implementing a small habit than by going between the extremes of all or nothing.

Take a Bath

Effort level: Medium to high ⬤⬤⬤⬤◯

When we imagine self-care, we often imagine cucumber slices on our eyes and luxurious baths, right? And perhaps there's a reason for that—baths are true opportunities to pamper ourselves. But I think it goes deeper than that, too. Baths remind us to connect more with our bodies and our senses. Put on music or bring in a favorite book, and they become meditative and mentally rejuvenating, too. This is the kind of energy the Ace of Cups invites into your day—renewing, reflective, and soothing.

There's so many ways to turn your bath into the perfect self-care experience. As someone with a great deal of chronic pain, I'm personally very partial to Epsom salt.

But of course, there are whole stores dedicated to bath bombs and accessories. If you can, really take the time to dress up this bath and make it as relaxing as you'd like. Pour a glass of wine or scoop a bowl of ice cream. Light candles. Put on an audiobook or a favorite playlist. Make this your opportunity to renew yourself and emerge refreshed.

Two of Cups

The Cups speak of connections that run deep, and perhaps none so strongly as the Two of Cups. This is a card for love that lasts. While the Lovers stand for sudden strong attractions or connections, the Two of Cups is what happens when those strong beginnings have weathered many ups and downs together. This card is for romances that survive past the fading of the honeymoon phase, for friendships that grow and shift with you as the years change you, and for self-love that is solid and enduring.

When this card appears in your daily reading, draw strength and comfort from your inner circle. You know who they are—the people whose company recharges you. Reach out to them when you need them. And, in turn, nourish those relationships back. Be that sacred space where your loved ones can recharge when they need it. Odds are that they rely on you just as much as you rely on them.

Affirmations

I AM beloved and loving.
I CAN trust my loved ones.
I WILL rely on my loved ones and be reliable for them.

Reflections

Who in my life do I feel closest to?

Don't take this question at face value. It's tempting to give the easy answer—the people you live with, or the people whose company you keep the most often. But push past the easy answers and be honest about the souls who you truly feel the most open with, the most fully yourself with, the most vulnerable with. If you were by yourself and having an anxiety attack, who would you call or text to help you stay grounded? If you landed a huge career success, who would you want to share that joy with first? If you were undergoing surgery, who would you want to be at your bedside? The people who appear on this list (and the people who don't) may surprise you. Go deeper. Examine what makes those people so important.

How can I better support my loved ones?

Relationships are meant to be a give and take. When a relationship is too one-sided, it isn't sustainable. It's important to feel comfortable asking for what you need in a relationship of any sort, and it's just as important to set boundaries to keep yourself emotionally healthy. But it's also important to not grow too comfortable in a long-term relationship, to make sure you aren't taking your dearest loved ones for granted. How can you make those you hold dear feel supported and loved by you? It could be as simple as remembering to ask about the status of a project they've been working on for weeks, or as complex as planning a weekend getaway. What steps can you take to celebrate and cherish the people you love the most?

What does intimacy mean to me?

When you are truly intimate with someone, what does that look like? This can certainly have a sexual and/or physical layer for some relationships, but you can be intimate with someone in a completely platonic context as well. A simple and somewhat silly example from my life: I have hardcore insomnia, and it's difficult for me to fall asleep in the presence of anyone else. A major sign of how close I am to you is whether I can drift off while you're in the room. My spouse, immediate family, and several of my dearest friends would fall into this category. What signs make it clear that you're on intimate terms with someone in your life? Or to put it another way, how do you express your intimacy?

 **Actions**

Tell Someone Why They Matter to You

Effort level: Low to medium ●●○○○

There are straightforward ways of saying that someone means a lot to you—telling them, "I love you," for instance. But when was the last time you told someone why? It doesn't have to be eloquent or poetic. It can be as simple as looking your partner in the eye and saying that they make you happy every day. It can be giving your parent a call and letting them know that you still employ a lesson they taught you as a child. It can be leaving a greeting card at your coworker's desk to tell them that they brighten up your workweek. Go beyond "I love you" or "thank you" and articulate the why and the how.

I think it's also easier to do this with immediate family and romantic partners, in some ways—we have a societal script for these sorts of conversations. To a certain extent, we're expected to express affection to our life partners, to our parents, and to our siblings. But for other platonic relationships, such as friends and colleagues, we aren't armed with the same understanding of how to voice appreciation. I have a close friend (we'll call them Milo) whose personality is similar to mine in many ways, and I realized recently that my conversations with Milo has helped me gain a deeper understanding of my own anxiety and how to navigate it. So—stay with me here—that's exactly what I told them. "One of the reasons I'm so glad we get coffee every weekend is because being around you helps me level out my anxiety from the workweek," I said. And I think it meant a lot to Milo to hear.

Not only does saying these things out loud brighten the recipient's day and make them feel loved, but it also brings their importance into sharper focus for you, too. Nobody wants to feel taken for granted and taking the time to say why someone means the world to *you* will mean the world to *them*.

Make a Gift for Someone

Effort level: Medium to high ●●●●○

My mom is an amazing knitter. Her knitting needles have turned out everything from cozy blankets to tiny stuffed animals and everything in between. Every now and then people will ask why she doesn't try to sell her creations, and she always answers, "I only knit for my loved ones."

There's something especially touching and meaningful about receiving a gift that was handmade, isn't there? Part of that special factor is, of course, the degree of thought that goes into it—the gift-giver had to think of what you in particular would like and want. But that's not the whole of it. After all, a lot of thought can go into the selection of a store-bought gift as well. My mom articulates it best when she says that a handmade gift represents time. The person who makes a gift for you has poured their precious time into the gift, and that is something that can never be returned or regifted.

What skills can you use to make a special gift for someone you love? Whether it's as simple as baking a batch of their favorite cookies or as complicated as painting a piece of artwork for their home, pull from your hobbies and talents to make a gift that will bring a huge smile to their face. Save it for a special occasion or give it to them right away as a just-because gift. Whatever you choose to make and however you choose to deploy it, the act of making and giving a gift to someone is its own form of intimacy.

Three of Cups

The Three of Cups is your community, the people who make up your home base. While the Two represents the strong threads that connect you to each of your treasured loved ones, the Three is the quilt that all of you make up together. It's the breath that you subconsciously stop holding when you're in the presence of your family (not necessarily your blood family, but the people who make you feel most at home—whatever and whoever that means). It's knowing that if you fall, not just one but many loved ones will be there to catch you and set you on your feet again.

When the Three of Cups arrives in a daily reading, tend the garden of your community. Celebrate all the extraordinary individuals that populate your inner circle. Plan an evening out with your friends or a visit home to see your family. If you feel a lack in this area, examine how you might fill it up. Do you need to take advantage of opportunities to make new friends? Do you need to rekindle a relationship with a cherished family member that has grown distant? What actions can you take to feel truly confident that there is a community behind you?

 ## Affirmations

I AM a cherished friend.
I CAN trust my community.
I WILL make time for my friendships.

 ## Reflections

What does friendship mean to me?
Our friends play different roles at different points in our lives. When we're children, our friends are the people we sit next to in school and who we invite for sleepovers. If we go to college, friends are roommates and classmates who we see almost daily. As we

branch away from our foundations, friends may be coworkers or parents of our children's friends. How do you remain connected to your friends when your life becomes increasingly busy and complicated? What do those friendships mean to you, and how do you make them a priority?

What communities am I a part of?

Community has so many meanings, doesn't it? For instance, I am part of communities as broad as the LGBTQ+ community and as narrow as a tiny coven with two of my closest friends. How I interact with these communities is completely different, of course, but at the end of the day this much is true: I feel connected on some level to everyone else in the LGBTQ+ community, and I feel connected to my coven-mates. Both of these communities are deeply meaningful to me. What communities are you a part of? What role do those communities play in your daily life? How do you reaffirm your connections to these communities? How do they enrich your world?

What do I do when I'm lonely?

The time we spend alone is precious and important. But sometimes we feel alone when we'd rather be in someone's company. When you feel isolated or cut off, what do you do? Do you have loved ones who you can reach out to when you need them? If you're stuck in a moment of being alone, how do you manage the loneliness? What self-care measures do you take? If you can't think of anything you usually do, brainstorm ways that you might address moments of loneliness next time they come up. As is often the case, it's easier to formulate a self-care plan ahead of time, rather than waiting until you're already feeling alone and overwhelmed.

 *Actions*

A Toast to You

Effort level: Low to medium ●●○○○

The imagery of the Three of Cups often features three people lifting their glasses, cups, or other drinking vessels in a toast to each other. The energy is one of camaraderie and shared celebration. They are proud of each other, reveling in the unique magic that each of them brings to the table. It feels good to be acknowledged for who you are and what you contribute to your little corner of the universe. And while the Three of Cups encourages you to share these moments with others, it doesn't mean that you can't give yourself these moments as a gift.

If you'd like to be fancy about it, you can pour yourself a glass of something celebratory like wine or sparkling grape juice. But this can also be a special moment that you claim for yourself during your morning coffee, or even over a glass of water to keep yourself hydrated during the workday (see the Ace of Cups). If you're in a space where you can speak aloud without feeling self-conscious, do so—but if not, say the words in your mind. "I'd like to propose a toast to myself," and take the time to state what the toast is honoring. What have you done that deserves celebration recently? If a friend *were* there in the room with you, what would they be proud of you for? It doesn't have to be a momentous accomplishment. If you're toasting yourself for getting out of bed on time for work even though you felt like calling in sick and going back to sleep, that's your toast! Because you know what? That's an accomplishment, no matter how small and insignificant it may seem to you.

Maybe this will seem silly or even arrogant. We aren't taught to own our accomplishments—more often, we're expected to just look ahead to the next deadline, the next task, the next obligation. But the Three of Cups invokes not just you but the community behind you. They are celebrating you and lifting you up even when they aren't physically with you. They would want you to take a moment and acknowledge your accomplishments. Summon their energy and pat yourself on the back. You've earned it.

Spend Time in One of Your Communities

Effort level: Medium to high ●●●●○

As we explored in one of the reflections above, community can mean many different things. When the Three of Cups turns up in a daily reading, it's a great time to reconnect to one of the communities you're a part of. But again, that can take a million different forms! Maybe it's going to a meetup of people who share one of your interests or identities. Maybe it's going to church or visiting a side of your family that you don't see often. It doesn't even have to be spending time in a physical location. For example, when I'm feeling left out because of my chronic pain, I hop on to one of my online fibromyalgia groups and read/comment on posts written by other people who understand the challenges of this illness. It's deeply comforting and, most importantly, makes me feel much less alone.

No matter how actively you participate in them, you are a member of countless communities, big and small. How can you spend time in one or more of those groups? If you aren't sure what communities you can count yourself in, take some time reflecting on the question above. Then reach out to one of them. Your presence can be virtual or physical. It can be loud and proud or it can be quiet and shy. You don't have to be planning the church potluck to spend time in your church community, after all.

Four of Cups

The Four of Cups arises when things have become stale or stagnant. No matter what your current situation is—even if it is full of abundance—you find yourself wishing for a change. The passionate feelings that carried us through the Ace, Two, and Three of Cups have become dull and flat...or perhaps they haven't changed at all, but you've grown so accustomed to them that they feel dull and flat. I often think of the Four of Cups as the period that comes after the honeymoon phase of a new relationship. The fireworks of new love have simmered down into something steadier and quieter, and the heart may find itself craving those intense highs again.

When you pull the Four of Cups in your daily reading, ask yourself if you are growing complacent. Is this restlessness and boredom a sign that you need to shake things up and add something new to your routine? Or is it a symptom of taking your world and your loved ones for granted? The Four of Cups can point to either, so be just as honest with yourself as you are curious. The change you need could just as easily be a change of attitude as a change of pace.

Affirmations

I AM grateful for what I have.
I CAN sit with disquiet and discover what's underneath.
I WILL take time to contemplate.

Reflections

What is drawing my attention away?
Sometimes if we're trying to focus on something relatively mindless (or even if we're trying to focus on something engaging!) we have particular thought patterns that tend to tempt our attention off the path to Granny's house. For example: most of us are guilty

of losing ourselves in plans and predictions about the rest of the day, our outstanding to-do list, and how to get as much done as we possibly can. But sometimes there are specific subjects or even obsessions that keep capturing our interest. Think about how hard it is to focus on anything else when you're nursing a new crush, for instance! So if you're struggling to focus right now, ask yourself what you keep catching your mind wandering to instead. Is there something you can do to scratch that mental itch (e.g., if you're obsessing about a particular item on your to-do list, would it make more sense to pause your current project and take care of that to-do item first)? If not, how might you gently remind your brain to shelve this topic for now?

When am I most prone to boredom?

Is there a particular part of your day when you tend to grow restless? Really consider the last time you felt this way. Can you pinpoint where that feeling was coming from? What did you do to address it? Perhaps it was something as easy as getting up and taking a few laps away from your desk, or perhaps it was much more involved and elaborate. Boredom can be a sign that you need a mental hiatus from whatever you're currently working on. But it can also be a call to look deeper and push past the surface of your thoughts. If there's a part of your routine where boredom often sneaks in, there may be some deeper workings at play—a need that you aren't acknowledging, a mental itch that you aren't scratching, a wish that you aren't voicing. If you identify that pattern, how can you stay curious about its origins the next time it repeats itself?

What do I need to reflect on right now?

Continuing on the theme of the previous question, chronic apathy may be a warning that you need to do some soul-searching. What do you need to really sit with and reflect on? As one example, perhaps a goal that you were pursuing with gusto has stalled out and left you feeling deflated. You aren't happy with where you are, but you're still smarting too much from the letdown to reconnoiter. The result? Boredom and restlessness. Again, this is just one possibility. What is your boredom trying to tell you? Sit with it and let it tell you what areas need your contemplation.

 *Actions*

Make a List of Your Boredom-Busters

Effort level: Low to medium ⬤⬤◯◯◯

As may be evident if you've read enough of these card entries, I'm a big fan of making lists of ways to manage challenging feelings. When I'm in the middle of a terrible chronic pain flareup, it's a lot harder to come up with ways to make myself feel better—so having a pre-assembled toolbox full of comforting activities is tremendously helpful. I find this to be true for any number of flareups, whether it's my mental or physical health that's suffering. Boredom is no exception!

I've talked a lot about boredom being a sign that some reflection needs to be done, but sometimes boredom is just boredom, too. If you're feeling the need to do something but can't decide what, how nice would it be to have a list of activities ready-made? I'll sometimes keep a running list of movies and videos I want to re-watch—that way if I can't decide on something to throw on while I work, I have a list to refer to. You could do the same thing with books to read, albums to listen to, games to play, etc. This could even extend to activities you want to try, or that you want to do more frequently, such as taking a walk outside or knitting.

As you create this list, I would encourage you to make sure you have a range of activities in terms of energy and time commitment. If your list is full of time-consuming or high-intensity activities, you may find it more demoralizing than helpful if you're just looking for something quick to get your brain out of a rut. Similarly, if you've got a two-hour block of time to kill and your list only includes short videos, you may get fed up with them after one or two and wind up bored all over again. So fill your list with a variety of activities and ideas. Future bored you will be grateful.

Find a Good Place to Contemplate

Effort level: Medium to high ⬤⬤⬤⬤◯

I cannot articulate how much a change of scenery can make a difference when you're in a rut. If you're feeling stuck, the places where you're stuck are probably only going to make you feel even MORE stuck. When I'm in a creative low, I'll pack up my laptop and go someplace completely different. I've planted myself in the whale exhibit at my local aquarium, armed with a notebook and a pen, and gotten more writing done than I ever could have at home. It doesn't have to be someplace as dramatic as an aquarium, of course—it could just be the nearest park or coffee shop. But shaking up your surroundings can do a world of good in shaking up your mental pathways.

So if you're sick of your current routine and you're looking for a change of pace, look for a change of place! (Sorry.) Find someplace new to go, whether it's around the corner or across the country. Get out there and really pay attention to how you feel as you go on your journey. If any new insights or possibilities occur to you, take note of them. Write them down if it helps you keep track of them. If you feel an intuitive pull to do something unexpected, listen to it. Let your thoughts come and go as they may, and again, pay attention to anything that may address your current situation or routine.

Five of Cups

As the halfway point through the pips, the fives are often the fulcrum of each suit's challenges and pitfalls. The Five of Cups is no exception—it stands for the kind of crushing, all-encompassing grief that blots out the sunlight and makes you forget what joy ever felt like. Most variations of the Five of Cups depict three cups that have been broken or overturned, but two cups remain upright and full. This reminds us that when we've lost something or someone precious to us, the fog of mourning can obscure what yet remains.

When you find the Five of Cups in a daily reading, there are deep, painful feelings that demand to be felt. Attempting to mask those feelings behind pleasantry or a false smile will only delay (and in all likelihood, prolong) the sorrow. Yet at the same time, the Five of Cups asks us to hold on tight to what we haven't lost. In grieving for our three overturned cups, we should not forget to be grateful for the two cups left to us.

 ## Affirmations

I AM acquainted with sorrow.
I CAN balance grief and gratitude.
I WILL feel what I need to feel.

 ## Reflections

What have I lost?

I think it's kind of charming that we use the word "lost" to describe such a broad category of absence. With the same word, you can misplace your favorite pen in an Uber, and you can mourn your beloved grandmother who died when you were twelve. Loss can be as tiny as an insignificant object you put in the wrong place or as vast as a loved one. So when I ask what you've lost, answer with anything that comes to mind, big and small. It doesn't have to be a cherished family member whose presence you miss every day, although it certainly can be. What losses have you endured, either recently or in your life as a whole? What impact do those losses have on your day-to-day?

What do I miss?

This may seem like an obvious extension of the previous question, and in some ways it is. But at the same time, you can lose something that you don't miss much. You might misplace something and go for years without noticing its absence. Or at the other end of the spectrum, if you have certain blood relatives who you were never close to, their death might be sad in a general sense, but you may not actively miss them. And too, you can miss people or things or even periods of time in your life that aren't gone, just distant. I live halfway across the country from my family, and I miss them even though I text and video chat with them regularly! What do you miss right now? A college friend who you've fallen out of touch with? A stuffed unicorn you carried everywhere as a child that got lost the last time you moved homes? Again, think as big or as small as you'd like with this question. Humans ascribe meaning to everything, and there's nothing trivial about missing a possession that meant something to you.

What do I still have to be thankful for?

Few cards remind you to be grateful with such urgency as the Five of Cups. When we're in the midst of profound sorrow, it's all too easy to overlook the remaining good in our universe. And again, this isn't meant to nullify or dismiss the sadness. The Five of Cups asks us to validate both our grief and our gratitude. Both are important and worthy of your attention. No matter how much sadness you're carrying, take a moment to think about what you're thankful to have in your life. A roof over your head? A support system of loved ones who remind you to take care of yourself even in dark times? A furry family member who keeps you laughing even when you don't much feel like it?

 **Actions**

Write to Someone You Miss

Effort level: Low to medium ●●○○○

Every year on the anniversary of my dad's death, I write a letter to tell him how I'm doing. Sometimes I believe that he can read what I've written. Sometimes I think he's been watching the whole time and already knows what I'm writing about. Sometimes I'm not sure he's out there at all. Regardless, the ritual of writing a letter to honor him is deeply comforting for me. It makes me feel more strongly that he's part of my life even though he's no longer alive, and that soothes the ache of missing him.

You could just as easily write a letter to someone who's still alive but isn't part of your life anymore. Maybe it's a childhood friend who moved away when you were young. Maybe it's a family member you've cut off communication with, but whose presence you nonetheless miss. Maybe it's a beloved pet! Even though you're writing "to" someone, ultimately this activity is for *you* and nobody else. So don't second guess it—whoever comes to mind first is probably the person you should address your letter to. And try not to edit or censor yourself, either. This doesn't need to be literature for the ages, and it doesn't need to be merely sentimental, either. Just because you miss someone doesn't mean you might not have complicated feelings about them (such as in the case of a toxic family member who you no longer speak with). If an unexpected feeling emerges, like anger or bitterness, let that come out in your letter, too.

Make a Person-Based Gratitude List

Effort level: Medium to high ●●●●○

When you think about what you're grateful for, do you ever ascribe specific reasons for your gratitude? I know when I first tried keeping a gratitude journal, I lost interest because it felt repetitive. Of course I'm going to say I'm grateful for my spouse more days than not. Boring and obvious, I thought. I only really got into gratitude journaling once I started listing why, specifically, I was grateful for that person on that particular day. "I'm grateful for my spouse for making me tea when I wasn't feeling well today."

"I'm grateful for my spouse's goofiness making me laugh." And so on. It makes the gratitude more tangible, somehow.

For this activity, I suggest that you take it one step farther. Choose someone whose presence is a constant in your life—a partner, a child, a sibling—and spend a few moments listing all the reasons you can think of to be grateful for that person. Does their smile always brighten your mood? Do they bring dinner on their way home from work when you need a pick-me-up? Can you always count on them for a hug, or an encouraging text message? Write it all down, the big stuff and the small stuff. Or if you aren't in a writing mood, at least make a mental list. You can do this for as many loved ones as you'd like, but try to focus on one person at a time. My only caveat: if you are in the middle of grieving a recently-deceased loved one, I'd avoid using them as the object of your gratitude list. If you want to write to them, do the first activity (write to someone you miss) instead. The purpose of *this* activity is to get you out of the heartspace of your sadness (away from the three overturned cups) and focus your attention on the people who are supporting you through your grieving process (the two upright and full cups).

Six of Cups

The Six of Cups is all about memory and nostalgia. It's about looking to your past not merely as a source of wisdom and experience, but as a wellspring of emotional strength. Your story isn't a flat sequence of facts in a dusty history book—it's a dynamic, living, breathing part of you, and it flows in your veins every moment! The people who came in and out of your life, the situations you lived through—all are touchstones that you can access whenever you need them.

This card invites you to reach back into your memories and cherish what you find there, good and bad. Take a trip down memory lane and linger wherever you pass something of particular significance. Honor the people who made you who you are. Cherish your moments of triumph and love. When you find a memory that is painful or uncomfortable, remind yourself what you learned from the experience. You are the sum total of everyone who has loved and hated you, every day you've soared or fallen flat, and every emotion you've held in your heart. Don't be shy about revisiting those pieces of your past.

 ## Affirmations

I AM made of memories.
I CAN honor my history.
I WILL look to the past for guidance.

 ## Reflections

What have I inherited from my relatives or ancestors?
It's something of a cliché to worry that you're turning into your parent, right? And when you have a fraught relationship with one or both of your parents, I can certainly see why this might be a concern. But if you have one or more immediate relatives (not just

parents) who you admire, this question can get you thinking about positive ways that you see them in yourself. And if you have immediate relatives whose presence in your life is more negative than positive, you might use this question to consider what habits or mannerisms you've inherited that you want to break or soften.

If you aren't comfortable applying this reflection to any of your living relatives, another way to go about it is to consider your ancestors instead. Were they survivors of oppression or trauma? Did they travel great distances or endure profound hardship? How do you see their qualities in yourself? Or how might you weave those qualities into your awareness going forward?

How can I invite nostalgia into my everyday life?

A common piece of mindfulness/meditation wisdom is that you should endeavor to stay in the present moment. And while there is a lot to be gained from tethering yourself to the here and now, there's also something to be said for mindfully looking back to moments of joy and belonging in your past. The danger is when we get so caught up in replaying memories (especially painful ones) that we completely miss out on the here and now. So how might you inject conscious, intentional nostalgia into your day? Here's an example: my dad had a ton of goofy catchphrases and reference jokes that we lovingly refer to as Dad-isms or Ralph-isms. Now that he's gone, I find it profoundly meaningful to quote him in my daily life. It brings that feeling of bittersweet, loving nostalgia, and it makes me feel that he's a part of my present moment, even if he isn't physically with me. How might you find little moments of mindful nostalgia like this?

What about the present moment will I want to remember in the future?

This is almost the opposite of the previous question. Take a moment to look around. Even if there's a lot about your present situation that you'd like to change, I bet there's at least one element of your world that you could remember with fondness. It might be as mundane as the cozy little nook in your bedroom where you go to recharge after a long day, or it might be as significant as your relationship with a beloved sibling. This question reminds you to take nothing for granted—it's a slightly different angle on the traditional gratitude list. What about this moment, this current second of life that you're living, might you look back on with nostalgia someday?

 **Actions**

Invite Someone Older to Share Their Memories

Effort level: Low to medium ● ● ○ ○ ○

A note I want to make right at the top: I recognize that not everyone has living older relatives to talk to, or they may have older relatives who are alive but not safe or comfortable to engage with. If that's the case for you, feel free to adapt this activity as you see fit. Talk to any relative who exceeds you in years, or talk to an older somebody who isn't related to you, or even just choose someone who comes from a distinctly different background than you. The only reason I specify "someone older" here is because people in their later years are often in a stage of remembering and indulging in nostalgia, and because they often love nothing more than to share those memories with their loved ones.

All of that being said, this is an opportunity to listen openheartedly, discover tidbits from an unfamiliar time or place, and (if you're talking to someone who you're close with) maybe even learn something new about someone you love. They might choose to reminisce about a Big Moment in their lives—a wedding, the birth of a child, a trip—or they might pick something smaller and seemingly mundane. I love finding out about tiny little character quirks or quiet life moments in my grandparents' histories.

If you aren't sure how to start this conversation—especially if you don't often ask this person to share—here's a few suggestions.

"Hey, Uncle David, I know you grew up on a farm. I was just wondering what that was like for you."

"Mrs. Johansen, can you tell me what your husband was like when you first met him?"

"I'd love to hear some of your favorite memories from when you were a kid."

Even if it feels a little awkward to ask, most people love to talk about themselves and their memories. Chances are that the conversation will start to flow naturally enough.

Decorate with Pictures or Symbols of Ancestors

Effort level: Medium to high ●●●●○

Do you ever look through photos of your family members from when they were your age, or even younger? For me, there's always a strange sense of surreal nostalgia. Surreal because I never knew my parents or grandparents at this age, and nostalgia because I can still see the person I know in their features and expressions. But it's only been recently that I've started bringing photos and relics that remind me of my relatives into my own house and decorating with them. I personally have a special ancestor altar where I'm slowly collecting symbols and talismans. But there are any number of ways you can bring reminders of your ancestors into your living space.

As with the above exercise, if you don't know much about your distant relatives or you aren't connected to them, you can customize this activity to work for you. If you feel a connection with a culture or ethnicity from your genetic makeup, you might select symbols that signify that culture or ethnicity for you. (For example, my dad's side of the family are Ashkenazi Jews, so even though I'm not religiously Jewish, I feel a strong connection to the Star of David.) If you don't have strong ties to your cultures of origin, you might consider other sorts of kinships. If you're part of the disabled community, are there particular disabled trailblazers who you feel strongly connected to? If you're an artist, are there artists whose work has inspired yours? Get creative and introspective as you consider what person or group you identify with, and then what images or symbols might be meaningful to place somewhere in your home.

Seven of Cups

Welcome to the Seven of Cups, where we are swept away by so many beautiful fantasies that we find ourselves overwhelmed with choices. On the one hand, fantasy can be a lovely thing. We all need a little fantasy from time to time. But on the other hand, we can find ourselves so immersed in our fantasies that the real world becomes intangible and distant. Our judgment can become clouded, rendering decision-making nearly impossible. (A note here that I use the word "fantasy" as a catch-all to mean any piece of imagination or fiction—not just the genre by the same name with magic and swordplay.)

While some tarot guides will tell you that the Seven of Cups is a warning against illusions of all kinds, I take more of a middle-ground stance. When this card appears, I see it as a reminder to keep your feet firmly planted on the ground as you dream. Fantasy and escapism have an important place in our lives as long as we navigate them with clear eyes. If a fantasy is helping you recharge or bringing you simple joy, that's one thing. But if you're using your fantasy to hide from important decisions, the Seven of Cups may indeed be a warning to take a step back and reassess.

Affirmations

I AM clear-eyed.
I CAN see things for what they are.
I WILL be mindful of illusion.

Reflections

What fantasy worlds do I find comfort in?
Each of us has different fiction that we prefer to lose ourselves in. Maybe you can watch all the *Lord of the Rings* movies on loop and never get tired of them. Maybe you have a

shelf of Harlequin romance novels that you always turn to on a bad day. Maybe you log into MMORPGs and spend hours levelling up your character alongside online friends. Whatever the case, take a moment to consciously call these fictional worlds to mind. How long have you loved them? What about this story, genre, medium, world, etc. makes it so appealing to you when you need to get away from the "real" world for a bit? If you had to describe it to someone who never tried it before (or even someone who actively disliked it) how would you describe the familiar sense of relief and comfort you experience when you disappear into this alternate reality?

How do I know when I'm indulging in too much escapism?

As I've said, I don't believe there's anything wrong with wanting to hit the pause button on reality by opening a book, turning on a movie, or playing a videogame. However, there is certainly a point at which it becomes a means of avoidance rather than a healthy break. Can you think of a time in your life when you used fiction or fantasy to dodge responsibility or avoid feelings? (My therapist definitely called me out on this when I was watching the same YouTube videos over and over to keep from facing my grief.) Are you aware of any warning signs when you're starting to hide behind your favorite fantasy worlds? If you notice those warning signs popping up, how might you course correct?

What big choices do I currently have to make?

The Seven of Cups is often a heads up that we're feeling overwhelmed by a myriad of choices. Are there any decisions hanging over your head that make you feel swamped by choices? How might you actually begin the process of sorting through your options? Or, to ask it another way, what is one step you could take right now that might help you arrive at your decision?

 *Actions*

Make a Pro/Con List

Effort level: Low to medium ●●○○○

You've probably made a pro/con list while trying to reach a decision before. Or if you haven't, you've at least had people advise you to do so. As someone who makes almost all of their decisions from my heart and gut instead of my head, I'm often resistant to this method. It seems too logic-driven, reducing an emotional decision to a laundry list of advantages and disadvantages. However, I DO believe in the power of writing things down. And especially when you're feeling overwhelmed by choices, the classic pro/con list can genuinely help you untangle your thoughts from each other.

So if you're like me and tend to make your decisions intuitively rather than logically, here's my suggestion. As you sit down to make your list, don't think of pros and cons as solely objective, clinical advantages and disadvantages. As much as we'd like to believe we can be objective when necessary, the truth is that we're emotional creatures, and we attach feelings to everything we do and think. So I encourage you to actively include your feelings in your list! If you know that one option is the more logical one but another option seems way more fun, write that down in the pros for the option in question. If you have a strong gut instinct that one option is the right one, write that down. If you know a loved one is really pushing you toward one option and you're hesitant to disappoint them, write that down. We do ourselves a disservice when we try to completely remove emotions from our decision-making equation, because whatever decision we arrive at, we're going to feel some type of way about it. So, making those emotions part of the deciding is, in my opinion, more genuine and more constructive.

There and Back Again

Effort level: Medium to high ●●●●○

The Seven of Cups cautions us not to hide behind fantasy to avoid making decisions. In this exercise, I invite you to turn that danger on its head. Call to mind a situation where you feel overwhelmed with choices, or where you're caught between two or three choices that seem equally advantageous. (This might even be a good activity to try if you've already attempted to make a pro/con list and it's only made you more confused.) Pick one of your options to start with and settle in someplace where you won't be disturbed or distracted for a bit.

Now, take that powerful imagination of yours and use it to fully immerse yourself in a world where you choose option A. Really allow yourself to fantasize about all the little details, all the ripple effects that might occur in this reality. If you go with Job Offer A instead of Job Offer B, what will your commute be like? How much more stress would you be liable to bring home with you? Would you need to fill out your wardrobe with more appropriate workwear? Take your time and explore all the impacts of option A that you can think of. Once you feel that you've exhausted your imagination in this arena, bring yourself back to the present day. You may want to take a moment to jot down any insights, questions, or thoughts that arose. Then, when you feel ready, go through this same process for each of the other options you're caught between.

Naturally, the effects you've imagined may not be what come to pass in real life. But it's still worth exploring the effects that *you* imagined as you try to arrive at a decision. For one thing, this exercise may get you thinking about details that you hadn't considered before. And even if it doesn't, you may discover that you're lingering in one option much longer than the others, or that you're unfairly imagining negative or positive effects for one of the options. This, too, is useful to know—it may help you recognize that you're leaning toward one option more than you initially believed.

Eight of Cups

If the Seven of Cups represents illusion, the Eight often points to disillusionment. Perhaps you recently made a decision that hasn't panned out the way you hoped, or perhaps you've learned something about a situation that's soured your view of it. Whatever the case, you've reached a point where your Right Now isn't at all what you thought it was going to be, and you're feeling a pull to step away and reassess how to move forward…or whether to move forward with this enterprise at all.

When the Eight of Cups visits us, it's confirmation that it is indeed time to excuse ourselves and reconnoiter. The *Numinous Tarot* by Cedar McCloud illustrates this as the moment you step outside to get some air from a loud, overwhelming party and decide that you don't want to go back inside after all. There's no shame in deciding that something isn't for you, and there's no shame in allowing yourself to feel disappointed or disillusioned by the reality of something you were initially excited about. Give yourself the gift of that space to take stock and, if it feels like the right move, to walk away altogether.

Affirmations

I AM aware of my limits.
I CAN recognize when I'm not satisfied.
I WILL step away to recalibrate.

Reflections

What do I need to release?
In the Hanged Man, we explored whether there were any places where we might loosen our grip on controlling some aspect of our life. Now, I invite you to consider whether there's anything that needs to be released completely. Maybe you can finally donate

those ice skates that have been gathering dust on the off-chance that you might get the itch to go skating again. Maybe you can delete the number of that "friend" who only ever texts you when *they* need emotional support. It may be something small, or it may be something as huge as evaluating whether your current job or romantic relationship is good for you. Where are you holding on tightly to something which is no longer serving you? What would it mean to let go of that something? What steps would you need to take to do so?

How do I navigate disappointment?

We all suffer letdowns and setbacks—in our jobs, in our relationships, and in our personal development. When one of your plans doesn't pan out or a success you anticipated falls flat, what do you do? Are you quicker to point the finger of blame at others or at yourself? Do you find yourself demoralized and unmotivated to regroup, or does the setback reinvigorate you to try again? What emotions typically accompany disappointment for you? Anger? Sorrow? Anxiety? And how can you sit with those emotions as you accept the disappointment?

How can I check in with myself more regularly?

The Eight of Cups is often a reminder to check in with yourself. You may be trudging through something on autopilot, or you may just have gotten good at ignoring your own internal messages. Consider this card the universe's way of checking up on you, since you haven't been so good at doing it yourself lately. How can you remember to tune into your emotional radio station more frequently throughout the day? It could be as simple as asking yourself, "What am I feeling right now?" anytime you catch your own eyes in the mirror, or taking five minutes before bed to breathe and observe what's going on in your body. There's no one right way to have these conversations with yourself—what's important is to have them with some regularity.

 *Actions*

Watch a Sunset

Effort level: Low to medium ●●○○○

We go into each day with a litany of plans, schedules, and expectations. By the day's end, it's not unusual for us to feel we didn't accomplish everything we hoped to. Then we fall into bed already running through our checklist for tomorrow. "Okay, but how does watching a sunset fix that?" I hear you asking. The answer is, it doesn't (any more than ANY of the reflections or activities in this book "fix" anything). But it can provide a tiny moment of ritual at the end of the day, reminding you to let go of the ups and downs of the last few hours and enjoy the peacefulness of the day coming to a close.

It's pretty easy to look up what time the sunset is going to happen on any given day in your area. If you need to, set an alarm to remind yourself to stop whatever you're doing. Settle yourself in front of a westerly-facing window, or even better, find a place outside where you can sit or stand comfortably for a few moments. I'd also encourage you to silence your phone so you can be fully present, if possible. With notifications from calls, text messages, and social media buzzing in your pocket, it can be that much harder to take this time for yourself.

As the sun sets, allow yourself to think back over the day. Congratulate yourself for the things that you accomplished, and consciously release the things that are yet to be done. Trust that you did everything you were able to do today, and that you will do the same tomorrow. In the meantime, you are here, enjoying a sunset and saying good night to your day. Let yourself enjoy the moment you are in and set your intention to rest well tonight so that you can rise with tomorrow's sun and tackle your to-do list at that time.

Make a List of Things to Leave Behind

Effort level: Medium to high ●●●●○

This can be a surprisingly emotional exercise, so I encourage you to only undertake it if you're in a good headspace for deep self-reflection of this nature. Settle in with some blank paper or a notebook and a writing utensil. (Although I'm all for using technology most of the time, I think it's better to have a physical piece of paper to work with in this case. Even though you may want to revisit this list from time to time, I don't feel there's much to be gained from having it instantly accessible on your laptop or phone. This isn't a list you want to enable yourself to obsess over.)

At the top of the page, write something like, "What I'm Ready to Leave Behind." Then, taking as much time as you need, free write whatever comes to mind. This isn't unlike the reflection prompt above (What do I need to release?) but you can think of this as an actionable list rather than an invitation for reflection. Bear in mind that this list isn't meant as a means of beating yourself up ("I KNOW I need to stop drinking soda all the time, so I'll put that on the list!"). It should be a space for you to consciously admit what relationships, activities, and even self-images are no longer serving you. A space where you can say, "I've been holding onto this even though I'm not getting anything out of it. I'm ready to let go."

Here's an example that may illustrate the intent of the exercise. When I first came out as non-binary, there were certain gendered relationship words that I wasn't ready to stop using. I had identified with words like "daughter" and "sister" for my whole life, and I cherish the relationships that they refer to. So even though I was using a new name and non-binary pronouns, I still didn't mind when my dad talked about me as his daughter, or when my brother affectionately called me sister. For a while, that was right for me. But as time has passed, I've more fully inhabited words like child and sibling, and I've become more comfortable with those words replacing their gendered alternatives. (I am, of course, not advocating that this should be ANYONE ELSE'S journey! I'm just sharing my personal experience with growing out of some words and into others.) So if I were to undertake this exercise, I might add to my list that I'm ready to let go of seeing myself as a daughter, granddaughter, niece, and sister. Those words served me well for a long time, but I've changed enough that I'm prepared to leave them behind.

Nine of Cups

One of the loveliest cards to turn up in a daily reading (or most readings, for that matter!), the Nine of Cups heralds wishes fulfilled. There are other cards in the tarot that signify hard work coming to fruition (looking at you, Six of Wands and Seven of Pentacles), and while the Nine of Cups can certainly encompass the rewards of a job well done, it more broadly stands for that moment when you realize you've gotten something you wished for as hard as you possibly could. You dreamed, you hoped, and now here you are.

It's worth noting that the Nine of Cups doesn't often grant its wish-granting magic to those of us with unclear hopes and murky dreams. If you're drawing this card today, it's because you set your sights high and you held out hope. That combination of clear intentions and openhearted hoping is truly powerful. The Nine of Cups celebrates mindful, hopeful intentions like no other card. And if you're reading this and thinking to yourself, *What the heck? I haven't gotten any of my wishes fulfilled lately,* your dream come true may be closer than you think. Make sure you're taking the time to regularly visit with your heart's fondest wishes, and the Nine of Cups will likely come through for you.

Affirmations

I AM deserving of everything I wish for.
I CAN shoot for the moon.
I WILL give voice to my greatest wishes.

Reflections

How can I make my dreams come true?
I know I just said that there are other cards that represent the rewards of hard work, and that's still true. But you need dreams and fantasies just as much as you need the hard

work. Think about your biggest, wildest dreams, the things that you fall asleep imagining. Are you taking any steps to bring those dreams closer to reality? If not, what steps might you take? Do you have support from your loved ones in chasing this dream of yours? How might you recruit their help?

What am I satisfied with in my life?

Looking ahead and making wishes is good for the soul, and it can help us identify what we want and how to get there. But it's equally important to look around at your present day and acknowledge what dreams have already panned out. If you're happily partnered to someone(s), can you recall dreaming of a Special Someone when you were younger? Imagine what you might tell that younger version of yourself! If you have a job or a home that makes you happy, can you trace back when you started fantasizing about a job in this field or a home you could decorate however you wanted? Maybe it's something seemingly smaller (but ultimately no less important)—for instance, if you have a furry, feathered, or scaled family member who has kept you company for years, what did you picture your life with them might be like when you first brought them home?

How can I cultivate gratitude?

There are other questions in this book designed to get you thinking about *what* to be grateful for (including, to some extent, the question just before this one). But it's worth considering, too, how to invite more little opportunities for gratitude into your daily life. There's a reason practices like the gratitude journal and saying grace over meals are so widespread—both set aside mindful but brief moments in the day to acknowledge what you're thankful for. It may very well be that neither of these practices fit for you. In that case, what else might you try? Is there a particular song that makes you feel humbled and seems to put the world in perspective for you? Is there a tree outside your office window that reminds you of the beauty of life? When you hug your partner or children, can you hold a little more thoughtfully onto that rush of love and joy?

 *Actions*

Read Poetry

Effort level: Low to medium ●●○○○

What does poetry have to do with wishes and the Nine of Cups? Well, first of all, the Cups are the suit of emotion and feeling, so I honestly think reading poetry could be an appropriate activity for the majority of the Cups. But in particular, it fits for the Nine. Poems have a way of taking a feeling we're having or a thought we're grappling with and distilling it into verse. Whether the words rhyme or not, there's an incredible art to making a poem say so much with so little. And second of all, what do we say when we're wishing on stars as children? "Star light, star bright, first star I see tonight," etc.…isn't that a poem? Wishes and poems have more in common than we think.

You can use any number of websites that curate regular selections of poetry if you're looking to browse or you aren't sure what to read. Or if you have a favorite poet in mind, look them up or pull out one of their books. And I recommend keeping a notebook or other writing implement nearby. Reading poetry has a way of dislodging thoughts (and maybe even wishes) unexpectedly, and you'll want to be prepared if this happens.

Make a Wish

Effort level: Medium to high ●●●●○

I think there's a secret power in the childhood tradition of wishing on stars, dandelion seeds, coins tossed into wells, and anything else that seems even remotely magical. We as a culture (or maybe as a species) are not always taught how to name what we want— or, at best, we aren't taught to do it well. We either swallow our desires until they fester deep in our souls, or we overwhelm our loved ones with our wants and expect them to make things happen for us. Either way, we get lost somewhere between recognizing the things we're hoping for and giving a voice to those hopes.

Not so with wishing on stars (or coins, or so on). We can make a wish as huge and seemingly impossible as we want, and we can say it out loud to a universe that is in no danger of being overwhelmed by the strength of our wanting. Noticing and naming our wants and needs is so important to our self-care, and if you're someone who (like me) struggles to ask your loved ones for what you need, making a wish might help you dip your toe in the water before you sit down with a human being to make your wishes known.

A quick true story for you to illustrate how deeply I believe in regular wish-making. Early on in our friendship, my dear friend Olivia (who is always immaculately dressed) noticed that the clasp of my necklace had ridden down to the pendant. Without thinking, she moved it back up to the back of my neck for me. Mock offended, I called her out for depriving me of the wish I could have made. (My mom always taught me that if the clasp of your necklace touches the pendant/charm/etc., you can make a wish, kiss the clasp, and then move it back into its proper place. No idea if that's a widespread Wishing Protocol or just a thing I've inherited from my mom, but I still do it.) Olivia was bemused in the moment. But the next gift-giving occasion, she presented me with a jar full of "wishing stars" that she had meticulously folded out of origami paper. It remains one of my most cherished possessions to this day.

Be a starry-eyed child. Go outside at night to wish you may and wish you might. Pick a dandelion and blow the seeds into the wind. Throw a coin into a pond. And own that wish burbling up inside of you.

Ten of Cups

With our wishes fulfilled in the Nine of Cups, we want nothing more than to share our successes and joys with our loved ones. And here we come to the peak of the Cups' journey: having embraced and integrated our feelings (the dark along with the light), we can come to rest within the comfort of our family, our community, our tribe. There is a profound contentment in the Ten of Cups; it makes me think of family movie nights snuggled together on the couch, of standing coffee dates with our dearest friends, of spiritual communities that feel like home the second you walk across the threshold.

When this card comes up in a daily drawing, take it as an invitation to spend some quality time with your people—the ones who recharge your spiritual and emotional batteries, whoever that might be. If you're unfortunately not living with people who fit this category for you at the moment, do whatever you can to connect with the people who do. Set up a Skype call with your college roommates, plan a family dinner or brunch, take your kids to the park and play hide and seek with them. The relationships where we can be 100 percent genuine, the people and activities that nourish our souls—those are the pieces of your life that the Ten of Cups points to insistently.

 Affirmations

I AM fulfilled.
I CAN take solace in my soul family.
I WILL seek out the company of those who recharge me.

 *Reflections*

What does joy look and feel like?

In the reflection questions for the Sun, I ask what brings you joy. There is some overlap with this question, but it's asked in a fundamentally different way: when you are joyful, how do you know? Is there a kinesthetic/somatic feeling in your body (your heart feeling lighter, your shoulders relaxing, etc.)? Does your tone of voice become markedly different? Has a loved one told you that they've noticed something specific you do or say when you're feeling genuine joy? And on the flip side, how can you tell when one of your loved ones is joyful? Do the laugh lines around their eyes become more pronounced? Do they smile or laugh more easily? How does their joy affect you?

What actions can I take to be more understanding?

The people you love may not always be able to understand you, but the people who you count among your tribe are always willing to *try*. For instance, I can't stand the taste of onions. My spouse, a consummate foodie, puts onion powder in everything they cook themself. They probably can't understand how anyone could *not* like onions. And yet, when they make dinner for both of us, they're always happy to make a separate onion-free helping for me.

How might you spend more effort or energy on at least trying to understand your loved ones? Do they have hobbies or passions that are entirely unappealing to you? Do they have friends that you, for whatever reason, don't get along with? How might you better support them, even in the things that you don't have in common?

How do I define my family?

When I use the word "family," I am not necessarily referring to the people who are biologically related to you. Perhaps you are lucky enough to have biological family members that you're close with—if so, that's wonderful. But you may feel a stronger kinship to your romantic partners, your deepest friendships, your spiritual community, etc. Your definition of family is for nobody but *you* to determine. I'm fortunate to have close relationships with my mom, brother, and grandparents, but I would also include my spouse and several dear friends as part of my family. Who fits into the category of family for you?

 ## Actions

Reflect on What Roles Your Loved Ones Play in Your Life

Effort level: Low to medium ●●○○○

In Western culture, we put a *lot* of priority (and pressure) on romantic connections to be the most significant and important in our lives. And I'm not here to try to downplay how wonderful and fulfilling romantic relationships can be! But I think we culturally underestimate how meaningful other types of relationships (like platonic love between siblings, deep friendships, and longtime collaborators) can be. Each of our loved ones brings something unique and needed into our lives. For instance, my dear friend Olivia and I are almost as opposite as two human beings can be. I often tell people that Olivia helps me learn to be more assertive, and I help her learn to be more thoughtful. This has been deeply formative in the moments in my life when I most needed to find my courage. Meanwhile, another dear friend Milo has a personality that is (sometimes absurdly) similar to mine. The closer I've gotten to Milo, the better I've been able to understand my own anxiety, and the kinder to myself I've learned to be. These are two of the people I feel the closest with, and they add wildly different but absolutely cherished elements to my world.

Consider the people who make up your tribe. For the purposes of this exercise, try to let go of the relationship titles that you associate with each of them—spouse, friend, sibling, and so on. Think instead of what each of these people brings to your life. Is one of them especially skilled at making you laugh? Does one always seem to know just what to say when you're sad? Does one of them just give really great hugs? What new things do you discover about yourself when you're with each of them—what pieces of your personality do they bring out? How do each of the people in your inner circle enrich your world?

Plan Family Time

Effort level: Medium to high ●●●●○

No matter what your life is like and who you include in your definition of family, it's easy to orbit around your loved ones and allow moments of connection to just sort of happen when they happen. And certainly those little unplanned moments—singing a dumb pop song together during the morning commute, for instance, or finding yourself in a spontaneous tickle war—have their own value. But it's important to also have pre-planned, intentional family time. I think this is one reason the family dinner is so sacred to so many people. It's a part of the day that's set aside for connecting with your folks.

If you're lucky enough to live in the same house as several members of your family (and again recall that I don't only mean blood relatives when I say "family"), a family dinner is a pretty straightforward way to spend some planned time together. My college roommates and I would plan occasional family dinners where we all cooked, ate, and tidied up together; there's just something about making and sharing a meal that brings you closer. You can also invite folks who don't live under your roof but still make up part of your inner circle. I know of families who have regular weekend brunches with grandparents, aunts and uncles, and family friends.

All of that said, a family meal is far from the only way to spend some intentional time with your family! Part of this book was written during the COVID-19 pandemic, and boy did we all have to get creative about ways to connect. I've held long-distance game nights with my friends and family. I've read a favorite book aloud to my mom and brother over the phone. One of my friends and I started a mini book club for just the two of us. Anything goes. The important part is the planning of an activity that will be fun, engaging, and meaningful for everyone involved (for example, if you have a family member with chronic pain, maybe don't plan a day of hiking if you want them to feel included). Other than that, the sky's the limit!

THE COURT OF CUPS

Folks in the court of Cups are the connective tissue that keeps relationships, families, teams, and communities together. As you might expect from the suit of feelings, these people can be moody, but they are also the most in touch with emotions—theirs, as well as others'. They may have a gift for putting their finger on the exact source of conflict between two people, intuitively seeing past the surface of an argument and identifying each party's fundamental needs. They also tend to take on the emotional energy of the people around them, so learning to establish and maintain boundaries is critical for members of the Cups court.

Some words to describe the court of Cups: *intuitive, emotional, caring, deep, spiritual, dreamy, soulful, expressive, romantic, moody, affectionate, thoughtful, kind, hospitable, open, sentimental, collaborative, introspective, nostalgic, wise.*

If a member of the court of Cups appears in your daily reading and you'd like to take a field trip to someplace that might invoke their energy, here are a few suggestions:

- A lake, river, beach, or even a swimming pool, to invoke the Cups' element of water
- A family member or good friend's home, to invoke relationships and camaraderie
- A graveyard or cemetery, to invoke nostalgia and introspection (especially if you can visit the resting place of someone you personally knew or someone you're related to)
- A poetry reading, to invoke romance and expression
- A spa or massage parlor, to invoke self-care and kindness

Page of Cups

The Page of Cups is the poster child for wonder. They appreciate the beauty and majesty in everything and everyone they see. And if you've ever read Antoine de Saint-Exupéry's incredible book *The Little Prince* or watched the gorgeous film adaptation, you know exactly what this Page is like. (And if you haven't, consider that an extra suggested activity when you draw this card—both versions of the story are beautiful beyond words.) The Little Prince is an openhearted, inquisitive boy who feels everything deeply and articulates his feelings with profound simplicity. If the members of the court of Swords are often guilty of speaking their mind bluntly, the members of the court of Cups speak from the heart, for better or for worse. The Little Prince is not only direct about his feelings, but also able to connect them to nature and the world around him with the ease and grace of a poet. When the narrator dismisses the Prince's concerns about his beloved rose, he flies into a rage that quickly spirals into inconsolable sorrow. And when he loves, he loves so powerfully that it burns brightly within him: "What moves me so deeply about this sleeping little prince is his loyalty to a flower—the image of a rose shining within him like the flame within a lamp, even when he's asleep," (149).

At first glance, the Page of Cups may seem like a naïve youngster who looks on the bright side of everything. Don't be fooled. Just because this Page sees the wonder in everything doesn't mean they're immune to the world's darkness. As with the Little Prince, when the Page of Cups is sad or angry, they feel it just as deeply and overwhelmingly as they feel their joy and curiosity. With a tendency to believe the best in everyone, it's easy for the Page of Cups to fall prey to energy vampires who lean on them for emotional support but don't offer the same in return. And because they trust their heart above all else, they may follow their emotional impulses without thinking them through (like the way the Little Prince runs away from his planet in a moment of overwhelming frustration). And that's where this Page may surprise you. They often have profound insight (especially when it comes to matters of the heart) that seems out of step with their usual bright-eyed innocence. This insight is hard-won, born from the times they've had their hearts broken or used. But rarely do these bad experiences stop them from gasping in awe at a sunset or falling in love like a ton of bricks.

 ## Affirmations

I AM an open book.
I CAN embrace the wonder of the world.
I WILL wear my heart on my sleeve.

 ## Reflections

Who in my life reminds me of the Page of Cups?
What aspects of the Page of Cups do I see in myself?
What aspects of the Page of Cups would I like to cultivate in myself?

 ## Actions

Do Something Unexpected to Brighten Someone's Day

Effort level: Low to medium ●●○○○

Nobody loves tiny moments of beauty and joy like the Page of Cups. They can fall into a reverie over a fall leaf drifting perfectly past their window, or the aroma of their favorite tea brewing. And as much as they love these moments for themselves, they're even more delighted to bring these moments to their near and dear. Remember that Cups are not only the suit of emotions, but also the suit of relationships. When you can inject a little dose of joy into a loved one's day, you're in the sweet spot of Page of Cups energy.

This exercise has a lot in common with the random acts of kindness exercise from the Six of Pentacles. But where that activity is meant to be truly random to benefit a stranger, this can be more focused. Is there someone in your life who could particularly use a pick-me-up? Choose someone who you know well enough to really tailor your activity to them. Where random acts of kindness are usually designed to be generic enough that they'd suit any stranger who receives them, this can get much more honed in. If you know your sibling is overwhelmed at work, you could cook their favorite meal to surprise them. If your friend who lives across the country is having a tough day, you could send them a selfie wearing the t-shirt that they gave you for your birthday. It doesn't have to be an enormous grand gesture to brighten up someone's day.

For that matter, a kind or meaningful word can put a smile on someone's face just as easily as a small gift or act of service. One of the most poignant moments in *The Little Prince* comes from a moment when the Prince's friend the fox is bidding him farewell, and he decides to give him the gift of a secret. That secret—that your heart is what sees the essential things in life—becomes a defining truth for the Prince, one that he passes on to the book's narrator later on. If you're not sure what to do for a loved one or you aren't in a position to buy or do something for them, take a moment to tell them something you admire or appreciate about them, or share a quotation that you think they'll find meaningful. It will probably make them smile just knowing you thought about them.

Admire the Beauty of Something

Effort level: Medium to high ●●●●○

Our world is filled with miraculous, uncannily beautiful things. But when we're caught up in the stress and bustle of our day-to-day lives, it's easy to forget to pause and appreciate these tiny marvels. It may be cliché to say "stop and smell the roses," but that doesn't make it less true. If there's a colorful flower bush just outside your front door, how often do you actually notice it and admire it as you're running to catch the bus to work or trudging inside after a long day?

You can truly choose any subject for this exercise—the only guiding factors should be A) is it something that you see frequently enough that you tend to overlook it, and B) is it something that strikes you as beautiful? Maybe it's the leaves of a tree that peeks into your bedroom window. Maybe it's your family pet who keeps you company at night. Maybe it's a ring that you wear every day. Whatever you've chosen, make yourself comfortable in a place where you can spend at least five to ten minutes looking at your subject. If you'd like to journal about your observations, have writing tools on hand. It may be helpful to set a timer for yourself, but it's not necessary.

Almost as if you're meditating, bring your focus to your subject. Use as many of your senses to observe it as you can. If it's a small enough object, for example, you might pay attention to the tactile sensations as you pick it up and turn it over in your hands. If it's a flower, you might honestly stop and appreciate its aroma. If you're journaling as you go, write down anything that strikes you—tiny details that you might not have noticed before, or particular elements that seem especially meaningful to you at the moment. If your mind wanders, gently return your attention to your subject. With so many obligations and activities pulling at us, it can feel unnatural and even a bit hedonistic to luxuriate in the beauty of something like this. But I've found that it's quite the opposite. When I take a little time to appreciate the wonders of the world around me, I become more engaged in my day-to-day activities, too. One small beacon of beauty can illuminate a swath of dim tedium around it. As the Little Prince tells the narrator, "When you look up at the sky at night, since I'll be living on one of them, since I'll be laughing on one of them, for you it'll be as if all the stars are laughing. You'll have stars that can laugh!"

Knight of Cups

Many tarot books will introduce you to the Knight of Cups as a beret-wearing, poetry-writing tortured artist. And this is certainly one manifestation of the character. But I'd like to nominate a different sort of character to represent this Knight: Flynn Rider from Disney's *Tangled*. At first glance, Flynn may not seem like an especially romantic soul—he starts the film as a swashbuckling, snarky thief. But take a closer look. Over the course of the movie, not only do we see him fall for Rapunzel so hard that he gives up everything to protect her, but we also learn who he is beneath the façade of the charismatic bandit. He confides in Rapunzel that he was an orphan who discovered a book about Flynnigan Rider, a charming and talented rogue, who Flynn admired so much that he modeled himself in his image, even borrowing his name. "He had enough money to do anything that he wanted to do. He could go anywhere that he wanted to go. And for a kid with nothing… I don't know, it just seemed like the better option." Flynn may not act like a romantic, but he absolutely is one—falling in love with ideas and archetypes as much as he falls in love with living, breathing people like Rapunzel.

The Knight of Cups is often an artist in one way or another, since art provides them an outlet to express their deepest emotions. They may be prone to a melodramatic streak because they feel everything so deeply. (If you aren't convinced that Flynn Rider is a perfect Knight of Cups, take a look at his first line of narration in the movie: "This is the story of how I died." Instant melodrama.) In romance, they're liable to fall hard and fast. In relationships, they may struggle to set healthy boundaries. These are often highly empathic people who take on too much for their loved ones. But the flip side of this is that the Knight of Cups is usually a loyal and attentive family member or friend. Just be prepared to weather the occasional intense mood swing, since this Knight can flit from the highest high to the lowest low in a surprisingly short span of time.

 ## Affirmations

I AM a romantic.
I CAN always learn more about myself.
I WILL set boundaries when I need to.

 ## Reflections

Who in my life reminds me of the Knight of Cups?
What aspects of the Knight of Cups do I see in myself?
What aspects of the Knight of Cups would I like to cultivate in myself?

 ## Actions

Listen to Love Songs

Effort level: Low to medium ●●○○○

Sometimes on Valentine's Day I'll listen to a playlist of love songs—say what you will about the holiday being a commercial ploy, but there is something nice about leaning into the hopeless romantic part of myself on a specific day. It's almost like listening to Christmas songs in December. But you don't need any particular reason to listen to romantic music. And if you feel like you do need a reason, consider the appearance of the Knight of Cups reason enough.

The good news is that no matter what style of music you enjoy, it shouldn't be hard to find love songs in that category. A truly staggering percentage of songs are, in fact, love songs—or they at least deal with love-related themes like breakups or unrequited love. So whether you're a country music fan who was recently dumped by a longtime partner, or a lover of metal who's experiencing the first blushes of new romance, you can almost certainly find music that caters to you. Search Spotify or YouTube or your music service of choice and you'll probably find existing playlists put together by folks with similar tastes.

If you want to take it a step further, you could make your own custom playlist to match your exact romantic pulse at the moment. You could include songs that aren't romantic in and of themselves, but that remind you of your beloved or beloveds. You could shift back and forth between wildly different genres and styles. You could even make a playlist that charts your unique history with relationships and dating, starting from your first conscious crush and leading all the way up until now. (Visit the Eight of Wands for more ideas about creating custom playlists.) But whether you take hours to put together a detailed playlist or you just give a quick listen to "At Last I See the Light" from *Tangled*, including a love song or two in your day is the perfect way to incorporate Knight of Cups energy.

Write Yourself a Love Letter

Effort level: Medium to high ◉◉◉◉◯

Some might argue that the art of the love letter is dying out in the age of smartphones and email. I'd make the argument that it isn't dying as much as it's transforming—of course we use the tools that allow us to communicate and connect with each other instantaneously. I'm reasonably confident that if they'd had access to the internet in pioneer days, for instance, they absolutely would have used it to stay in touch with their faraway family members. But be that as it may, there is an inherent romance in pen and paper communication. Why not use that romantic medium on ourselves for a change?

For this exercise, I encourage you to be as dramatic, flamboyant, and poetic as you see fit. If there's ANY card that endorses wholehearted, over-the-top wordsmithery, it's the Knight of Cups. Does it seem silly or even embarrassing to write yourself a gushy love letter? Imagine yourself as a third party, if it helps—someone outside of yourself who's developing an intense crush on you and needs to get their thoughts and feelings on paper. Talk about the things that you appreciate or admire about yourself. If you're struggling to come up with anything, look at your accomplishments and experiences that you're proud of. Searching for objective facts about the things you've done may be easier at first than complimenting your personality traits or attributes. Are your kids relatively happy and healthy because of the care you've taken in raising them? Have you reached any of your career goals? Are you consistently praised for your sweet potato casserole on Thanksgiving? ANY of these facts might be noticed by someone who was secretly admiring you, so write about them in your love letter.

For bonus points, you might consider tucking this letter away and reading it when you're feeling down on yourself. Or seal it off and mark it to be read on a specific date in the future, like a time capsule in letter form. As uncomfortable as you might be writing these things to yourself, you might be surprised at how meaningful they are after you've stepped away from them for a bit.

Queen of Cups

If you grew up with Winnie the Pooh, it should come as no surprise to you that Kanga is my choice to represent the Queen of Cups. She is the quintessential mother character, so much so that she doesn't only nurture and care for her son Roo, but many of the other characters in the Hundred Acre Wood such as Piglet and Tigger. But despite initial appearances, Kanga isn't simply a mother, either. She's a fundamentally goodhearted person (er…kangaroo?) who gives love and wisdom freely, but she has a sharp side as well: "A Kanga was Generally Regarded as One of the Fiercer Animals…it is well known that, if One of the Fiercer Animals is Deprived of Its Young, it becomes as fierce as Two of the Fiercer Animals," (92). The Queen of Cups is attuned to their feelings in a deep yet sustainable way. They know when to be protective and fierce and when to be soft and affectionate. And like a good mother, this Queen will not attempt to shield their children from difficult learning moments. Kanga doesn't usually go along with Roo and the others when they have adventures with Christopher Robin. But she's always there waiting with food and strengthening medicine when her brood returns.

Where the Page and Knight of Cups can sometimes get swept away by the intensity of their emotions, the Queen knows how to stay centered in their heart without becoming overwhelmed. They're those people who hold groups together by seeing everyone's point of view and keeping the peace. If your friend group has a "mom friend," they're likely very attuned to this Queen of Cups kind of energy. But while the Queen of Cups is certainly empathic, they have enough experience and wisdom to set boundaries and hold them steady. They aren't as likely to burn themself out by giving and giving until they're running on empty. In dark moments, this Queen might use their natural empathic skill to turn manipulative or to blatantly disregard other people's boundaries because, in their mind, they've spent so much time taking care of others that they deserve some extra consideration. This is truly a rarity, though. Most of the time, the Queen of Cups is cheering from the wings as you face your demons.

 *Affirmations*

I AM a kindred spirit.
I CAN share my warmth.
I WILL reach out.

 *Reflections*

Who in my life reminds me of the Queen of Cups?
What aspects of the Queen of Cups do I see in myself?
What aspects of the Queen of Cups would I like to cultivate in myself?

 *Actions*

Reach Out to Someone Going Through Tough Times

Effort level: Low to medium ●●○○○

We've talked about the challenge of asking for help when you're struggling many times in this book. The Queen of Cups offers an invitation for you to stand on the other side of this struggle. Do you know anyone who's having a hard time right now? You probably do, even if it isn't something dramatic like a divorce or a death in the family. Who do you know with seasonal depression, for example? Or who do you know who's just started a new job—even a job they're excited about!—who's anxious to make a good first impression? If you're truly coming up short, take a quick peek at your social media. You'll almost certainly find someone opening up about something they're going through.

It's important to know up top that your goal here isn't to get a gold star for offering help to someone. This isn't an opportunity to swoop in with some grand gesture to show the world what a wonderfully supportive person you are. Think of it instead as establishing an open line for someone who may or may not need to use it. My favorite way to accomplish this is by prefacing my check-in with something like, "Hey, I know you're having a tough time, so no need to respond if you're not feeling up for it!" I know when I'm in a dark period, sometimes even mustering the energy to shoot back a quick "thank you" is impossible—but it still means everything to me that someone thought of me enough to reach out. Just make sure that whatever you offer (whether it's space to talk or stopping by to visit, etc.) you're able to follow through with it if your friend takes you up on it.

Here are a few scripts you can start with (especially if the person you're contacting is someone you don't speak with super regularly):

"Hey _____, I saw on Facebook that you've been having a hard time with your depression recently. I just wanted to let you know that you're loved, and if you need someone to vent to, I'm always available. But no worries if you aren't up for talking at the moment, either."

"_____, I'm so sorry to hear about the loss of your uncle. I know how close you two were. I'm sure you're completely overwhelmed right now, but I wanted to check in because I know how hard it is to lose a loved one. If you're ever up for it, I'd love to hear some stories about your uncle. And in the meantime, I'm here if you need me!"

"Hi _____, I saw in the group chat that you're feeling really anxious about the state of the world right now—I think it shows what a caring person you are, but I know it's overwhelming. If you want to talk about anything, or if you just want someone to distract you with goofy conversation for a bit, I'm always available. Love you."

Identify a Boundary You Need to Set or Enforce

Effort level: Medium to high ●●●●○

Boundaries. Are. Hard. It's hard when you accidentally run into someone else's boundary and they have to ask you to adjust your behavior, and it's even harder when you're the one having to set and enforce your own boundaries. It can feel like you're letting someone down, or even that you're cutting them off altogether. But boundaries are as much about self-love as they are about loving others. Even if it feels like you're disappointing someone, you are actually being kind by articulating your needs clearly, rather than letting them be run over and stewing in resentment.

Even if you're a relatively stoic person who sets boundaries regularly, there are probably areas in your life or people who you love that toe the edges of your limits—even if you aren't consciously aware of it. It might be as small as asking your partner to stay out of the bedroom for twenty minutes in the evening so you can meditate without interruption. Or it might be as daunting as setting limits on when and how you talk to a toxic parent.

Whatever boundary you choose for this exercise, I encourage you to take it slow. Even if it seems like a small adjustment in the first place, be patient with yourself. It's much, MUCH harder to voice a boundary in the moment than you think. Especially when someone you love is standing there looking at you expectantly. Or crying. Or yelling. So if you cave in at first, don't beat yourself up. Look for ways that you can start small. If the boundary you want to implement involves limiting your communication with someone, for example, you may not want to start by totally cutting them off. Start with only talking to them for a half hour when they call, and when the time is up, firmly excuse yourself from the conversation. Or start with only visiting them once a month, instead of every weekend. Choose small starting places that feel achievable, and then ramp up from there once you feel comfortable with the changes you've already made.

King of Cups

Brace yourself, we're about to talk about one of my favorite characters in all of fiction. When you start watching *Avatar: The Last Airbender*, Uncle Iroh seems like your average wise-old-mentor type. He loves tea, he's a bit of a goofball, and he's full of wise little anecdotes and sayings. But the more you get to know him, the more you realize the depth of his character. The brother of the show's main antagonist, Uncle Iroh has more or less abandoned his nation in order to accompany his nephew, the dishonored and banished Prince Zuko. Iroh has had the opportunity for power and wealth in his long life, but after a devastating personal loss (which I won't spoil for you just in case you haven't seen the show—trust me, it's worth the watch) he directs all his energy into nurturing Zuko's heart and soul. The King of Cups is a person who has experienced incredible pain and incredible joy, and they are capable of weathering both with grace and mindfulness. Iroh is certainly an emotional character—we see him weep, explode in fury, and beam at the simple things like a good cup of tea—but he's able to experience these feelings, sit with them, and eventually return to the calm, wise uncle who tells Zuko, "In the darkest times, hope is something you give yourself. That is the meaning of inner strength."

Full disclosure: the King of Cups is the card that I associate the most strongly with my dad. It's the card that's leapt out of my decks over and over again at times when I've missed him the most. So, if I'm a bit biased toward this card, I hope you'll forgive me. The King of Cups is the rock of their family, the foundation of support and love upon which everything else is built. If you've ever had a parent or grandparent who tells you to follow your dreams, or a teacher who encourages you to develop your writing or follow your interest in history, you know the King of Cups. This isn't to say that this King is perfectly calm and dispassionate at all times—they've experienced all of life's joys and sorrows, to be sure. But as Cedar McCloud says in *The Numinous Tarot*, this King "does not try to stop the storm, but tries to understand where, when, and why it will strike so they can meet it in full strength," (116). And ultimately, the King of Cups knows how to build a family (of blood or of chosen loved ones) that will provide support when they need it.

 ## Affirmations

I AM a mentor.
I CAN rely on what I've learned.
I WILL guide my loved ones.

 ## Reflections

Who in my life reminds me of the King of Cups?
What aspects of the King of Cups do I see in myself?
What aspects of the King of Cups would I like to cultivate in myself?

 ## Actions

Cook a Meal to Share

Effort level: Low to medium ●●○○○

If you have a loved one who enjoys cooking, you know very well that food can be an effective (and delicious!) love language. As satisfying as it is to cook something comforting or hearty for yourself, there's even more satisfaction to be found in cooking for the people you care about. It doesn't have to be wildly elaborate to be meaningful, either. I'm not a big foodie (being a picky eater will do that to you) but even so, when my partner goes out of their way to make anything—even a simple side dish—that they know I'll like, it means the world to me.

The only real caveat to this activity is that you should make sure you know your guests' culinary limitations before you make something. You wouldn't want to spend hours making chicken noodle soup from scratch only to discover that one of your dinner guests is vegetarian. Don't feel like you need to make something special and custom for each person (unless you really want to!) but remember that the purpose of this activity is to be inclusive, not the reverse. If one of your guests is watching everyone else eat, it won't be much fun for them—nor will it be much fun for you, the apologetic host.

Other than that, though, go as simple or as lavish as you'd like! Make surprise pancakes for your roommates to wake up to. Set up a taco bar for your coworkers. Bake cookies for your partners and kiddos to eat together. Then sit back and enjoy the feeling of sharing a full belly and full heart with your near and dear.

Acknowledge Your Negative Feelings

Effort level: Medium to high ⬤⬤⬤⬤◯

We're EXCELLENT at distracting ourselves when we're feeling uncomfortable feelings. Having an anxiety-inducing kind of day? Go for a run with loud music to drown out the pit in your stomach! Feeling sad after a breakup? Binge your favorite Netflix series and eat a pint of your favorite ice cream! And sometimes that's the best thing you can do—we can't spend all our time wallowing in our darkest feelings any more than we can spend all our time reveling in our joy. But be that as it may, if we keep stuffing those negative feelings in the closet, eventually they'll all come spilling out like so many toys we were hiding from our parents instead of cleaning our rooms.

It can be tough to slow down enough to acknowledge the resentment or nervousness or grief that may be lurking beneath the surfaces of our minds. A good starting place might be to consider a situation that's currently stressing you out or frustrating you. Find someplace quiet to sit with your thoughts for a bit, and bring your attention to that situation. Notice what comes up. Rather than immediately jumping into problem-solving mode or trying to distract yourself, pay attention to the mental and physical cues you receive. Do your shoulders tense up? Does your stomach clench? Do you find yourself obsessing about how you might fix things or what you did wrong? Don't try to squash those reactions, but don't cling to them, either. Notice them. Acknowledge their presence. Then keep paying attention. You may find yourself shifting between many quick physical or emotional responses. Or you may remain in the same steady feeling for a while. There isn't any right or wrong way to feel or think in this moment. Just be with the feelings as they come and go.

Ask yourself, "What do I need right now?" It may be that you just need to tell yourself, "I'm allowed to feel this way." Or you may need to do something to re-center yourself, such as meditating or some sort of physical exercise. Or you might need to give yourself that distraction, which is perfectly reasonable after sitting with uncomfortable feelings for a while. Be kind to yourself and listen to what your gut tells you it needs. It often knows better than your head does.

THE SUIT OF SWORDS
Contemplate and Communicate

The Swords are the suit of the element air. It governs the mind, the voice, and communication, and it is also often associated with matters of career. Sharp wit and sharper tongues are common in this suit—if you've ever found yourself drawn into a heated debate (or started one yourself!) you know the texture of the Swords. Be prepared to face the hidden recesses and darker corners of your mind. The Swords can provide clarity and insight, but they won't pull any punches when it's time to confront the truth.

Some words to describe the suit of Swords: *communication, consideration, intellect, truth, logic, empowerment, reason, problem-solving, philosophy, ideas, messages, decisions, mental health, order, language, conflict, discourse, ambition, curiosity, clarity.*

If Swords keep popping up in your daily readings, the universe is telling you to take a step back and pay attention to the workings of your own mind. Perhaps external events, either in your personal life or in the world at large, are flustering your thoughts. Or it may be your thoughts themselves that are sending you off-balance. Either way, the Swords invite you to examine your mind with curiosity and scrutiny. Mindfulness, meditation, journaling, and therapy are all closely associated with this suit. However you choose to do so, if these cards are appearing regularly in your readings, it's a sign to spend some intentional time with your mind. And if you avoid it for too long, you may find yourself plunged into the darker side of the realm of Swords: anxiety, insomnia, analysis paralysis, and nightmares.

Ace of Swords

Whenever I draw the Ace of Swords, I picture one of those black-and-white films with a mad scientist holding up a test tube of some physics-altering potion and shouting, "EUREKA!" Which is maybe a tad dramatic, but the important thing here is the eureka. The Ace of Swords signals clarity and discovery, a moment of sharp realization when you see things clearly. As the suit of the mind and the voice, the Swords herald pure truth. The Ace cuts through any hemming and hawing, any uncertainty you may have had, and reveals the core of things.

Seeing this card in a daily drawing is a sign that you have (or you're about to have) more clarity about an issue you've been chewing on for a while now. Or, alternatively, an unexpected truth bomb is about to fall right into your lap. Whatever the case, the Ace of Swords asks you to watch with clear eyes and an open mind. It doesn't promise that the answer it reveals will be easy, or that it will be what you wanted to hear. But it does promise to point to the truth, no more and no less. What you do with that truth is up to you.

 Affirmations

I AM insightful.
I CAN discover new things all the time.
I WILL keep asking questions.

 Reflections

What do I want to learn?
Is there a language you've always wanted to become fluent in? What about a skill you've always wanted to cultivate (something like juggling, or growing succulents, or repairing cars)? Or maybe there's a subject you've always been vaguely interested in, something

that you'd like to find out more about? (I thought I wanted to become a pet psychologist when I was a kid, and although that desire made way for different goals as I grew older, I'm still fascinated by animal behavior.) Don't worry about whether you have the time or money to pursue these interests—for the purposes of this question, just let yourself unearth all those subjects, topics, and talents you're curious about delving into more deeply.

How can I invite clarity into my life?

The clarity of the Ace of Swords is not a conclusion hastily jumped to. It may have taken a great deal of study and thought to arrive here. Or even if your eureka moment came as a surprise, the foundation has likely been quietly assembling itself beneath the surface of your awareness. With this in mind, how might you invite more of this open-eyed clarity into your daily life? If you're of an inclination to charge into decision-making, how might you remind yourself to pause and consider next time? If you're a more reserved type, would one of your current conundrums benefit from being discussed with a trusted loved one? There is no single path to clarity. The Ace of Swords encourages you to try on different mindsets and invite unfamiliar thought processes into your brainspace.

How do I define truth?

We like to think of truth as something unquestionable and absolute. And no wonder—it's uncomfortable at best to recognize that almost nothing in our world is certain. A family member of mine was once told in a dream, "Truth, like beauty, is in the eye of the beholder." Think of how many people define their spiritual beliefs or non-beliefs as Unquestionably True, for instance. But I'm not asking you to make a list of things that are your truths (though that could be a useful exercise in itself). Instead, reflect on how you determine what is true and what is not. Do you put more stock in your gut and intuition, or in your logic and reason, or do you rely on some combination thereof? Do other people (in your life, in your community, in the world in general) figure into your process of determining truth, or do you mostly depend on yourself alone? What happens when something that you considered true is challenged? What about when it is completely disproven?

! Actions

Learn Something New

Effort level: Variable, low to high ●○○○●

I'll freely admit that this is just the enacted version of one of the reflections above. But I can think of very few cards that encourage us to devour new thoughts, ideas, and experiences more than the Ace of Swords! If the Ace of Swords were a person, they would absolutely be a teacher. Probably an elementary school teacher, the kind who was somewhat strict and intimidated you a little bit, but who took as much time as you needed to understand a concept and was genuinely delighted when the lightbulb went off in your head.

This is another one of those activities that can be as quick or as involved as you make it. If you don't have much time to spare today, take five minutes to find and read an article on a topic that interests you. If you've got a little more time, watch a documentary or fall down a Wikipedia rabbit hole. And if you truly have the ability and the gumption, you might consider committing to something more long-term. Research sewing classes that you might take in your area. Get the Rosetta Stone program for the language you're hoping to learn. Browse through one of the many websites that offer video courses on everything from bicycle repair to social media marketing.

And own the fact that you can want to learn about something just for the pure joy of it! With everyone developing side hustles and turning their hobbies into small businesses these days, it can be easy to look at everything through the lens of "how would this look on my resume?" And while that's certainly worth considering, sometimes you just want to learn Japanese because you want to learn Japanese. Or you want to take that cake decorating class because it looks fun. The Ace of Swords encourages you to learn for the sake of learning first and foremost.

Read a Book

Effort level: Medium to high ●●●●○

(A book besides this one, I mean.)

You know that book that's been sitting on your nightstand for the last eight months? The one that your cousin got you for your birthday that you keep meaning to start but you just haven't had the *oomph* to crack it open yet? Yeah, you know the one. Or I bet there's a book that someone has recommended to you, or a book that you loved as a kid but haven't reread in ages, or a book that one of your favorite authors recently released that you haven't had a chance to pick up yet. My point is, even if your to-be-read list isn't twelve miles long, you probably have a few books that you've been meaning to dig into.

If the Ace of Swords has made an appearance in your daily reading, today might be just the day to tackle one of these books. And listen, as much as the Ace of Swords (and all the Swords, really) love intellect and deep thought, this activity isn't meant to be snobby. Pick up that romance novel that whisks you away and gives you warm fuzzies. Pick up that children's book that reminds you of a time when your kids would snuggle on your lap and let you read to them. Pick up that *Peanuts* anthology that you've reread so much the pages are ragged. Don't genre-shame yourself out of reading something you'll enjoy just because it isn't an informative nonfiction book or a piece of "classic" literary fiction. Grab that book (or that e-reader, or your headphones if you're an audiobook sort of person) and settle in.

Two of Swords

Have you ever felt completely stymied when trying to make a decision? Maybe both options feel equally good, bad, or neutral. Or maybe one option is the logical choice, but the other is tugging at your heart. Perhaps people are urging you toward one choice but your gut tells you the other is the right one. Whatever the case may be, this is when the Two of Swords tends to appear in your life. The character in this card is typically blindfolded. Maybe they think that this will allow them to weigh each sword by feel alone, or maybe it's a sign of how narrow their vision has become, caught between two swords and unable to choose between either.

When the Two of Swords appears in a daily reading, you may be on a precipice like this, struggling to choose between two or more options before you. Even if there isn't a tangible life decision that you're grappling with, there may be some sort of internal debate that you're having with yourself. The bottom line is that you feel arrested in the moment of choosing, and you're looking for some guidance or cosmic push to decide which option to go with.

Affirmations

I AM decisive.
I CAN pull myself out of a stalemate.
I WILL make decisions carefully and wisely.

Reflections

Do I make decisions more often with my heart or my head?
As is usually the case when we try to oversimplify these sorts of things, the answer to this question is probably not a binary one. You probably make some decisions by overthinking them, and others by going with your instincts. An example: my mom always

thought she was a person who made her decisions with logic. She made pro/con lists, considered every angle, and so on. My dad was the one who pointed out that for big, life-altering decisions like when to have kids, the lists and data went out the window and Mom went with her gut. That's an important thing to know about yourself when you're in the middle of a Two-of-Swords stalemate! The more you understand your unique process, the more consciously and mindfully you can apply it to your current decision. Is there one way or another that you tend to lean? In what situations do you find yourself switching from logic to emotion, or vice versa?

How do I manage feeling stuck?
There are few states of being that I hate more than feeling stuck. I'm patient as long as I know I'm moving toward something, even if that movement is slow. But when it feels as if I'm in a holding pattern, I have to remember to be extra kind to myself. Do you have specific self-care practices for times like this? Think back to times in your life when everything has been on hold—perhaps when you were between jobs and looking for new employment, or waiting for a hospitalized family member's condition to improve or worsen—and recall what you did to keep your feet on the ground. If you can't think of anything you *did*, think instead about what you *could* have done to make yourself feel a bit better.

How can I better compromise with myself?
There are whole books dedicated to the art of compromising with other people—family members, friends, coworkers—but we don't often consider the art of compromising with ourselves. I think we're all pretty familiar with this sort of thought process: *I'll just watch **one** more episode of the show I'm bingeing, and then I'll get up and do the laundry.* Call it bargaining if you like, but it's a form of compromise. When you make these sorts of deals with yourself, do you follow through? Or do you tend to just repeat the same promise for one more episode, and then another, and then another? How might you hold yourself accountable for the compromises you make with yourself?

 *Actions*

Set a Deadline for Making a Decision

Effort level: Low to medium ●●○○○

There's certainly such a thing as impulsive decision-making, but there's also such a thing as putting off a decision until it festers someplace deep inside our psyche. If you're guilty of saying "just let me sleep on this before I decide" multiple times in a row, one way to circumvent yourself is to set a hard and fast deadline for making your decision. Sometimes this deadline is preordained for us by outside factors, but if there isn't an external time limit already in place, why not set a time limit for yourself? Be fair when you do this—if you're weighing something like which city to move to, you should allow yourself plenty of time to do your research. The goal here isn't to induce panic as the clock ticks down; after all, it's simply a method of holding yourself accountable for making the decision. It's not unlike creating a goal for yourself. The most effective goals usually have an element of time-limitation to them.

Once you've selected a date, put it in your calendar or to-do list app of choice so you have a visual reminder someplace. If need be, set smaller deadlines or goals for the time between now and your Decision Deadline to help it feel less overwhelming (e.g., "by next Saturday research one-bedroom apartment prices in Missoula," "within two weeks call Angie to ask them about their experience living in Omaha," and so on). And do your very best to stick to the deadline you've set for yourself, as much as you would stick to a deadline at work or in school.

Get Outside Perspective

Effort level: Medium to high ●●●●○

Some of us include everyone in our inner circle in decision making, and others work everything through in the privacy of their own mind and only inform their loved ones after they've reached a conclusion. There is (as I keep saying in this book) no right or wrong way here. But even if you're a serial advice-seeker such as myself, you can still get stuck if you've exhausted your usual sources of outside-input. And if you're a keep-it-mum-till-the-decision-is-made type, this exercise especially applies.

Getting an outside opinion when you're struggling to reach a decision can be surprisingly helpful, and not for the reasons you might think. Sometimes your best friend will bring a completely new and unexpected insight to the table, or your grandparent will reassure you in just the right way, and that in itself will help you make up your mind. But other times, just the act of talking through the options will help you sort out what you want. Or sometimes your loved one will make a good case for option A, and in disagreeing with them you'll realize why you've been gunning for option B all along.

It can be tough to let someone into a moment of vulnerability like this, especially if it's a larger decision that will impact your life in a major way. But if you choose your confidant with care, it can truly make a world of difference. And if you already tend to ask your inner circle for advice on decision making, I challenge you to ask someone you wouldn't typically ask for their take. Not someone who you don't trust, but maybe someone who you don't usually go to first. They likely have a fresh perspective that you haven't considered yet.

Three of Swords

Sometimes when we make decisions or enact bold changes in our lives, there are pieces—and people—who must be left behind. And these do not always go quietly. In the Three of Swords, we find ourselves facing heartbreak, betrayal, or jealousy. People we trusted have cut us to the quick, and situations we thought would never change have fallen away. We are left to reckon with all the hurt and distress of the aftermath. I often think that the Three of Swords finds us attempting to intellectualize our way through an emotional shock that might otherwise belong more to the suit of Cups. We'd like to believe that we can think ourselves out of a painful time, but sooner or later we must feel the feelings of that painful time, too.

When you draw the Three of Swords in your daily reading, you may be grappling with deeply uncomfortable feelings like the squeeze of jealousy, the anguish of heartbreak, or the rug-pulled-out-from-under-you sensation of betrayal. As tempting as it may be to distract yourself or trivialize your emotions, make sure that you're taking the time to sit with them and acknowledge their validity. Even the most rational among us cannot logic their way through everything. We are emotional creatures by nature, and the Three of Swords reminds us that painful, traumatic experiences must be faced through a synthesis of head and heart.

 Affirmations

I AM a survivor.
I CAN endure tumultuous times.
I WILL allow myself to be angry.

 *Reflections*

How do I manage strong negative feelings?

We've danced around related questions with other cards, but with the Three of Swords we may be experiencing a maelstrom of "negative" feelings—grief, fury, heartbreak, jealousy, and on and on. Each of them carries its own unique flavor, but they all have in common that we tend to shove them aside and try to ignore them when they come a-knocking. No matter how upset you are, you can't spend 100 percent of your time sobbing uncontrollably or screaming at the walls. But you also can't put a lid on your feelings forever—sooner or later they'll spill over. When you're in the thick of an uncomfortable emotion (or several at once!) how do you strike the balance between feeling what you need to feel and functioning in your day-to-day life?

How can I befriend anger?

There isn't a solid script for anger in our culture. We're taught that we must either repress it indefinitely (which leads to passive aggression and unexpected boil-overs) or that we have no choice but to explode on hapless loved ones. And yet, anger can be a powerful ally when we learn to befriend it. It encourages us to protect ourselves, our loved ones, and our communities. What is your relationship with anger? Do you tend to push it away, or do you tend to cling to it long after its shelf life? How can you better navigate your anger, when it comes up? (For further reading on this topic, I cannot recommend Lama Rod Owens' *Love and Rage* enough.)

What heartbreak have I endured?

Heartbreak doesn't just mean losing a romantic partner (although that's a type of heartbreak that almost all of us experience at one time or another). It can also mean losing a friend, a family member, a home, a job, and on and on. This question isn't unlike one we pose for the grief of the Five of Cups, and there's certainly a great deal of overlap between heartbreak and loss. When a romantic partner leaves us, or when we're fired from a job we loved, there's a grieving process involved. But often the grieving is complicated by anger, betrayal, jealousy, and self-blame. When has heartbreak manifested in your life? What has the grieving process looked like for you? What did it have in common with other losses you've experienced, and where did it differ?

Actions

Break Something

Effort level: Low to medium ●●○○○

We've all done the thing where we grab a pillow and punch it, bang it into the couch, and just generally take out all our feelings on something soft and unbreakable, right? Sometimes this can genuinely help you let off steam, but I've found that sometimes when I'm especially upset, I actually *want* that tangible feeling of breaking something. Now, I'm not telling you to hurl your phone out the window or put your fist through the TV. I'm suggesting that you find a small, safe, and satisfying way to shatter something that doesn't much matter anyway.

This may take a bit of creativity on your part. You need to find an object that doesn't matter and a place to do the breaking where you won't harm anyone (including yourself). As an example, I might grab a glass out of the cabinet that I (and my housemates!) don't care much for, go out on my balcony, and drop the glass directly onto the cement. This is a contained space, and a small enough object that the pieces aren't likely to scatter into unfindable corners. I'll still get the kinesthetic satisfaction of breaking an object, but in a controlled, contained environment. A lightbulb inside a paper bag could accomplish the same thing.

The aftermath of this exercise is just as important as the exercise itself, of course. Make sure you thoroughly clean up after yourself, and make sure you do it in such a way that you won't cut your fingers or feet, for heaven's sake! A handheld vacuum can be your best friend in this situation. And as you clean, consider the parallels with whatever difficult emotions you're weathering right now. You can experience the full intensity of your anger, heartache, or jealousy, but do so in a way that is healthy for you and everyone around you. Don't hurl all your feelings at your loved ones, any more than you'd hurl a glass at them! But in safe, contained environments, experience the depth of your emotions. And then carefully, gently, and kindly clean up after yourself.

Don't Bottle It Up

Effort level: Medium to high ●●●●○

The opposite of throwing your feelings at anyone around you is completely bottling them up. I'm the champion of swallowing my anger. I'll let things go that could be easily addressed if I just brought them up the first time they annoyed me, over and over, until I'm a festering volcano of resentment just waiting to erupt. Is this any healthier than exploding at the slightest inconvenience? Absolutely not. So just as it's important not to unleash your full wrath on anyone at any time, it's important to have safe and healthy methods for expressing anger.

I'm a big believer in asking before I vent my frustrations to anyone, even my most trusted loved ones. You never know when they're going through a bad day, too, and I don't want to overload them. I'll introduce my need to vent but leave them an out if they need it: "Hey, I'm feeling really frustrated with such-and-such situation—do you mind if I gripe about it for a few minutes?" If they say no, I find someone else to talk to (or even just journal about it. Journals NEVER get overloaded).

Are you the type to avoid these sorts of conversations like the plague? I feel you. It doesn't come naturally to me, either. But believe me when I say that holding it all inside your brain and heart forever is untenable. Sooner or later, that unexpressed anger or hurt will spill over onto someone through passive aggression or outright explosions. Better to talk through it in a more stable and controlled space like this. Even if the only person you're "talking" to is a journal, there's a release in acknowledging that you're upset. Even if the thing you're upset about is kind of unfair or petty. Those feelings are real, and whether you mean to act on them or not, giving them a voice can help you release them.

Four of Swords

We've been through a great deal after the heartache of the Three of Swords. With the Four of Swords, we're ready for some well-deserved rest. Perhaps we've arrived here exhausted and beaten-down, or perhaps we're self-aware enough to take a break before we get too overwhelmed. Regardless, the Four of Swords is a space for us to rejuvenate our bodies as well as our minds.

When you draw the Four of Swords in a daily reading, you are cordially invited to take a breath, take a nap, or take the day off. We put a lot of pressure on ourselves in every aspect of our daily lives, but the Four of Swords is an opportunity to release that pressure. Everything on your to-do list will wait five minutes, or five hours. And if you're so wiped out that you're doing a half-assed job on everything anyway, you're actually making a smart decision by choosing to recover some mental energy. Give yourself a break. You unquestionably deserve it.

 ## Affirmations

I AM worthy of rest.
I CAN separate my worth from my productivity.
I WILL relax.

 ## Reflections

What do I need to truly relax?
Relaxation for me may look like over-stimulation for you. Everyone has different methods of taking their brain off the hook and recharging their internal batteries. What helps you unwind? Is it a soothing bubble bath? A favorite movie or book? A walk through your local park? Beyond just the external trappings of relaxation, what do you have to take care of in order to feel capable of relaxing? Do you need to ask a partner to keep an eye on the kids while you rest? Do you need to put your phone in do-not-disturb mode?

Do you need to set your work email's vacation response? What typically gets in the way of your efforts to relax, and how might you circumvent those obstacles?

How have I been sleeping lately?

Our sleep quality is such an easy tell for how stressed out we are or how our physical health is faring, isn't it? And again, it differs from person to person how much sleep we need. I feel like death if I don't get a minimum of seven hours, but I know people who can manage just fine on five, and on the other end of the spectrum I know people who can sleep for ten solid hours and wake up feeling just as tired. Only you know what a good night's sleep looks like for you. Thinking about the last week or so, have you been waking up feeling refreshed, or have you needed to hit the snooze button five or six times before dragging yourself into the kitchen for coffee? Has it taken you any longer than usual to fall asleep at night? Have nightmares woken you more frequently? If you consider this question and find that you're sleeping more poorly than usual, what ways might you improve your quality of sleep?

What does recovery look like?

This is a bit of an abstract question. Think of times in your life when you've been coming out of a bad spell—not the bad spell itself, but the aftermath. How can you tell that you're gradually healing? You may have tiny habits and mannerisms that act as tells for how your mental health is faring. Here's an easy one for me: the more often I catch myself singing as I go about my daily routine, the more I know that my mental health is in a good place. If I'm having a bad anxiety day or I'm in the thick of a sad time, I rarely sing out loud. If you can't think of any little signs like this, consider asking a significant other or someone else who lives with you or spends a lot of time around you. They can almost certainly tell the difference between you healing and you floundering.

 *Actions*

Rest Up!

Effort level: Low to medium ●●○○○

I probably don't need to give you much explanation for this one. No other card in the tarot says with such insistence and clarity, "Hey, you look exhausted. Why don't you go lie down for a bit?" You can read all kinds of research on the benefits of the power nap, if you're so inclined. If you don't usually have trouble falling asleep during the day, the power nap (of 20 minutes or thereabouts) is accessible to you. If you're among those of us who have a harder time conking out on command, you may need to set aside more time to wind yourself down and get a full REM cycle in.

Here's another tip from a consummate insomniac, though: don't put too much pressure on yourself to sleep. My brain is like a cat or a petulant toddler—the more I let it know that I *want* and *need* it to shut down for a bit, the more it refuses to do what I ask. My most successful naps have been the ones I've approached from the side instead of head-on. Instead of telling myself, "Okay, I have thirty minutes to CATCH UP ON ALL THE SLEEP I MISSED LAST NIGHT. GO GO GO!" I simply tell myself, "Okay, here's an opportunity to rest." I get a book or put on some soothing music, and if I don't end up falling asleep, it's okay. I still recharged a bit. But oftentimes, I do doze off because I didn't jinx myself. So consider this exercise an invitation to rest, which may include sleeping if you're inclined and able, but also isn't required to. Even just making yourself comfortable and slowing down your brain for a bit can do a lot for your energy level.

Take an Intentional Day Off

Effort level: Medium to high ●●●●○

"Aren't all days off intentional?" I hear you asking. And the answer is no. Most of us have weekends off from our day jobs, but we fill those days with chores and obligations and everything we can think of. For this exercise, I challenge you to do just the opposite. Take a day off from work (either a weekend day that you already have free, or a legitimate vacation day during your usual workweek) and do your best to keep that day as open and free as you possibly can.

When your day off arrives, let your gut instincts be your guide. Do you feel like turning off your alarm clock and sleeping late? Do it. In the mood to make a batch of pancakes for yourself and your family? Why not? Interested in spending most of the day curled up on the couch reading that novel that's been waiting for you? Nothing's stopping you. The key is to let yourself follow your desires and let your spirit lead you from one activity (or non-activity!) to the next. The one caveat here is that you should remain mindful of any impulses to work. It's one thing if cleaning is a de-stressing, relaxing activity for you—in that case, absolutely take the time to deep clean the kitchen. But if you're being pulled to clean by guilt, or that nagging feeling that you should be using this time "productively," resist the urge. Turn away from the shoulds and turn toward the cans. "How can I be spending this time to rejuvenate myself?" Not, "How should I be using this time to accomplish something?"

Five of Swords

As always, the Five brings tidings of conflict. In the case of the Swords, the conflict is especially grandiose and painful. Where the Five of Wands indicates an unwillingness to compromise among collaborators, the Five of Swords stands for the kinds of arguments that grow out of fundamental differences in opinion. It often appears when disagreements turn into hateful battles. There's likely someone in this argument who has an unfair advantage or who's fighting dirty—it may be someone else, or it might be you. It can also indicate oppressors and privilege; for example, if a white person engages a person of color in a debate about race relations, the white individual is coming into the argument with the weight of white privilege behind them, whereas the person of color has their own rights on the line.

When you pull this card, be mindful of any disagreements you encounter during the course of your day. It's not that you should avoid conflict at all costs, but if conflict arises and you engage, you may find yourself in over your head. Or you may be the one causing undue pain to the person you're arguing with. The Five of Swords asks you to be sure that you're fighting on equal footing. Be Peter Pan offering to help Captain Hook to his feet so that they can continue their duel fair and square. Don't be Captain Hook looking for any opportunity to cheat.

 Affirmations

I AM dedicated to equality.
I CAN use my voice to enact change.
I WILL choose my battles wisely.

 *Reflections*

What is the difference between self-preservation and self-interest?

Sometimes you have to take care of yourself first, and when there's a battle raging around you, you may need to make decisions to protect yourself first and foremost. But of course, there's also such a thing as acting too selfishly. Where and how do you draw that line? Is there a time in your life when you made a choice to protect yourself at great cost to someone else? What did you learn from the experience? Is there a situation in your current daily life where you struggle to distinguish self-preservation from selfish behavior?

When am I prone to selfishness?

You may be the most caring, self-sacrificing person on the face of the planet, but you still have moments of selfishness because you're still a human being. Can you think of those moments when you're most likely to be a bit self-absorbed? Here's a small example from my own daily life: I catch myself getting instantly defensive when someone points out one of my shortcomings or notices that I didn't do something I said I'd do. I immediately reach for excuses. It's something I'm aware of, and I'm consciously trying to break the habit. But this is a form of selfishness; when I make excuses, I refuse to take accountability for myself and my actions. Do any similar moments or mannerisms come to mind for you?

How can I work for equality?

I probably don't need to tell you, but if we want the world to be a safe, fair, and welcoming place for everyone, we have a lot of work yet to do. And you don't have to write to Congress or march in giant protests to do your part for equality. Maybe you sign petitions, or donate money, or maybe you quietly educate your less socially conscious family members. Are there things you're already doing to make the world a fairer place? What else might you do?

 ***Actions***

Apologize to Someone

Effort level: Low to medium ●●○○○

Apologizing well is NOT easy. When we know we've harmed someone (especially someone we care about), we all tend to let our shame and guilt do the talking for us, with results ranging from vaguely defensive to flat-out victim-blaming. This kind of apology also often turns into what my dad called the "I'm sorry I got caught" apology—not true contrition for the harmful action, but shame at being caught red-handed. The best and most impactful apologies include acknowledgement of wrongdoing and a genuine promise to improve the hurtful behavior.

Is there someone you know you've hurt recently? It doesn't have to be a major disagreement—just think if you hurt someone's feelings or overstepped your bounds. Find a time when you can talk to the person in question (ideally choose a time when you can be one-on-one), let them know that you recognize you hurt them, and that you don't intend to make the same mistake again. They may want to explain why your behavior was harmful, and if they're being respectful, you should do your best to genuinely listen—after all, if you better understand where they're coming from, you're less likely to repeat your harmful behavior.

Finally, remember that you don't have to flagellate yourself for a good apology. (As a matter of fact, going overboard can turn a well-meant apology into a pity party for you, the harmful person!) Don't repeat over and over, "Oh my god, I'm a terrible human being for doing this to you. Can you ever, ever forgive me?" That's not a good look. A simple invitation to discuss may be all you need: "Hey, I know that what I said yesterday hurt your feelings, and I want to apologize for that. Would you be open to talking about it a little, so I understand how to avoid hurting you in the future?"

Confront Your Privilege

Effort level: Medium to high ●●●●○

When the concept of privilege is introduced, it often prompts a lot of resentment and outright hostility. But the Five of Swords insists that we pay attention to our privilege.

You almost certainly have one or more identities that are privileged by society: maybe you're white, or male, or straight, or cisgender, or able-bodied. Even if you're none of these things, you might have privileges that are less discussed or considered—were you raised by both your parents in a stable, loving environment, for example? Do you belong to a mainstream religious community like a church?

Spend some time reflecting on one or more of your layers of privilege. There are any number of resources on the internet for this sort of work. There are books coming out all the time about white privilege and male privilege in particular. Or you can approach your privilege from a more individual point of view—for example, if you're white, you could seek out an article or blog written by a person of color and pay close attention to their descriptions of struggles you haven't faced. It's uncomfortable work, to be sure, but there's no overstating how necessary this work is to heal our world. I also recommend having a like-minded friend or loved one to do this work alongside. If your research brings up feelings of guilt or anger, it can help to talk it out with someone, but you absolutely shouldn't put the onus on a person from the oppressed community. Instead, choose a fellow white person, man, heterosexual, etc. to discuss your findings and feelings with.

Six of Swords

There are two words I associate strongly with the Six of Swords: journey and underway. Our home base is far behind us, but there is still a way to go before we reach our destination. The Six of Swords is the true midpoint when turning back would take just as much effort and time as pressing on. It can be an uncomfortable time when doubts about the journey mingle with homesickness. But it can also leave your heart buzzing with excitement as you realize that there is no turning back now.

You may be in the midst of a long process or transformation. The goal may seem as distant as the place you started from, and you may be overwhelmed with a mixture of anticipation, doubt, weariness, and eagerness. It's a strange place to be, halfway between here and there, but all you can do is embrace this liminal moment and continue forward. Let the Six of Swords serve as a reminder that your journey is a worthy one, whether it's a tangible movement from Point A to Point B or more of an internal transformation.

Affirmations

I AM on my way.
I CAN be patient with the journey.
I WILL recognize where I come from and where I'm headed.

Reflections

What journeys am I on right now?

Don't let the word "journey" fool you into thinking that you have to be traveling for the Six of Swords to be relevant. If you're practicing a challenging piece of music for an upcoming concert, you're on a journey. If you're working to incorporate more exercise into your daily life, you're on a journey. If you're fighting to feel more self-love and build your self-esteem, you're on a journey. Through this lens, you're probably on quite a few journeys all at once. What comes to mind? What transformations or practices are you in the middle of?

How can I coexist with doubt?

Doubt is deeply uncomfortable for most of us, and you may feel tempted to squash your feelings of uncertainty when they arise. But at its root, doubt is like life's spell check—it reminds us to double check our work and make extra sure we're ready before we leap. It can certainly be allowed to run so rampant that we end up paralyzed, but we all need a healthy bit of doubt so we don't charge after our every impulse. When those whispery doubts pop up in the back of your mind, how might you welcome them without completely ignoring them or allowing them to put you into analysis paralysis?

What negative situations am I leaving/have I left behind?

Sometimes our journeys are characterized by homesickness, and we're like Orpheus trying desperately not to look over our shoulder as we move ahead. But sometimes we're leaving behind something that we've been trying to escape for quite a while. Is this the case for you right now? Or if it isn't, when have you actively removed yourself from a negative situation? What was that journey like? Did you have mixed feelings, or was it a profound relief?

 *Actions*

Look Over Old Photos

Effort level: Low to medium ●●○○○

If you want a quick and relatively easy visual of how much you've changed, go back and look at some pictures from a few years ago. Thanks to the smartphones most of us carry around, you probably have at least a few selfies from years past, even if you don't tend to take a ton of pictures. Let me tell you, even just glancing at my college pictures—which wasn't *that* long ago—makes me think, "Who the heck is that?!" (You may want to give this activity a pass if you tend to look at *any* photos of yourself with an unfairly critical eye, or if you have any dysphoria about seeing your younger self.) It's important to note that this exercise isn't encouraging you to dunk on past-you. It's meant as an opportunity to acknowledge how much you've grown and changed over the years. Nothing is static, and the Six of Swords asks us to keep in mind that every journey shapes who we are.

A personal anecdote that might help you look back on your older self with fondness rather than criticism: once, I turned up some of my childhood writing projects and became more and more embarrassed for younger-author-me as I read. When my mom found me in the middle of this time-traveling-shame-game, I wailed, "Am I going to look back on the stuff I'm writing *now* with this much disgust?" Mom shrugged and said matter-of-factly, "Maybe you will, but if you hadn't written this stuff as a kid, you wouldn't have improved at all. So what's the alternative—just not writing ever again?"

So, as you detour down memory lane with this exercise, do your best to celebrate how much you've grown and changed without putting down your past self for where they were then. You wouldn't be the you you're celebrating if you hadn't been that you then. (And that may win the prize for the most confusing sentence I've ever committed to paper.)

Pay Attention to the Journey during Your Commute

Effort level: Medium to high ●●●●○

When you make the same trip back and forth every weekday, the scenery tends to fade into the background pretty quickly. Even if you're lucky enough to be within walking distance of your job, you probably have your headphones on and your head in the clouds as you walk. (The only exception here is if you happen to work from home. If that's the case, apply this same logic to another trip that you make frequently, like to the grocery store.) But Six of Swords energy is all about the travel itself, not the arrival. So during your commute today, try to spend at least part of the time actively paying attention to your route rather than distracting yourself with music or podcasts or just mentally planning for the day ahead as you drive, ride, or walk.

If this seems like too tall or broad an order, you can approach this activity with the mindset, "I'm going to notice and remember *one* particular thing from my commute today." Maybe you'll make eye contact with an especially enthusiastic sign spinner as you wait at a stoplight, or maybe you'll realize that the library you pass every day is closed for renovations, or maybe you'll just admire how beautifully the trees are changing colors. The *what* isn't as important as the noticing itself.

Seven of Swords

The Seven of Swords speaks in hushed undertones, and often does so behind someone's back. It is a sign of secrets and deception. Whether you are the one acting deceitfully or the one being deceived, this is a card that cautions us to recenter ourselves on truth and honesty. It may be time for us to confront someone who isn't being straight with us…or it may be time to come clean about a lie that we've told. Or we may be telling lies for our own protection—honesty isn't *always* the best policy, but dishonesty does always come at a cost.

When you draw the Seven of Swords in a daily reading, perhaps you're feeling caught in a web of lies, or perhaps you've just told one recent lie that has you feeling guilty. Maybe you're lying to protect yourself and it's weighing on you. Maybe you have a gut instinct that someone is being less than truthful with you. Or maybe you're completely in the dark as yet, and the untruth is so subtle and well-camouflaged that it's in position to blindside you when it comes to light. There are any number of ways that deception may be influencing your current situation, but the Seven of Swords is a sure sign that there are bent truths, half-truths, or untruths hanging in the air around you.

 ## Affirmations

I AM honest.
I CAN take care of myself without hurting others.
I WILL consider how my actions impact those around me.

 ## Reflections

Where can I be more honest with myself and others?
You don't have to be actively telling lies to benefit from deeper honesty. Most of us have moments when we bite our tongues, wanting to say how we're really feeling but afraid

of the fallout that might result. Where and when might you allow yourself to speak more openly? Maybe there's something your significant other has been doing (or not doing) that bothers you, but you haven't felt right about speaking up. Maybe there's a situation at work that you've been meaning to discuss with your boss. Maybe you need to sit down and consciously confront a truth about yourself that you've been avoiding! Spend some time reflecting and/or journaling about areas of your life that could use an infusion of honesty.

Are there secrets I'm holding onto needlessly?

There are as many reasons to keep secrets as there are people to keep them, and make no mistake, some of those are valid and important reasons! But just as often, we keep secrets because we feel loyal to a person or situation that's years out of date by now, or because we fear the consequences of sharing, or because it makes us feel powerful to have information that nobody else has. Sometimes, kept secrets cause more harm than secrets shared. Now, I'm certainly not encouraging you to betray someone's trust or go behind their back if they've asked you to keep something in your confidence. But say a friend has told you information about their romantic relationship that feels deeply troubling, and you aren't sure whether to talk to someone to get them help since that would betray their trust. Or say you're still keeping a secret about a long-gone grandparent that's weighing on you. There are circumstances where these secrets might be shared in a contained environment, and that might make you feel that a weight has been lifted. (Therapists, coaches, and counselors can be perfect for this, but in the absence of any of those, try to choose a loved one to speak to who only knows the secret-teller vaguely, or through you.)

When in my past was I deceptive?
How has my view of that time changed since?

Can you think back to a time when you were hiding parts of yourself or misrepresenting the facts of a situation? What were your reasons for doing so? Who did the deception impact, and how? And has enough time passed that your perception has shifted? Maybe a childhood white lie felt enormous and guilt-inducing, but with the wisdom of adulthood you can see how ultimately inconsequential it was. Or conversely, maybe it didn't seem like any big deal at the time, but now you can look back and recognize how deeply it hurt someone. Try to bring an objective eye to this question. Be neither too forgiving nor too harsh with your past self.

 *Actions*

Admit That You Were Wrong

Effort level: Low to medium ●●○○○

One of the most significant behaviors my mom modeled for us as kids was a willingness to admit when she was wrong. That may not sound like a big deal, but you would not believe how many parents I've met who refuse to acknowledge ANY wrongdoing to their children. When my mom sat my brother and me down and told us she was sorry for something she'd done wrong or a mistake she'd made, we learned not only that it was okay to make mistakes, but that it was okay to talk about them. What a rarity in the world we live in, right? How many celebrities, politicians, and other public figures can you recall off the top of your head who have genuinely admitted to messing up or misspeaking?

In the entry for the Five of Swords, one activity invites you to apologize to someone you've wronged. This is obviously a related exercise, but not identical. Admitting that you were wrong may be the first stop on the way to apologizing, and if this activity draws you toward apologizing to anyone impacted by your mistake, by all means, do so. But before you can seek forgiveness for something you did wrong, you have to be able to acknowledge its wrongness to yourself. This is, on its face, a solitary exercise. The wrongdoing may be years old now—in fact, it's often easier to admit to our mistakes once we've gotten some distance from them. You may choose to journal about it, or you may simply spend some time reflecting on the situation in question.

As always, this exercise isn't an invitation to beat yourself up mercilessly or slide into a chasm of self-deprecation. We all make mistakes. Feeling ashamed of your mistakes is just as unproductive as being too proud to admit to them. The best thing you can do for yourself is admit that a mistake was made and resolve to take whatever action may be necessary to prevent it from happening again.

Release a Secret

Effort level: Medium to high ⬤⬤⬤⬤◯

Letting trusted loved ones into the innermost workings of your heart and mind can be terrifying. Even you aren't an especially private person. I'm not someone who consciously keeps many secrets about myself—I'm a very "front stage" sort of human, as my mom would say. But there are still pieces of my psyche that I don't voice to anyone besides myself very often. For me, these are often the pieces that feel too needy or fragile to foist on anyone else, even my family. So "releasing a secret" for me might translate to telling my spouse that I've been feeling particularly anxious for the last few weeks, and I could use some extra hugs.

If you are more of a private person than me by nature, you may have a more obvious secret to share. And listen, this prompt isn't telling you to run onto the street and yell your darkest secrets to random passersby. It could be as small-scale as telling your significant other or best friend something they've never heard about you before. Choose someone who you know will love you unconditionally or choose a secret that feels relatively low-stakes or choose both.

On the other hand, if this card has popped up at a time when you really are ready to let go of a big secret that's been weighing on you, the Seven of Swords may be the nudge you're looking for. But please make sure that you're taking care of yourself as you do so. Ask for the support of your closest loved ones, take your time, and carve out a space and time where you can regularly withdraw and recharge your batteries.

Eight of Swords

The Swords are the suit of intellect and the mind, and sometimes the mind is just as skilled at creating problems for itself as it is at solving problems. With the Eight of Swords, we are caged in by anxiety and terror. Whether there is true danger in our current situation or not, we feel absolutely paralyzed and incapable of freeing ourselves. If you've ever had the kind of panic attack that freezes you in place and convinces you that any movement or action will make things catastrophically worse, you're familiar with the energy that the Eight of Swords carries with it.

In a daily reading, the Eight of Swords may warn you that an anxiety storm is on the horizon. Or you may already be in the thick of that storm, and this card may make you say, "Well DUH," out loud. Or perhaps there isn't anything intense looming, but there's a quiet worry that's been gnawing at you from the background of your thoughts, growing increasingly more uncomfortable bit by bit. (If that's the case, the Eight of Swords is probably warning you to sit down with that worry and figure out how to navigate it before it turns into a full-blown anxiety paralysis scenario.) But the most important message of the Eight of Swords is this: within your grasp is the power to cut through your mental bonds and emerge from the quagmire of panic. The Swords may feel as though they're hemming you in, but at any moment you can snatch one up and use it as a weapon to free yourself.

 Affirmations

I AM my own liberator.
I CAN escape from turmoil within and without.
I WILL break unhealthy cycles.

 *Reflections*

Are there any situations that I'm keeping myself trapped in?

People are remarkable at getting used to just about any situation, no matter how awful it seems. Not that it becomes less awful once you're accustomed to it, of course, but the rawness and newness wears off. And sometimes, we let ourselves become comfortable with our discomfort. Have you ever remained in a relationship that clearly wasn't going anywhere (or was clearly not good for one or both of you) because at least that relationship was familiar? Or resisted looking for a new job even though you hated your current one, because the uncertainty of job hunting seemed even more daunting? These are just a few tangible examples, but there's any number of other ways that we can languish in a bad situation because we prefer the devil we know. What current situations come to mind as you consider this question? What steps might you take that you're resisting, even though they could alleviate the uncomfortable situation of the present?

What is my relationship with anxiety?

It legitimately took me until my mid-twenties to recognize the fact that yes, I have anxiety. Because I wasn't having regular panic attacks or struggling with social situations, I assumed that I couldn't possibly have anxiety…right? Yeah, no. I firmly believe that all mental health issues exist on a spectrum (just like everything else in human existence, right?). Everyone has moments of extreme anxiety, even if they don't necessarily meet the criteria to be diagnosed with clinical anxiety. Same with depression, trauma, and so on. When you're dealing with nerves or feeling especially jittery, what do you do? Do you know what symptoms you experience, physically and emotionally, when you're particularly anxious? Do you have any practices that you already use to navigate these moments? If not, what might you try?

What makes me a survivor?

I don't think there's any such thing as a person who isn't resilient. We wouldn't have made it this far as a species if we weren't a stubbornly persistent bunch of creatures. We all have different methods of enduring, and one person's surviving might look like another person's drowning. But even in our darkest and most self-destructive moments, even if the survival method we're utilizing is deeply unhealthy, we're trying to protect ourselves in one way or another. What makes you a survivor? When you've gotten through tough times, what traits have you called upon to help you? Is it your optimism? Your courage? Your ability to make and keep close friends who you can reach out to when you're struggling?

 **Actions**

Journal Your Anxieties

Effort level: Low to medium ●●○○○

I return to writing-related activities quite often in this book, but I've seen firsthand (with myself and my clients) how powerful the simple act of writing something down can be. A great deal of anxiety's power over us lies in its ability to trap us inside our own minds. Often, when a fear is shared with someone else, it loses some of its sway on us. And journaling is a middle space between keeping a thought contained in your own mind and fully voicing it to another person. Thoughts and feelings are squishy, abstract things that float around in our minds and hearts. When we distill them into words on a page, we give ourselves the opportunity to sort through them—and that's often the first step toward navigating them with greater clarity and ease.

The incredible writer and sociologist Brené Brown has a method I love in *Rising Strong as a Spiritual Practice*. When you're feeling overwhelmed by a situation, you sit down and write what "story" you're telling yourself. For instance, if you just got into a small dispute with your partner and you're rehashing it over and over in your mind, you might write, "The story I'm telling myself is that this small fight is the beginning of something much bigger. My partner is going to get more and more frustrated with me and eventually they'll leave me." Don't censor yourself because something seems too absurd or too dramatic. This is the other beauty of writing: you don't have to justify even the wildest of your anxious fantasies. Yet at the same time, putting those words on paper allows you to acknowledge to yourself that you're catastrophizing. You can let yourself write out all the worst-case scenarios you're fearing, then take a good long look at them and say to yourself, "Okay. This is unlikely to be the outcome, and I can recognize that without blaming myself for worrying." You might also start your journaling with a phrase like, "Right now, I'm worrying about…" or, "I keep thinking about…" Whatever it takes to get you openly sharing with yourself about your current worries, anxieties, and fears—even if it's literally just free-writing a bullet-point list of the things that are bothering you today.

Try Martial Arts

Effort level: Medium to high ●●●●○

If you've never tried a martial art before, you may associate it with self-defense and not much else. And the self-defense factor is the first reason that I've chosen it as an activity for the Eight of Swords. Knowing how to defend yourself in the event of a physical attack is a skill that, ideally, everyone should have at least a basic understanding of. But martial arts can provide so much more than this. It can help you develop your physical strength, endurance, balance, and flexibility. It can introduce you to a community of friends if you take an in-person class. And (perhaps the *biggest* reason I chose it for the Eight of Swords) it empowers you with the awareness of your own strength and physical ability to stand up for yourself. One of my closest loved ones has PTSD, and their regular tae kwon do practice has been instrumental in building their self-confidence and trust in themself.

You don't have to sign up for an eight-week class or invest in expensive gear to try a martial art on for size. YouTube has any number of mini tutorials and exercises you can explore in every discipline under the sun. There are online classes if you want to dive a little deeper but aren't ready to try an in-person class. And don't write off the possibility of martial arts if you're someone with chronic pain or living with a disability. I use an online video series that's specifically designed to teach tai chi to people living with arthritis, fibromyalgia, and other chronic pain conditions, even if you need to remain seated throughout the practice. It's been enormously rewarding to realize that I can exercise my body in a way that actually feels good instead of terrible.

So yes, when you're in a particularly anxious moment in your life, martial arts can provide a sense of physical safety by teaching you to protect yourself. But it can also build your stamina emotionally and physically. And it can remind you that you are powerful enough and strong enough to protect yourself in ANY circumstance, no matter if the threat is physical, emotional, or spiritual.

Nine of Swords

What happens when anxiety is left to fester, rather than consciously navigated? It seeps deeper into the psyche, and there it metastasizes, spreading its influence over your subconscious. When we find ourselves feeling overwhelmed and hopeless, when our nights are tormented by chronic nightmares or insomnia, we may be under the influence of the Nine of Swords.

While every card in the tarot is part of a sequenced story to some extent, the Eight and Nine of Swords are so intertwined that I *still* occasionally must return to my reference books to remind myself of the particular nuances of each. If the Eight was a warning, the Nine is what happens when that warning goes unheeded. If you've pulled the Nine of Swords in a daily reading—especially if it seems to come out of nowhere and you aren't sure how it applies to your life—I recommend incorporating elements of the Eight of Swords' reflections and actions as well as those below. Taken together, these two cards are a firm reminder that you hold the power to rescue yourself from the darkest depths of your own mind.

Affirmations

I AM safe.
I CAN resist hopelessness.
I WILL comfort myself.

Reflections

What do I do when I wake from a nightmare?
There are few feelings worse than jolting awake from a bad dream. Especially if you live alone, nightmares can hijack your rational mind and leave you feeling unsafe and insecure even if you know intellectually that everything was "just a dream." Do you have a particular practice to help yourself re-center before you try to get back to sleep? And

if not, what practices *might* you try out next time a nightmare wakes you? If you share a room with a loved one, are you comfortable waking them for a quick hug or a word of reassurance? Is there someone you know who keeps odd hours who you might text message or call quickly? Would getting up and getting a drink of water, pacing, or reading a few pages of a book help you? These are just a few ideas to get you thinking—the purpose here is to brainstorm ways that you might help yourself feel more comfortable and reassured.

How to I soothe myself when I'm overwhelmed?

This isn't unlike the above question but differs in how you arrived here. Nightmares are usually abrupt, where feeling overwhelmed can creep up on you—sometimes over the course of many days, sometimes in just an hour or two. Whether you're swamped with work, worried about keeping up with your family's needs, or just feeling generally stressed out, what methods do you employ to calm yourself down? In my opinion, these practices can fall into one of two categories. One is self-soothing practices (think things like listening to music, taking a bath, reading a book, etc.) and the other is organization or management of the source of overwhelm (think breaking down your tasks into a to-do list, talking things out with a trusted loved one, etc.) Take a few moments and consider both of these categories, and come up with at least one or two suggestions for yourself.

What am I processing right now? How does it affect my everyday life?

Very early on in my relationship with my therapist, I stated that I didn't feel like I was getting anywhere in grieving my dad and I needed to "process" it better. She asked me what I meant by processing. To be honest, I think what I meant at the time was "I'm not feeling better yet and I don't like it." (No duh, Sherlock: your dad just died.) The fact of the matter is, we're all processing a million things, all the time. And there's no way to section things off from each other—if you're dealing with the emotional fallout from a fight with a loved one, it will impact how you manage stress at work, for example. What's happened recently that's still impacting your emotional and mental landscape, for better or for worse? Can you think of ways that it's affected other aspects of your life, even ones that are seemingly unrelated?

 **Actions**

Meditate

Effort level: Low to medium ●●○○○

If you're reading this book, I'd say the chances are high that you've tried meditation at one point or another—or if you haven't, you've certainly at least been advised to try meditation by a teacher, healer, or another author. I'm not here to try to convince you of the validity or importance of meditation, but I do believe that the Nine of Swords is a grave reminder to check in with your own mind from time to time, and meditation can be a powerful method for doing so.

That being said, meditation doesn't have to be a long, motionless spell if that isn't what works for you. Meditation can be as simple as spending a couple of minutes focusing on your breathing. It can be going for a walk and noticing your surroundings rather than listening to music or staring at your phone. It can even be an activity that helps you slow down and pay attention to the current moment—cross stitching, for example, is an activity that I find incredibly meditative under the right circumstances. The active ingredient in meditation is that willingness to stay present and mindful. If the stereotypical mental image of meditation (sitting on the ground with your legs crossed and eyes closed, intoning *"ommmmm"*) makes you wrinkle your nose, try a walking meditation or a short, guided meditation to help you pay attention to your breathing. (A quick internet search can turn up any number of free guided meditations of varying lengths.) Anything you do to pause and spend a few minutes with your own thoughts can balance out that subconscious, bone-deep darkness that the Nine of Swords carries with it.

Create a Calming Bedtime Routine

Effort level: Medium to high ●●●●○

As someone who suffers from chronic insomnia, I can attest to the significance of having a nightly routine. Even if I don't fall asleep when I want to (which I usually don't), my quality of whatever sleep I DO get is still better when I'm in bed around the same time every night. That being said, I'm not necessarily one of those people who believes that you absolutely have to lock your phone in a strongbox at night if you want a prayer of sleeping well. I've tried going weeks at a time where I put my phone on silent and leave it in a drawer, and not only does it not improve my ability to fall asleep, sometimes it actually seems to make my insomnia worse. My compromise (which seems to work well) is setting boundaries about which apps I'm allowed to use after a certain hour. Calming, low-key games that help me wind down are fine. Social media and YouTube, which tempt me to stay up for just one more post or one more video, are no-gos.

I'm sharing all of this to illustrate that your bedtime routine should be *yours*. If watching the same movie every night or listening to the same playlist helps you relax as you prepare for sleep, that's what you should do. If showering *right* before bed is a surefire relaxation technique for you, do it. And by the same token, if there are activities that are frequently recommended as nighttime fail-safes but aren't effective for you, don't do them. (While some reading before bed works for me, I can't let myself pick up a fiction book after 8:00 PM or so. I *will*, inevitably, stay up to devour it whole.) Experiment with different routines and activities until you find something that works for you and you alone—and then commit to sticking to it every night, to the best of your ability.

Ten of Swords

The Ten of Swords is the manifestation of the phrase, "When you hit rock bottom, there's nowhere else to go but up." We've endured every wound, heartbreak, anxiety, and danger the Swords have thrown at us, and in the final number card in this suit, we are cast into a pit so dark and deep that it seems impossible that we'll lift ourselves out of it. But the secret gift in this card is the knowledge that there is no farther to fall. We've not only reached the worst our journey has to throw at us, but we're also getting through it. There is, truly, no other place to go but forward or up.

When the Ten of Swords appears in your daily reading, you may have reached one of those worst case scenarios that you worried about. A huge, life-altering sucker punch has caught you in the gut. Or, alternatively, you may be in the thick of a particularly bad spell of depression or anxiety that seems endless. Although this card may seem like a harbinger of worse times, I encourage you to take heart from its appearance. It acknowledges how bleak your current situation is, yet it reminds you that nothing lasts forever, not even bad times. When we're tumbling, there's no way of knowing where the fall will end or whether there will be a way to get up again. Once we've reached the bottom of the pit, we can begin to reconnoiter and plan our escape.

 Affirmations

I AM capable of recovery.
I CAN emerge from the darkest times.
I WILL take care of myself as I recover.

 ## Reflections

How do I manage pain?

We like to divide pain into categories (especially in the medical realm)—physical pain, emotional pain, mental pain, etc. My experience has been that you can't cut these categories off from one another so neatly, any more than you can cut your body off from your spirit or mind. When I'm having an especially bad fibromyalgia flareup, of course it negatively impacts my mood; and when I'm struggling with anxiety, the physical tension makes my chronic pain worse. So when considering this reflection, I encourage you to interpret "pain" in every sense of the word. When you're going through a tough time (physically, emotionally, mentally, spiritually, etc.), what do you do? How do you ride out the storm? What is your relationship with the pain itself?

What does endurance mean to me?

The Ten of Swords teaches us that sometimes, all we can do is endure. It's not about being happy, or even pretending to be happy. That's a big piece of my definition of endurance—allowing myself to be unhappy, but remaining grateful that I'm breathing. What's your definition? Are there times in your life that you can look back on and see true endurance in yourself? Are there people you know who seem to have a knack for enduring hard times (at least from the outside)?

What have some of my darkest moments been?

Only undertake this reflection question if you're in a healthy enough mental space to do so. Revisiting our darkest times can obviously be triggering, so if that's even a remote danger for you, skip this question and return to it at a time when you feel more centered and capable. But when you're going through something difficult, it can be empowering (or at least comforting) to look back on other hard times you've made it through. You are hardwired to survive. If you think back to other dark moments in your life, how does your current situation feel? Be wary of simply comparing. It probably won't help to say to yourself, "Wow, I'm being a big baby—this should be MUCH easier to deal with than that!" But looking back and recognizing, "Hey, that was really, really tough, and

I made it through," can remind you that you're still just as capable. So what moments come to mind? Can you recall what you felt like? How long did that situation from your past seem to go on? How does it feel to look back on it now?

 *Actions*

Create a List of Empowering Words

Effort level: Low to medium ●●○○○

As someone who is much more verbally oriented than visually oriented, sometimes I find vision boards or visualization activities to be more frustrating than inspiring. I consider this activity the verbal equivalent of creating a vision board. Rather than collecting images that fit a theme, you gather words. I think this activity is best done by hand in a journal (or even on a whiteboard if you have one handy), but in a pinch you can type the list up and print it out.

Choose words that make you feel powerful, inspired, excited, or just generally fill your heart and get your blood pumping. You can include words that might make anybody feel empowered (think words like strength, endurance, or joy), but you can also include words that are very specifically empowering for you and you alone. Perhaps words that are linked to particular experiences in your past that remind you of your personal wellspring of power. For example, the word "practice" might show up on my list of empowering words because my ability to consistently hold to a practice (whether it's a daily practice of writing, my spiritual practice, etc.) builds my confidence and makes me feel capable.

Shoot for a minimum of ten words, but feel free to add as many as you like. Once the list feels complete (at least for the moment), find someplace to display it. This can be a list you return to and read when you need an emotional pick-me-up, especially if you're going through a rough patch. You might even jot the words down in a notes app on your phone so you can glance at it when you're not at home!

Ask a Loved One What Makes You Strong

Effort level: Medium to high ⬤⬤⬤⬤◯

When you're struggling to endure through a difficult situation, it probably doesn't feel like strength from the inside—it just feels like survival. In the privacy of our own minds, it's easy to focus on all the balls we feel we're dropping, rather than noticing and acknowledging how much energy and strength we're summoning. The people who love us are in a much better position to notice that strength. I remember during one of my worst chronic pain spells, my mom casually mentioned how strong she thought I was, and I was genuinely flabbergasted. I felt anything but strong in that moment. Only now that I'm on the other side of that experience am I able to look back and acknowledge that yes, I was showing remarkable strength.

This activity may seem like fishing for compliments, and it will probably feel awkward (which is why it's the medium-to-high effort activity for this card), especially if you don't often talk to your loved ones about this sort of thing. I recommend you come at the conversation with full, open honesty: say something along the lines of, "Hey, I'm going through a really hard time, and you know me better than I know myself sometimes. Do you think you could remind me of what you admire about me/what you think my strengths are/how I've been strong in the past?"

It may be worth writing down what they say after the conversation, too—that way you can revisit it and you have a concrete reminder of what your loved ones see in you. These things are too easy to forget when we're feeling knocked for a loop.

THE COURT OF SWORDS

The court of Swords is populated by sharp-minded thinkers, tireless analyzers, and fearless communicators. These are folks who apply their intellect to any problem they come across with equal intensity, whether it's global injustice or how best to organize their desk drawers. They're also highly resilient—the journey through the Swords is, in many ways, the most intense of the four suits. Therefore, these court members must be capable of weathering all manner of storms from without and within.

Some words to describe the court of Swords: *analytical, clear, communicative, intellectual, logical, blunt, insightful, perceptive, curious, graceful, vigilant, vocal, sharp, poised, sophisticated, self-sufficient, ambitious, fair, dedicated, clever.*

If you're looking for some places to visit to invoke the court of Swords, here's a few ideas:

- Someplace overlooking an inspiring view, to invoke the Swords' air energy
- A library, to invoke writing and knowledge

- A science museum, to invoke learning and discovery
- An event featuring someone speaking or lecturing, to invoke discourse and communication
- Your favorite coffee shop, to invoke intellectual energy and a shared space of work

Page of Swords

Sharp as a knife and just as cutting, Elizabeth Bennet is the perfect example of intellect and curiosity, which is exactly what the Page of Swords stands for. She's a brilliant woman who quickly and efficiently analyzes everyone and everything around her, and she refuses to keep her insight to herself (which is especially bold, given the time period that she hails from). The flip side of this is, of course, that she assumes her insights to be correct no matter what. Elizabeth's fearless (and sometimes tactless) outspokenness certainly leads her into some untrue assumptions and sticky situations in *Pride and Prejudice*. But ultimately, she learns to reassess when necessary. I think one of the many themes of Jane Austen's book is that a truly great mind is willing to explore and integrate the viewpoints of others. You might be the biggest genius on the planet earth, but you must still be open to learning and growing from the people around you. This is a lesson that Elizabeth fully inhabits by the end of her story, and it's a lesson that any Page of Swords should consider, too.

The Page of Swords is a seeker of capital-t Truth. This means that they're excellent non-linear thinkers and they'll often come up with unexpected or unconventional ideas, but don't worry—those ideas come from dedicated study and close consideration. This Page usually knows what they're talking about. In fact, that can sometimes be their downfall; the Page of Swords speaks their mind no matter what, even when their thoughts are blunt or even hurtful. But the good news is that this Page is a straight shooter. You'll know where you stand with them, for good or for ill. And if you want to learn something new or troubleshoot something in your daily life, there's no one better to have on your side.

Affirmations

I AM a student.
I CAN pursue the truth.
I WILL seek knowledge with abandon.

 *Reflections*

Who in my life reminds me of the Page of Swords?
What aspects of the Page of Swords do I see in myself?
What aspects of the Page of Swords would I like to cultivate in myself?

 *Actions*

Free Write

Effort level: Low to medium ●●○○○

The Swords govern communication, so the court members are often gifted speakers, writers, debaters, etc. The Page is still learning when and how to use their voice to its full potential—when to speak up, and when to hold their tongue. Free writing is, I think, the perfect middle ground between these two extremes. Writing is definitionally a more cautious and forgiving medium than speaking, since you have time to consider your words or even to erase them. But when you free write, you simply allow your pen or keyboard to follow your thoughts, doing your best not to censor or edit yourself as you go. It's almost like doing an audit of your current mental state.

There are many ways to go about free writing, but if you haven't done it before, there are a few methods I'd suggest. First, choose a topic you'd like to explore, an issue you're currently struggling with, or a situation you're hung up on. Frame this topic as a question (for example, "How do I feel about the delays to my project at work?" or, "What can I do to reconnect with my cousin?") and write it at the top of your page. Leave this question pretty broad and open-ended—a yes or no question typically doesn't generate anything much more than a yes or no. Then set a timer for how long you want to spend writing. Ten minutes is a good starting place if you're new to free writing, long enough that you can get at least a few paragraphs on paper but short enough that you don't flounder for too long if it's uncomfortable. Then put your pen to paper or your fingers to keys and just keep writing. Your only rule is to stop as infrequently as possible. Just let yourself write anything and everything that comes to mind, even if it's four lines of "I don't know what to talk about" over and over. Sooner or later, your brain will get bored of the repetition and give you something else to write about. Don't worry if you wander away from the original topic, or if the contents of your writing seem inane, silly, or free-wheeling. No matter what comes out of this exercise, you will almost certainly find little nuggets of thoughts that you didn't realize were top of mind.

Positive Honesty

Effort level: Medium to high ●●●●○

When we think of the more blunt or straightforward people in our lives, we probably think of people who offer constructive criticism freely and who are unafraid to speak their minds, even when it hurts someone's feelings along the way. And while there's certainly a time and place for honesty that calls out or calls to arms, why does honesty always have to be associated with brutality? Isn't it just as honest to tell a valued coworker that you respect their work ethic as it is to tell someone else that they need to step up their game? Why has brutality cornered the market on truth?

Because the Page of Swords has a reputation for speaking their mind in ways that can be hurtful or tactless, finding them in your daily reading can be a great invitation to speak your mind in a way that empowers and inspires. Look for opportunities to be straightforward with the people you value, respect, and appreciate. Tell your parent that their sweet good morning texts always brighten your day. Tell your boss that their guidance has helped you grow into a better employee. Tell your child that the stories they make up are incredibly creative. You don't have to grasp for saccharine things to tell people—this is an invitation to honesty. It might feel a bit awkward since we're often more accustomed to doling out criticism than compliments, but it shouldn't feel false. If there's one particular person you're struggling to find something positive about, let that person go for the purposes of the exercise. But I'll bet that there are at least one or two people in your daily life who you value in ways that you seldom share with them. This is your opportunity to do so.

Knight of Swords

When I think of the Knight of Swords, I imagine someone with the curiosity to pursue any question and the confidence to act on the knowledge they find. Fa Mulan possesses both. From the beginning of *Mulan*, she has the foresight to know that her aged father is unlikely to return from the war he's been called to. Her solution—let's just pose as a man and go in his place!—is the pinnacle of non-linear thinking. And over and over, she uses her wit to overcome the obstacles in her way. Whether she's facing a massive army or confronting her captain's bias against her when he realizes she's a woman, Mulan is always able and willing to consider every angle of a challenge. And yes, she sometimes gets in over her head, but even then, she uses her head to get out again.

All the knights are active doers, but the Knight of Swords is often two steps ahead because they have a gift for analysis and making quick connections. The Knight of Pentacles may have a polished plan and the Knight of Wands may be charging onto the battlefield, but the Knight of Swords lives somewhere between the two. They can adapt their plan based on new information at the drop of a hat (which the Knight of Pentacles may struggle with), and they are more capable than the Knight of Wands at stepping back and assessing when the moment calls for it. But while they don't have to be constantly moving like the Knight of Wands, this Knight does struggle to slow their mind down. They can easily spin off into anxiety or overthinking, especially if they aren't actively solving a problem. In a reading, their appearance may be an invitation to set your mind to a current challenge as if it's a puzzle to solve. But it may also be a warning that you've already given so much thought to your situation that you're fixating instead of trusting your solution.

 Affirmations

I AM an apprentice.
I CAN analyze the world around me.
I WILL put my knowledge into action.

 *Reflections*

Who in my life reminds me of the Knight of Swords?
What aspects of the Knight of Swords do I see in myself?
What aspects of the Knight of Swords would I like to cultivate in myself?

 *Actions*

Listen When You Might Otherwise Speak

Effort level: Low to medium ●●○○○

Cedar McCloud says of the Knight of Swords, "Often they don't leave much room for others to speak, and may even talk over others to get their point across," (72). We're all guilty of this from time to time, of course, but the Knight of Swords is particularly susceptible to it. There's usually no malice meant—it's just that they've done so much research and feel so confident in their understanding of whatever topic is at hand that they can't help but word vomit everything they know. The challenge for the Knight of Swords (and the Page, too, for that matter) is to see other people's opinions and ideas as a source of new information that's just as valid as any other source.

If you've drawn the Knight of Swords in your daily reading, take it as an opportunity to consciously listen when others speak. In situations where you might automatically interject your opinion or ideas, take an extra beat to pay attention instead of jumping in. Even if you tend to be more of a listener than a talker by nature, still look for at least one moment in your day when you can pause a little longer than usual. Maybe it's as small as letting your partner talk about the intricacies of their day without peppering in your own thoughts. Or maybe it's as broad as keeping quiet at a work meeting and truly listening to what your coworkers have to say, rather than taking every possible chance to contribute to the dialog. You might find that you notice something new or unexpected in your partner or coworkers' conversations. Or you might discover more about your own thoughts if you take more time to let them develop, rather than voicing them the second they cross your mind. Either way, you'll be bringing a deeper intellect and a more open ear into your day, and that is the Knight of Swords at their best.

Make a Personal Atlas

Effort level: Medium to high ●●●●○

We often think of wisdom and knowledge as exclusively the realm of books and classrooms, but the truth is that we learn from everyone and everything we encounter. Our minds are constantly analyzing, comparing, and storing away information about each experience we have, whether we're conscious of it or not. For instance, have you ever considered what you've learned from the places you've been? How the neighborhood you grew up in shaped the preferences that still guide you when you're choosing a new home, or how the restaurant where you and your partner had your first date has left an impression on your go-to comfort foods today?

This is an exercise that could quickly become overwhelming, so I suggest you choose a particular category of places and limit yourself to that category, at least at first. If you've moved from place to place a great deal, you might choose towns that you've inhabited as your category. You could select all the bookstores you've frequented over the course of your lifetime, or all the parks where you've gone hiking or camping. Or your category might be less place-specific and more emotion-specific—places where you've gotten bad news, or places you've visited with a partner.

If you're artistically inclined, you could create literal maps or drawings of these places with annotations. Or you could make a list in your journal of each place as it comes to mind, followed by a description of what you learned there or how it shaped you. As always, how this exercise plays out (and how involved you want to make it) is entirely up to you. But whether you wind up with three locations or thirty, spend some time ruminating on each of them. Really consider how your mind was impacted by that one house, or that special playground, or that forest clearing.

Queen of Swords

All of the members of the court of Swords are interested in objective knowledge, and the younger members are so devoted to this cause that they often pursue it to the detriment of those around them. The Queens of each court, meanwhile, are the ones who build and tend communities based around their respective realms. The Queen of Swords, therefore, is someone who seeks and protects the truth, but who does so to create and support their community. Garnet of *Steven Universe* is the perfect example of this Queen of Swords energy. At first glance, Garnet may seem as cool as a cucumber and aloof as an introverted cat. She leads her team with level-headed strategy. But look closer and you can see that Garnet's leadership is a synthesis of head and heart. Because she cares so deeply about her team, she can approach any challenge with the knowledge of each person's strengths and weaknesses. She knows when to push one of her team members harder and when to pull them back for rest or reassurance. Her knowledge doesn't limit itself to book smarts or battlefield tactics. Her knowledge includes the people she loves.

The Queen of Swords doesn't blurt out their opinions impulsively the way that the Page and Knight do, but don't let that fool you—their opinions can be just as sharp. The difference is that the Queen knows when to speak up and when to stay quiet. If you ask for their input, however, they will be happy to give it to you. Even if their opinion is mostly critiques, you can be sure that they're sharing this opinion because they want you to be the best version of yourself. And then again, the Queen of Swords understands the value of positive feedback, too. They value objectivity and aim to use their voice and mind for the good of their community. If the Queen of Swords appears in your daily reading, consider how you might benefit the people around you by applying your brilliant mind and eloquent tongue. As Garnet says, "You are an experience. Make sure you're a good experience."

 ## Affirmations

I AM a communicator.
I CAN trust my voice.
I WILL speak my truth.

 ## Reflections

Who in my life reminds me of the Queen of Swords?
What aspects of the Queen of Swords do I see in myself?
What aspects of the Queen of Swords would I like to cultivate in myself?

 ## Actions

Identify Something That Needs to Be Said

Effort level: Low to medium ●●○○○

We swallow our true feelings to maintain peace and order all the time. Even if you're a habitually outspoken person, I'm willing to bet that there are still things you'd like to say but don't feel that you can. Maybe you feel you're overdue for a raise but you're nervous to bring it up to your boss. Maybe your partner always leaves balled-up washcloths in the tub and it drives you up a wall, but it seems like such a small thing that you can't bring yourself to mention it. Maybe you're really missing your college roommate and you want to catch up with them, but they're always so busy you feel bad asking for their time. The Queen of Swords encourages us to be courageous and say the things that need to be said. It might feel incredibly uncomfortable to ask for a raise, or request that a partner change their cleaning habits, or reach out to someone you haven't spoken to in a while. But it will be much more uncomfortable—even painful—to spend months quietly fuming that your boss hasn't offered you a raise yet, that your partner never even *thinks* to put their washcloths in the laundry, that your friend has completely forgotten about your existence.

Now, this isn't an invitation to air all your dirty laundry from the past thirty years. Far from it. The Queen of Swords asks for honesty with good purpose. Good purpose alone might have you hiding your own needs and allowing your resentment to fester, while honesty alone might inspire unkind words that serve no purpose except hurting their target. But when you're honest *with* good purpose, you are willing to clear the path of communication. You address the elephant in the room even when it's embarrassing or uncomfortable to do so, because the outcome is a more spacious room for everyone. So what might need to be said today? Where can you find an opportunity to be kind with good purpose?

Host a Discussion

Effort level: Medium to high ●●●●○

There's something so romantic about the idea of a classic European salon. I don't mean a place to get your hair and nails done; I mean salon in the event sense of the word. A social gathering where intellectual conversation and the exchange of ideas was the order of the day. You've probably done some form of this in school discussion groups, although that was less of a social gathering and more of an assignment. Still, why don't we hold salons nowadays? You don't have to introduce a charged topic like politics or spirituality into a gathering to start a discussion—although if you and your fellow conversationalists enjoy heated debates, by all means feel free to take this avenue! But you can just as easily have a deep discussion about a recent scientific breakthrough on the news, or about a poem you read that moved you.

Of course, this can come about informally and unceremoniously—you might be having dinner with your family and suddenly find yourself in the middle of an involved discussion about the motivations of the antagonist from your favorite TV show. But you can also plan an elaborate and formal discussion group where you choose the topic or material ahead of time and guests can arrive prepared. However it plays out, remember to approach your discussion with open ears and an open mind. You may find new insights or ways of thinking that you never considered by truly listening to someone else's perspective.

King of Swords

Everybody's favorite brooding vigilante superhero is an obvious choice to represent the King of Swords. Although he might be a bit moody, Batman is a badass intellectual who (it's easy to forget) also has a profound sense of integrity. Although he is not unique in his origin story—many superheroes begin their careers after a personal tragedy—Bruce Wayne *is* unique in that he has no supernatural powers to aid him. His vow to protect humanity from evil-doers was never bolstered by radioactive spider bites or the power of alien suns. Instead, he relies on the bevy of gadgets he's invented and his skills as a martial artist to fight crime. The King of Swords has a wealth of knowledge and experience at their fingertips but is still more than capable of improvising and refining their technique at a moment's notice. Ditto Batman. He might come up against an enemy with powers he's never seen before and still come out on top, thanks to his clear and quick thinking. In a more negative light, after experiencing *so much* of the world, the King of Swords can sometimes become cynical and almost attached to their bitterness—and our pal Bruce certainly has his moments of cynicism. But ultimately, he holds a deep love for humankind, and he shows that love by keeping the residents of Gotham City safe.

Have you ever been in a heated debate with someone and thought you were winning because your opponent wasn't saying much, only to have them snipe your argument with a single eloquent response? That's the King of Swords in action. They know when to speak and when to remain silent. They're just as comfortable strategizing as they are stepping into the action firsthand. In the same way that the King of Cups has learned to trust their emotions, the King of Swords has learned to trust their mind and their thoughts. Remember that the journey through the suit of Swords is a difficult one. The King has been through this journey. They have confronted many of their own demons already, and it has made them a deliberate and mindful leader.

 ## Affirmations

I AM an intellectual.
I CAN be confident in what I've learned.
I WILL teach when I am called to.

 ## Reflections

Who in my life reminds me of the King of Swords?
What aspects of the King of Swords do I see in myself?
What aspects of the King of Swords would I like to cultivate in myself?

 ## Actions

Analyze All Aspects of a Current Situation

Effect level: Low to medium ●●○○○

When you're in the middle of a challenge, you may find yourself experiencing tunnel vision. Nothing else in your life feels as important or even as real as the issue at hand. The bigger and more stressful the situation is, the harder it may seem to make a decision or act on any decisions you make. The worst-case scenario here is that you feel stuck, absolutely mired in the challenge with no idea how to pull yourself out of it—and you may even shoot down anyone who tries to help or offers suggestions.

Now, to return to our character for this card, imagine Batman perched atop of a building in Gotham City at the beginning of a comic or movie. There's plenty of activity going on in the city below, and soon enough he'll descend into the true action of whatever plot point hooks him. But first, before he throws a Batarang or a punch, he has to get the lay of the land. He can't know what in Gotham needs his attention most if he leaps at the first flicker of trouble. He gets a bird's-eye (bat's-eye?…sorry) view, he assesses, and then he strikes.

With this in mind, take a moment and try to zoom out of whatever situation has a stranglehold on your thoughts. Rather than looking at it from the perspective of someone in the thick of it, look at it from the outside. How much will your actions impact you and the people around you, really? When you've spent two months deciding which family member should host the holiday party this year, it's easy to feel like the wrong decision will haunt you forever. And this isn't meant to dismiss your worry or thoroughness in making a decision! But remember that bird's-eye view—if the holiday party isn't absolutely perfect and flawless, will it *really* have disastrous consequences for you and your family? Even if you are dealing with a huge, life-altering decision, getting this zoomed-out perspective may help you recognize the parts of your life that can be counted on. Even if you must suddenly pack up and move across the country, for example, you have loved ones who will do everything they can to support you through the transition.

(There are a few other activities that this mental exercise may naturally lead you to—I particularly suggest the Worst Case/Best Case Scenario activity from the Tower and the "Pro/Con List" activity from the Seven of Cups.)

Write to Your Inner Critic

Effort level: Medium to high ●●●●○

The suit of Swords takes us to the highest peaks of our inner worlds as well as the lowest valleys. The King is someone who can sit with both the Ace of Swords surge of clarity and the Nine of Swords crush of anxiety. They know that while dark thoughts are unpleasant, they have no more power than any other type of thinking. It isn't that they're immune to that little cruel voice in the back of their mind—it's that they know how to listen to it, acknowledge its presence, and then keep moving forward anyway.

This activity asks you to write a letter directly to that little voice. Your inner critic. The constant whisper that tells you that you're not good enough, not attractive enough, not talented enough. Address this letter however you wish. Perhaps that voice has always sounded like a specific person from your life (a derisive teacher or family member, for instance) and you'd like to name your inner critic after them. But don't confuse this for writing a letter to anyone external—even if your inner voice *sounds* like someone you know, this letter is for the voice in your head. Nobody outside of it.

What would you say to that little voice? Maybe you have questions—why it feels the need to be so hard on you, why nothing you do ever seems to please it, etc. Maybe you have accusations—how *dare* that voice slow your progress and make you doubt yourself. Maybe you'd even like to lay your list of accomplishments at its feet as proof of your worthiness. What would you like to ask your inner critic? What would you like to tell it? And after you've written all the catharsis paragraphs of inquiry and fury, consider this: what function is your inner critic trying to serve for you? What might it be trying to protect you from? If you could ask it for something, what would you ask for? And what might it ask for in return?

THE SUIT OF PENTACLES
Ground and Nest

The Pentacles are associated with the element earth, and thus govern the home, physical materials and resources, and work. They are the most practical and patient of the suits. Here you will visit places that have been carefully built from the foundation up, meet people who are dedicated and grounded, and admire crafts and projects that have been years in the making. The Pentacles urge you to spend and save your resources mindfully—not just money, but time and physical energy as well. They invite you to make your home a welcoming and rejuvenating space for yourself and your loved ones. And they remind you that most worthwhile endeavors are marathons, not sprints; your dedication and patience are as necessary as your passion and intent.

Some words to describe the suit of Pentacles: *resources, material, community, foundation, stability, home, career, finances, manifestation, want, abundance, security, earth, senses, belongings, industry, physical, time, practice, labor.*

If you find yourself drawing Pentacles frequently in your regular readings, you should look to the spaces you occupy and the resources you possess or manage. Some major events that might be attracting the Pentacles into your readings include a move or renovation to your home, a financial challenge or a windfall, a change in career, or a loss of an object or possession. On a more internal level, you may need to reassess how to feel more comfortable in your home, how you're utilizing your resources, or what skills and efforts you're putting your time into. Whatever the case, the Pentacles are not a suit of urgency. They'd rather you take your time and make informed decisions or changes than rush into anything impulsive.

Ace of Pentacles

The Pentacles are the suit of home, hearth, and finances, and the Ace begins the journey of this suit by revealing a new opportunity for us to explore. It might be a new financial opportunity, a career change or advancement, or a physical move to a new home. Or (as with any card's meaning) it might be more subtle, such as a shift in the atmosphere of your home or a chance to collaborate with someone new at work. The key in the Pentacles is that this opportunity is not meant to be impulsively seized. All the Aces represent a new something in your life, but as the Ace in the suit of Earth, the Ace of Pentacles encourages you to approach this new opportunity steadily and patiently. Slow and steady wins the race, after all.

When the Ace of Pentacles appears in a daily reading, look for opportunities to present themselves in your daily life. But be sure to get your footing before you avail yourself of this chance. This card doesn't ask you to seize the opportunity so much as it asks you to meet it with deference and care. If you walk mindfully into a new situation (rather than sprinting or flinging yourself face first), you're more likely to reap the full rewards.

 ## Affirmations

I AM grounded.
I CAN connect with my roots.
I WILL begin each new endeavor from steady ground.

 ## Reflections

What makes up my foundation?

Everyone has resources to fall back on when times get tough. In one of my romantic relationships, for example, I struggled with the knowledge that I didn't have a lot of financial resources to contribute. But eventually I realized that I had other kinds of resources to share—my close, warm family which was delighted to welcome any of my romantic partners into the fold, for instance. Although the Pentacles are famously associated with finances, they can represent anything that solidifies the ground beneath you and keeps you rooted. What are your resources? In answering this question, leave no stone unturned. Look to your work, your skills, your personality strengths, your relationships, etc. Anything that helps ground you.

What do I need to prepare for?

If the major arcana cards associated themselves with specific suits, I think the Emperor would find their home in the Pentacles. The Emperor builds plans and structure to support your ambitions, and the Pentacles are the suit of plans and structures. So looking ahead, what do you have to plan for? If there's a big change coming at work, or if someone is about to move in with you, what do you need to do to prepare? Even if you only have "small" things planned ahead, there are probably things that need doing ahead of time. If you're getting a new bookshelf for your office, for instance, there are probably things you can tidy up or move aside to make space. What preparations might you be putting off that you can address?

How can I incorporate the wisdom of my teachers?

The Pentacles remind us to draw on everything we've learned in the past as we step wholeheartedly into the future. Think back to any teachers who have left a particular impression on you. These may be traditional classroom teachers, but they may also be people like parents, siblings, friends, bosses—anyone who you feel you've learned from. Take a few moments to call to mind the lessons they left you with. Then consider how those lessons might be useful in a current (or upcoming) situation. What might your teacher advise, if you could ask them directly? How might their lessons serve you as you approach any new opportunities in your immediate future?

 **Actions**

Connect with Your Body

Effort level: Low to medium ●●○○○

As the suit of home, the Pentacles can also represent your spirit's home—AKA, your physical body. So when the Ace of Pentacles makes an appearance, it can serve as a reminder to check in with your flesh and blood. You can't avail yourself of any opportunities without some connection between your mind, spirit, and body. Now, what form that connection takes (and how you choose to check in) can vary. Believe me, as a person who lives with chronic pain, my relationship with my body is a bit rocky. Sometimes it feels like my soul and my body are on opposing sides of a battle. But increasingly, a huge part of my spiritual practice is reaffirming my connection to my body and treating it as a friend who needs care. It's an ongoing process, but that's why I'm grateful for the Pentacles' reminder.

For a quick and straightforward exercise in this vein, try doing a brief body scan. Start at the top of your head and move your focus gradually downward, noticing how each part of your body is feeling. Try not to pass judgements about any feelings you experience, for good or ill. Give the same impartial attention to your relaxed shoulders as you do your achy lower back. If you need to, you can find any number of guided body scan videos and recordings online. On days when I'm feeling especially disconnected from my physical form, I'll do a full guided body scan that can last up to 45 minutes. But you don't have to spend 45 minutes to reestablish your connection to your body. Even a five-minute, self-guided scan will do the job.

Another method of checking in with your body is exercising! Whether it's stretching, going for a walk, or dancing in your living room, moving your body is a great way to get yourself on friendly terms with your meatsuit. Don't overdo it, of course, and be mindful of any physical limitations you have. Even if you're just doing a few seated stretches, movement will nourish your body—and by extension, your mind and spirit as well.

Connect to the Earth

If your body is the narrowest, closest circle of your home, the earth itself is the broadest (or at least, the broadest circle that you can connect to in an everyday manner). In a strange way, though, your relationship with the earth is subject to the same pitfalls as your relationship with your body—it's all too easy to fall into a rut of disconnection, moving through life without a thought to spare for it. In a very tangible way, the Pentacles encourage you to return to your roots, and the Ace is the purest reminder.

As with the suggestions for connecting to your body, there are a myriad of ways you can reaffirm your relationship with the planet we live on. One of my favorites is sitting in the grass and spending a few moments paying attention to the natural world. You can, of course, pay attention to the natural world through the vantage point of a window indoors. But there's something about sitting on the planet's floor rather than a man-made one, feeling yourself rooted to the soil, and breathing in the fresh air. Trees have a similar effect on me—all I must do is lean up against an old tree with a lot of personality, and my perspective feels fundamentally reattuned to the outside world.

If the weather doesn't permit outdoor activities today, get creative about bringing the outdoors to you. If you already have houseplants or succulents, take some time to tune into those—pay attention as you water them or just sit with them and notice what feelings arise. Bring something indoors from the outside, like a leaf, a stone, or handpicked flowers—and display it for a day or two. (Do be careful with this one, though—there are some outside-dwellers you may not want to invite into your space. I once brought a giant bag of acorns I'd collected into the house and later discovered that I'd also inadvertently collected a horde of acorn weevils.) The how isn't as important as the connection itself. You're looking for a way to invite the natural world into your day more mindfully and intentionally.

Two of Pentacles

Only when we are grounded can we navigate the many directions our lives pull us. In the Two of Pentacles, we begin to juggle multiple projects, responsibilities, goals, or skills. At its best, the Two of Pentacles affirms that we are indeed keeping all the balls in the air. In other cases, the Two may serve as a gentle warning that we're leaning too far into one aspect of our life. We may be in danger of letting balls drop on the side we're neglecting.

In a daily reading, the Two of Pentacles acknowledges that you have a lot on your plate. In a way, this card is the more down-to-earth, everyday version of Temperance from the major arcana: it speaks of balance, and of synthesizing the disparate elements of your life into a single multifaceted flow. Let it remind you that, while everyone's arrangement of work, family, leisure, etc. is unique to them, putting all your eggs in a single basket is unhealthy and unsustainable. If you feel yourself throwing all your effort behind one aspect of your life, the Two of Pentacles may be asking you to step back and realign.

 Affirmations

I AM a capable multitasker.
I CAN synthesize all my strengths.
I WILL balance my responsibilities.

 Reflections

What does flexibility look like for me?
While balance may look effortless from an outsider's view, anyone who's ever tried to stand on one foot for more than two seconds can tell you that it actually requires vigilance and the ability to make subtle adjustments. The ability to remain flexible and open

is a prerequisite for balance. When you're at your most adaptable, what does it look like? Can you think of a time in your life when you've shown remarkable flexibility? At your present moment, do you feel flexible or rigid? What might need to change to allow for more flexibility?

How is my work/life balance right now?

A "perfect" work/life balance is probably impossible to achieve (what does a perfect work/life balance even look like? Wouldn't it, too, be constantly changing?) but we can all benefit from looking at our current routine with a critical eye. Do you feel that you're leaning too far into one aspect of your life and thus neglecting another? Or perhaps you need to push yourself harder in one sphere right now (e.g., a big project is due soon at work, or you have a kiddo going through a rough patch at school) and thus need to mindfully take a few eggs out of another basket. If things feel pretty stable at the moment, how can you ensure that you maintain this grounded balance as busy periods come and go from each part of your daily life?

How do I feel about multitasking?

Left to your own devices, are you more of a natural multitasker or monotasker? That is to say, do you prefer to have several tasks that you're rapidly switching between, or would you rather focus all your attention on one task at a time? If you're a multitasker, how might you cultivate deeper focus from time to time? Or how might you become more comfortable with keeping your attention on a single thing at a time? If you're more of a monotasker, how might you navigate times when you have no choice but to multitask?

 *Actions*

Stand on One Foot

Effort level: Low to medium ●●○○○

Balance has been recognized as an important aspect of fitness in recent years, and one which deserves intentional cultivation just as much as flexibility and strength. There are all kinds of exercises that you can find to improve your balance, but if you want a quick and straightforward balance exercise, all you have to do is stand on one foot. I'll sometimes stand on one foot while I wait for food to warm up in the microwave—it's such a quick and accessible activity, you can do it pretty much anywhere.

As you work to keep yourself balanced, stay mindful and present. Sense when you're in danger of pitching to one side or losing your equilibrium and make those tiny adjustments to remain balanced. Recognize that, similarly, any aspect of your daily life that feels imbalanced may not need giant changes. Small shifts can have a surprisingly large impact on your sense of alignment.

If you want a "hard mode" version of this activity, try intentionally keeping yourself slightly off balance but maintaining equilibrium. (Again, this can be accomplished with small shifts—don't go throwing yourself wildly to one side or the other!) And of course, be careful. It might be wise to do this exercise in a location where you can easily stabilize yourself on a counter or wall. But you might be surprised at how capable you are of staying balanced even when you're consciously challenging yourself.

Balance the Day

Effort level: Medium to high ●●●●○

Look ahead at the things you have planned today. If it's a workday for you, your list is probably more responsibility-focused; if it's a day off, maybe you have more relaxation-related activities on the agenda. Whatever the case may be, apply the balance mentality of the Two of Pentacles to your plan for the day. If you have a busy workday ahead of you, for instance, how might you invite relaxation more consciously into your evening? Or if your day is more leisurely, what responsibilities might you spend some time tending to?

You may be wondering why this activity is marked as medium-to-high effort. When we think about work/life balance especially, we tend to look at the macro-level: "Am I spending enough time with my spouse?" or, "How can I find more time for my side hustle?" It's more infrequent that we consider the day-to-day legwork that balance requires, those micro adjustments that create lasting balance. Again, no day can be "perfectly" balanced, and some days demand that we put more eggs in one basket than another. But every day can benefit from this mentality of seeking balance, mindfully choosing when and how to invite in more relaxation or more responsibility.

Three of Pentacles

The Pentacles take us on a journey of practice and hard work, and when we reach the Three, we realize that no man, woman, or person is an island. Many depictions of the Three of Pentacles show three figures working together on a project, and this card can certainly encourage us to embrace the collaborative projects that come our way. But even if you're a solitary creature and you don't have many collaborations at the moment, you are still building on and learning from the work of others. Any course of study you undertake, any work that you pursue, you stand on the shoulders of those who came before.

When you draw this card in a daily reading, it may be time to check in with any teams you're a part of. How is your relationship with your coworkers, for instance? If you can't think of any teams that you're currently working with, the Three may be reminding you to remain open to collaboration. That collaboration could be with people who are an active part of your daily life, or it could be with the unseen teachers and guides whose work you're drawing from. Maintain the "beginner's mind," as it's called in Buddhist meditation and mindfulness practices, so that you can approach your work with the heart of a student, no matter how skilled you are.

 ## Affirmations

I AM a team player.
I CAN work well as part of a group.
I WILL learn from my peers.

 *Reflections*

How receptive am I to feedback?

When you're given constructive criticism of any sort, how do you respond? If you tend to take feedback personally or get defensive about your work, how might you maintain your confidence while still reacting with grace? If you generally don't pay any attention to feedback, how might you benefit from opening yourself up a bit more? Of course, not all feedback is useful or even fair. When you get feedback that genuinely isn't helpful (think "why didn't you just do it the way I would have done it" types of criticism) how do you respond?

How can I be more patient with my progress?

Goals can be a double-edged sword—they push us to achieve, but when we're unable to achieve in exactly the right way at exactly the right pace that we wanted, sometimes they turn into sources of guilt and discouragement. I find that when circumstances beyond my control (like chronic pain flareups, for instance) prevent me from meeting a deadline I set for myself, it actually sets me back even farther than if I'd been flexible with the deadline to begin with. In these moments, the greatest gift we can give ourselves is patience. When you're frustrated or disappointed because you aren't where you wanted to be right now, how can you cultivate patience for yourself?

What teams am I a part of right now?

Maybe you aren't in a soccer league, and maybe you're self-employed and thus don't work closely with a team during your day job. Even so, you're part of a few teams, no matter how much of a loner you consider yourself. Do you live with family members or roommates? You're all on a team maintaining the household. (Doubly so if you're a parent.) Do any of your recreational activities include a regular group of participants who meet consistently? That's team. Unless you live in the mountains in a cabin and have no family or friends whose company you keep, you're part of a team or two. What comes to mind? How healthy are the collaborations in the teams you're a part of? How do you contribute to each? What do you get out of each?

 *Actions*

Give Feedback Fairly

Effort level: Low to medium ●●○○○

In the reflections above, you were asked to consider how you respond to feedback. It's just as important to be mindful about how you give feedback to others. Whether you're giving constructive criticism to a work colleague or telling a loved one what you think of their creative project, your feedback can lift them up or cut them down. With that in mind, when you're given the opportunity to share your opinion with someone, here are a few things to consider.

While it's impossible to be entirely objective about anything, do your best to filter out comments that can be reduced to, "Well, I would have done it this way, so you should do that." A good rule of thumb when in doubt: ask a question first. For example, rather than saying, "This slide in the presentation seems out of place—you should put it at the end," you might ask, "What are you trying to communicate in this part of the presentation?" Once you have a bit more context for why they made the choices they made, you might agree with the way they assembled the presentation. And if you don't, you can say something like, "Knowing that, I felt a little lost in the transition into this slide." That lets them know that they may want to take another look, but it leaves it up to them to adjust (or not) as they see fit.

Don't *only* offer negative or critical feedback. You don't have to gush about something you think is poorly made or lie about something that you didn't enjoy. But think about how you'd feel if you showed something you made to someone whose opinion you valued and they only had negative things to say about it. If you have constructive criticism to offer, try to include at least one positive piece of feedback as well. Otherwise, how will they know what they got right? (And if you truly can't think of a single good thing you want to say, it may be best to stick to the old adage, "If you can't say anything nice, don't say anything at all.")

Do a Collaborative Project

Effort level: Medium to high ⬤⬤⬤⬤○

If you're the kind of person who thrives in groups and loves working with others, this may seem like an effortless activity—you may even be thinking, "I'm already doing like five collaborative projects!" On the other hand, if you're a deeply solitary person who prefers having complete control over all your work, just the thought of including another human in your projects might make your palms sweaty. I'm not suggesting that you go join a community theater troupe or start a giant new book club with all your Facebook friends. There are as many ways to collaborate as there are people in the world. The Three of Pentacles is simply an invitation to work alongside others.

If you're a person who generally prefers working alone, your collaboration could be as simple as asking your significant other to help you rearrange your reading nook. Or you might pick something you'd like to do just for fun and ask a loved one to do it with you. ("Hey, I've always wanted to try a pole dancing class. Would you go with me?") Choosing something completely new and low-stakes might take some of the fear out of collaboration, rather than choosing a high-stakes or existing project and surrendering some of your control over it.

If you're more of an extrovert and you already collaborate regularly, challenge yourself to collaborate on something you typically only do by yourself. Join a meditation group or explore exercise classes if you usually meditate or exercise on your own. If you're usually the chef for your family, ask them to join you in the kitchen for a family cooking night. Call someone who you don't normally solicit opinions from and ask for their feedback on something you're working on.

Four of Pentacles

Sometimes when we obtain, we're tempted to cling to what we've acquired. The Four of Pentacles suggests that we're clutching our resources too tightly to our chests. If we are in a period of financial stability or even wealth, we might be passing up opportunities to spend or donate. This may not come from a place of greediness—if we're accustomed to living in scarcity, it's hard to let go of that mindset even once we've reached a more secure place. Or the resources in question may not be financial; perhaps we are holding onto possessions that aren't serving us any longer.

In a daily reading, the Four of Pentacles asks you to take a hard look what you have. Are there places where you might let go a bit? Maybe you could be a bit less thrifty, or spend a bit more on the next gift-giving occasion for a loved one, or donate to a cause that matters to you. Maybe you can look at your possessions and decide to give away a few items that don't mean as much to you as they once did. And although the Pentacles tend to suggest matters of finance or materials, there might even be mindsets or relationships that you need to examine with a critical eye.

 *Affirmations*

I AM unburdened.
I WILL let go of material possessions.
I CAN make wise use of my resources.

Reflections

How can I step out of a mentality of scarcity?
I've seen words like "greediness" and "hoarding" associated with the Four of Pentacles, and while that is occasionally accurate, I much prefer seeing this card through the lens of

scarcity. Greediness suggests a hungry desire for wealth for its own sake, and to be honest, I've never read for anyone who seems greedy in that way. Instead, I read for people who have had to struggle and fight for every scrap of material stability they've ever had. And that experience changes your relationship with financial and material acquisition forever. If you find yourself in a position of abundance, you may yet be anxious to spend anything (especially on larger-ticket purchases) because you're still thinking in terms of the next possible scarcity. If this resonates for you, spend some time journaling or reflecting on how you might release that mentality a bit. And if you're currently living paycheck-to-paycheck, consider what you would need to feel a cushion between yourself and scarcity. It may not be possible for you to reach that stability right now but thinking about what you'd need to get there—how much money you'd want to have in the bank, what you'd need in terms of your home or your job, etc.—will prepare you to let go of that scarcity mentality when the time comes.

What am I clinging to that I could loosen my grip on?
Whether it's an object in your home, a twenty-dollar bill in your wallet that could be spent more freely, or a state of mind, there are almost certainly elements of your life that are no longer serving you. Here's an example to get you thinking. I have a relative who feels deeply responsible for keeping possessions in the family. Even if it's an object that doesn't have a great deal of sentimental significance (like a rocking chair from a relative who we weren't close to), she'll go out of her way to make space in her house (or try to guilt trip someone else in the family to do so) rather than donating the object. It makes it difficult not to feel guilty about giving the object away later. This is exactly what the Four of Pentacles is for: looking at what you have and weighing whether you truly need or want to keep it. What are you holding onto out of a sense of duty, or guilt, or simply because it's easy to shove it to the back of your closet and forget about it?

What does preservation mean to me?
On the other hand, while the Four of Pentacles asks you to turn a critical eye to your belongings, it doesn't ask that you become an absolute minimalist and get rid of all but the essentials. Some of our possessions are meaningful or significant, and it's up to each of us individually to define what that means. What do you own that you would like to

preserve forever? That you want to keep on your shelf or in your closet for as long as you live? And more broadly, what comes to mind when you consider the concept of preservation? What is worth preserving—not just objects, but ideas, traits, relationships, etc.?

 *Actions*

Prune Some of Your Possessions

Effort level: Low to medium ●●○○○

We touched on this in one of the reflection questions, and discussed letting go of things in the Eight of Cups. Odds are good that there's something in your house that could be reorganized or trimmed down. Maybe there's a collection of graphic tees shoved to the back of your closet that you haven't worn in years. Maybe there are books on your shelves that you've read once and will likely never pick up again. You know where those pileups and overflows are in your home. The Four of Pentacles' appearance in your daily drawing presents a great opportunity to do some paring down.

If it's a busy weekday or you don't have a lot of extra energy, you don't have to make this a gigantic undertaking. Choose one shelf to sort through, for example, or set aside a certain amount of time (say, fifteen to twenty minutes) and only spend that much time working. Even if you only find one or two things to get rid of, that's still a big step! In the process, you may rediscover things you'd forgotten you had, things that you want to start using or display more prominently. That's just as positive an outcome as finding a huge pile of things to get rid of.

You get even more Four of Pentacles energy and brownie points if you donate some of the stuff instead of just tossing it. This won't always be possible, of course—Goodwill probably doesn't want your half-used bottle of bath salts or that pretty set of lingerie you've worn a few times—but if you're able to, I highly recommend it. Making more space in your house is nice, but it's extra rewarding if you know that someone else will be able to use the stuff that's no longer serving you.

Donate

Effort level: Medium to high ●●●●○

Speaking of donating, the Four of Pentacles always reminds me to pay it forward when I'm able to. If you're fortunate enough to be in a position of financial abundance, now might be a great time to throw a few dollars at a cause you believe in or a person who's in need of support. The what isn't important, except in the sense that you should choose something that matters to you. Becoming a regular patron of an artist you love is just as Four of Pentacles as donating to the Trevor Project or the World Wildlife Fund.

If you aren't in a position to donate money, you can still donate your time by volunteering. Again, how you choose to volunteer and where you choose to do so doesn't matter, as long as you choose something that's meaningful for you. (Visit the "Volunteer" activity in Justice for more ideas!) You might even decide to "volunteer" by helping out a friend who's moving or tidying up the communal space at your office. The important part is recognizing that you have a resource to share (whether it's money, time, energy, etc.) and sharing it with an open heart.

Five of Pentacles

The Four of Pentacles saw us clinging too tightly to our resources in a mindset of scarcity, but the Five of Pentacles finds us in a moment of true scarcity. No longer are we holding onto things we don't need—now we are out in the cold, making every scrap count and every penny last. This card makes me think of the trope-y image of a young orphan with their nose pressed against the window of a bakery, drooling at the fresh-baked bread that they can't afford.

When this card appears in your daily reading, you may be weathering a particularly bleak period in your life. Your bank account may be low, you may be looking for work, or perhaps your current dwelling isn't providing the type of home you and your family need. You are feeling acutely without, and that lack may seem particularly sharp today. But there's a warning in this card, too; much like the Five of Cups, when our mourning blinded us to what we still had, the Five of Pentacles suggests that there may be sources of aid that you are failing to avail yourself of. These are lean times, so you shouldn't be afraid to call in a favor or lean on a support system until you're back on your feet.

 ## Affirmations

I AM resourceful.
I CAN weather barren times.
I WILL accept aid when I am in need.

 ## Reflections

What material/financial losses am I weathering?

It can be hard to admit that we're struggling with money, even to ourselves. Our society values financial success over almost all else; when we are dealing with financial loss, the cultural narrative is that it's our fault and we are fundamentally failing. Before you answer this question, take a moment to remind yourself that this situation is in no way a reflection on your worth as a person. With that in mind, it is still important to name what you're fighting. You can't very well manage your low bank account if you haven't checked it in days because you're afraid of seeing how empty it is. Or perhaps the loss has to do with a non-monetary resource—a job, a home, a beloved possession, etc. Name it, and be honest about what that loss is forcing you to reckon with. How is your life different without it? What challenges has it brought about?

How can I be kind to myself even during lean times?

Self-care has become synonymous with luxuries that aren't always accessible. If you're in a Five of Pentacles period in your life, you may not be able to afford indulgences like expensive skincare products or trips to the massage parlor. But naturally, this is a time when you could most use a little extra self-love. So how can you show yourself that same sort of kindness without spending much, if anything? What actions or habits could you incorporate into your daily routine to nourish yourself, mind, body, and spirit?

What resources do I have at my disposal?

The Five of Pentacles reminds us that there are places we can turn, even in desperate times. As an example, let's imagine that you've had to move into a smaller space that feels cramped and claustrophobic, and the resource you're missing is solitude. Rather than focusing on the lack of space in your home, consider where you might find that alone time that you're craving. Do you have loved ones or neighbors nearby who would let you co-opt a room in their home for an hour or two? Is there a park you could start taking regular walks in? You get the idea. Whatever lack you may be experiencing, there are resources that you haven't tapped into, and it's worth listing them out to remind yourself of the safety nets that you may have overlooked.

 **Actions**

Check Off a Responsibility

Effort level: Low to medium ●●○○○

I'm a big believer in the idea that self-care is more than just pampering yourself. It absolutely includes things like relaxing and prioritizing mental health, but it also includes taking care of business so that you can relax when the time comes. When you're in the middle of a lean time, it can be easy to let important things slide. If you're spending all your energy looking for a new job, for example, it may seem like cleaning the house is vastly less important. And to some extent, you have to be able to prioritize and address the most pressing challenges first. But on the other hand, if you come home from a day of grueling interviews to unwashed dishes, no clean laundry, and a filthy shower, it can add to that feeling that everything is out of your control.

Take a look around and see if there's a responsibility you could check off that wouldn't take a *huge* amount of effort. This isn't a time to tackle a giant project like reorganizing the entire house. Instead, call to arrange that doctor's appointment that you've been putting off scheduling. Or sort through that one overflowing drawer of paperwork that ramps up your stress level every time you open it. Knocking out a chore like this accomplishes two things. First, of course, it removes something from your to-do list, which may seem impossibly long when you're dealing with a time of scarcity. Second, and equally important, it gives you a small sense of agency. Stressful situations like financial uncertainty don't tend to stay in their lanes—they spill over into every square inch of your life and make everything feel insurmountable. But when you consciously accomplish a task that you've been putting off, or finish something that's been hanging over your head, you remind yourself that there are still ways that you can improve your day-to-day life, even on a small scale.

Tell Someone You're Struggling

Effort level: Medium to high ●●●●○

I was in college when some of the worst of my chronic pain started. All my closest friends knew that I was sick. They knew that I had left school for two semesters to try to get better, and they knew that I was taking a dizzying array of medications to try and soldier through classes now that I was back. And yet, when one of them asked me how I was feeling, my range of responses went from "I'm good!" (meaning "I'm having a low-pain day!") to "Hanging in there," (meaning "I am barely capable of standing up at the moment but I don't want to say that out loud, so let's just say that I'm managing even though I'm clearly not.") I don't know why it's so hard to admit that we're going through tough times—I suspect that part of it has to do with wanting to remain in control. Admitting that it's hard feels like admitting that it's out of our control. What I *do* know is that on the rare occasions that I sucked it up and told my friends that I was having a really rough pain day, it always, always made me feel better. It didn't take away the pain, of course. But it did remind me that I wasn't going through this alone. And oftentimes, they were able to help in ways I hadn't even thought to ask, like driving me to my next class or bringing me takeout.

If you're experiencing a tough time of ANY sort, I encourage you to let someone in on it. Whether it's a partner, a relative, or a dear friend, choose someone who you unquestionably trust, and someone who you'd want to support if it was them going through the rough patch. This isn't an invitation to dump all your woes on them for hours on end—that will probably wind up with both of you feeling drained instead of nourished. But it can be oddly empowering to sit down with someone you love and tell them, "Hey, I'm just having a really hard time right now, and I was wondering if I could share a little with you so I don't just let things fester in my brain."

If going out of your way to tell someone you're struggling sounds impossibly difficult, here's a slightly easier way to go about it. The next time a trusted loved one asks how you're doing, be honest. Don't couch your answer or sugarcoat it the way I described above ("Hanging in there!") and instead just say, "You know, this has been a tough couple of weeks." I'm not suggesting that you say this to the grocery store checkout clerk who asked how your day was going, mind you. But when someone you trust asks, they often genuinely want to know the honest answer. So this time, tell them. Be open to the conversation that follows. No matter what comes of it, you will have allowed a moment of honest connection into your solitary stress.

Six of Pentacles

Emerging from the scarcity of the Five of Pentacles, we are in a position to both receive and give generously! We are no longer too proud to accept help and gifts from our loved ones, and we are equally willing to share what we have. My absolute favorite depiction of this card is from my beloved *Numinous Tarot* by Cedar McCloud, where the Six of Pentacles is represented by a Little Free Library. I can't think of a more perfect symbol for the spirit of generosity than a place where you can leave books for others and claim books left by strangers.

When you draw the Six of Pentacles in a daily reading, make sure that you're open to generosity in your day. If you're offered a gift or a favor from someone, accept it graciously. And if you have an opportunity to give to someone, whether it's picking up a pint of your roommate's favorite ice cream to surprise them or giving money to a cause, take it. It's cliché to say so, but you'll truly get just as much from giving as you'll get from receiving, and the Six of Pentacles encourages you to do both with an open heart.

 *Affirmations*

I AM generous.
I CAN share the wealth.
I WILL give and receive gifts.

 *Reflections*

How can I open myself up to the generosity of others?
Do you often find yourself turning down offers of gifts or kindness from others? It's easy to fall into this pattern, especially in a culture that prizes independence over interconnectedness. "I couldn't ask you to do that!" or, "Oh, no, I'm fine, thank you!" And certainly,

there's a time and place to politely decline gifts or offers to help. But there's also a time and place to accept. When might those times come up in your daily life? When an opportunity to accept a gift or assistance appears, how might you do so with grace and gratitude?

How can I be a more giving person?

Before you reflect on this question, a quick disclaimer—it is entirely possible to be the kind of person who gives to others to an unhealthy degree by borrowing against yourself, and that is NOT the kind of giving I'm endorsing here. (As nostalgic as I am about Shel Silverstein's *The Giving Tree*, it's a perfect example of how to give so much that you take everything from yourself.) So consider this question an opportunity to examine not only how you might give to others more generously, but also how you might give to yourself. Do you tend to lean more one way or the other? How might you balance that out a bit more?

What wealth do I have to share?

I've hit on this point a lot in our exploration of the Pentacles, but the resources you have to share aren't just financial. Even if you're not in a position to give money at the moment, there are non-monetary sources of wealth that you can share with your loved ones or with people in need. Maybe you're an emotionally or spiritually grounded person and can hold space for your loved ones going through more turbulent times. Maybe you have enough free time that you can volunteer for an organization or cause that you believe in. Consider any aspect of your life where you feel not only that you have enough, but more than enough.

 *Actions*

Random Act of Kindness

Effort level: Low to medium ●●○○○

There are entire websites devoted to suggestions for random acts of kindness that you can do in any area of your life. I think the most well-known is paying for the order of the person behind you in a drive-thru or checkout line. But there's all sorts of ways to do tiny, good deeds like this. With services like PayPal and Venmo, you can anonymously send money to someone who could use a pick-me-up—even five dollars says "someone is thinking about you and wants you to grab a coffee or a cupcake for yourself." (This is a great option if you're shy about paying for a stranger's order in person.)

If you don't have money to spare now, think about other ways that you could brighten someone's day. In college, I spotted encouraging notes left as bookmarks and taped to vending machines during finals week when everyone was sleep deprived and stressed out. You could drop a postcard in the mail for someone who could use a smile. You could leave a complimentary comment on an artist's Instagram page.

The common denominator in random acts of kindness is doing something generous just for generosity's sake, and not for the potential recognition. Choose something that you can do anonymously, or at least with a low chance of being caught in the act. Doing the good deed should be its own reward, and you shouldn't be looking to be thanked profusely. Consider this a stealth mission of sorts—get in, do something good, and get out without being spotted as a good-deed-doer.

Give Someone a Gift

Effort level: Medium to high ●●●●○

There's a reason that receiving gifts is one of the five "love languages" identified by Dr. Gary Chapman, and it's not about materialism or greed. When you give someone a heartfelt gift, you're expressing that you know them well enough to know what they like. An expensive but generic gift isn't nearly as meaningful as a five-dollar button from your best friend's favorite obscure TV show. It's ultimately about the thoughtfulness and care in selecting the gift.

And if you don't have any money to spare on a just-because gift, consider making something. A handmade gift is representative of time spent instead of money spent, and time is a resource that we cannot earn back. So when you give a handmade gift, you're giving the gift of your time and energy. It doesn't have to be anything elaborate, either. I have cards that were handmade for me by friends that I've kept longer than some large-ticket gifts because of the degree of thoughtfulness they showed. Do a quick drawing, write a poem, or decorate a gift box and fill it with their favorite candy. It can be as simple or as involved as you want. The only rule is, as with purchasing a gift, make sure you're making something that the person would like, not something that *you* would like.

Seven of Pentacles

We've put in countless hours of blood, sweat, and tears, and with the Seven of Pentacles we begin to see the results of that work. This card usually heralds the impending realization of all our labor. The Pentacles are a practical suit that deal in resources and material progress, and the Seven assures us that everything we've worked for will soon be worth it. This card is often associated with farming or gardening, which is apt imagery—growing plants of any sort requires consistent work and no small amount of patience. But if we keep tending our fields and watering our gardens, we will eventually see flowers and produce bursting into bloom.

When this card appears in a daily reading, it usually means that your patience is due to be rewarded. You've held steady and put in a lot of work, and you've been waiting and watching for a long time now. Soon enough you will begin to see returns on all that effort. Alternatively, this card may serve as a gentle reminder that there is work that you have been neglecting, and if you continue down this path you will see no harvest this year. Either way, focus on the areas where you have long, steady work that needs doing or has recently been done. Those are where your effort will come back to you tenfold.

Affirmations

I AM reaching my aspirations.
I CAN see the fruits of my labor.
I WILL make sure my growth is sustainable.

Reflections

How can I trace my growth?
I've said this in several other entries, but it bears repeating: we're all kind of terrible at acknowledging the progress we've made. In the name of productivity, we're quick

to focus on the next unfinished project, the next deadline, the next item on the to-do list. The Seven of Pentacles asks us to remember when we began with nothing but an idea and a goal, and then to compare it to how far we are now. How can you ensure that you're acknowledging your progress? In what ways might you keep track of the work you've done and the steps you've taken? What might remind you to look back and honor all the effort you've made to get here? (For one idea, visit the "Start a pride journal" activity in the Chariot.)

What results am I seeing from my efforts?

Call to mind the areas where you've been putting in the most work and effort lately. What strides have you made? What tangible successes can you point to as a result of your work? I'm not just talking about obvious signs of success, such as getting a raise or moving into a nicer house (although those sorts of items certainly belong on the list). I'm also talking about things like, "I've been exercising consistently for the last two months, and I can finally lift my twenty-pound weights!" or, "I've almost filled up an entire journal with daily gratitude practice." Progress is rarely linear, and with so much on our plates, it's easy to overlook all but the most obvious, gigantic hallmarks of success. So take a few moments and list the results you can see from your labor, the big and the small. Often this is enough to remind you that the daily effort you make is well worth it.

What work remains to be done?

While the Seven of Pentacles invites you to reap the rewards of your work, it doesn't mean that the work is finished. If we return to the imagery of a field, the Seven of Pentacles tells us that the harvest is ready. Although we have tended our fields faithfully to arrive at this moment, the work of the harvest itself remains. Take this moment to examine any projects or efforts that you are currently in the middle of. What is still unfinished? Are there any unexpected or additional tasks that may arise in the near future? How can you prepare and plan for the work ahead?

 *Actions*

Assess the Direction of Your Effort

Effort level: Low to medium ⬤⬤◯◯◯

The more time and work we've put into something, the harder it can be to take a step back and objectively reconnoiter. I always hit this wall when I'm rearranging a bookshelf or a closet. I'll be two hours into taking things down, sorting them into new piles, and starting to put them back together, and invariably I'll realize that the new arrangement would work better if I undid half the work I just did and arranged things in yet a different way. And there's ALWAYS a part of me that wants to ignore that realization. I'm tired and sweaty and I just did two hours of work, and the last thing I want to do is backtrack. But more often than not, if I push through the frustration and stubbornness, the adjustment ends up working out MUCH better than my original plan.

Think about the areas where you've already put in a lot of work. Think about the work that's left to do. Then, as best you can, examine the project or endeavor with an objective eye. (It is, of course, impossible to be *entirely* objective about anything.) Are there ways that you could adjust your approach that might improve the outcome? Is there any place where it feels like you keep hitting a brick wall? If so, brainstorm how you might approach the challenge from a new angle. Be open-minded as you consider these prompts—there may be ideas that seem outlandish or possibilities that you're resistant to at first. Don't dismiss them out of hand. It may be that you're resisting them because you're attached to how much work you've already put into your original plan. Try to sit with each new possibility for a minute or two and truly consider whether it might be a better approach.

Plan Out a Long-Term Goal

Effort level: Medium to high ⬤⬤⬤⬤◯

Goals can be simultaneously inspiring and overwhelming. You have something Big and Important that you want to achieve, and imagining yourself achieving it is incredible— and yet, the amount of work that it will take to arrive there is daunting. When you only have a murky idea of some abstract future aspiration, you probably don't even know where to begin. And sometimes, the very act of hemming and hawing and deciding how to begin actually prevents you from beginning at all! The Seven of Pentacles reminds us that looking out at an empty patch of grass and imagining a beautiful garden will not get that garden growing. Even if you only plant one or two seedlings, you must roll up your sleeves and get to work if you want to have a garden at all.

Pick out a goal that you've been daydreaming about for a while now. Then sit down with pen and paper and begin listing all the things that need to happen, that you need to do, to achieve that goal. Don't try to organize the list yet, and don't spend too much time worrying about the nuts and bolts of each step. Right now you're just freeform brainstorming everything you can think of. So for example, say you've always wanted to start your own book club. Your list might include things like reaching out to other book club organizers for advice, assembling a reading list, etc. Include any step that comes to mind, big or small, complicated, or simple.

Once you've got a decent list (it doesn't have to be an *exhaustive* list) you can begin to organize. Arrange steps in an order that makes sense (for example, you probably want to bring together a few club members before you select the first book to read). Add any sub-steps that you think of as you go. If you're so inclined, you can set deadlines or estimated times you want to complete steps by. The important part is that you're creating a roadmap of sorts, something that you can refer back to when the goal feels too intangible and big to actually tackle anything. And before you put the list away, choose one of your first steps and make an agreement with yourself about when you want to complete it by. You don't have to set a hard-and-fast deadline if you work better without but do ask how you can hold yourself accountable for taking this first step.

Eight of Pentacles

No card more perfectly says "practice makes perfect" than the Eight of Pentacles. Here we are able to assess our skills and recognize how much we've improved. Recall a time that you started trying to learn something new, something like playing an instrument, or learning to knit, or trying a new form of exercise. At first it probably felt like you were impossibly clumsy at it. But as you stuck with it and put in hours of dedicated practice, your fingers or feet began to get the skills in their bones. And lo and behold, one day you realized that the once-impossible-seeming skill had become muscle memory. That's what the Eight of Pentacles is all about.

When this card turns up in a daily reading, it's a reminder to pause and recognize how hard you've been working and how far you've come. When practice has become a regular part of your routine, you might not notice the improvements you've made because you're so caught up in the day-to-day work of it. The Eight of Pentacles invites you to look back on that first day you picked up a cello or knitting needles and compare it to today. You are sharpening your skills every day you put in the work. Acknowledge the power in that.

Affirmations

I AM practiced.
I CAN hone my craft.
I WILL keep developing my gifts.

Reflections

What skills have I been working hard to hone?
This is one of those reflection questions where I encourage you to just freeform jot down anything and everything that comes to mind. The Eight of Pentacles is often associated

with skills that you practice with your hands—things like crafts, for example, or playing an instrument. Certainly, write down any activities like these that you participate in. But don't stop there. Are there practiced ways that you move your body, such as yoga or team sports? Include those in your list. Are there mental skills you've developed, such as meditation or learning a foreign language? Add them to the list. I even encourage you to include things that might not seem like skills but are *certainly* practices; things like remembering to stop and count to ten before speaking if you tend to get angry at your loved ones or taking regular time for yourself when your impulse is to give endlessly to others.

How can I be more confident in the skills I have?

Although there's always room for improvement, the Eight of Pentacles also asks us to have confidence in the skills that we've spent so long building. And there is a world of difference between arrogance and confidence—it doesn't make you an arrogant person to acknowledge that you've developed quite an aptitude for something. How might you nurture a sense of confidence in your skills and talents? If confidence isn't something that comes easily to you, what usually blocks you from feeling proud of yourself? How might you combat those blocks?

How can I avoid perfectionism?

Just as there's a difference between confidence and arrogance, there's a difference between hard work and perfectionism. It will serve you well, when developing a skill of any kind, to keep an eye out for areas where you could improve. But when that critical eye turns into the eye of a perfectionist, there's no room for error, and any misstep can become a weapon you use to beat yourself up. Does this sound familiar? Are you prone to perfectionism? If so, in what areas of your life or work do you tend to shift into perfectionist mode? How might you steer yourself away from this fruitless search for perfection?

 *Actions*

Do Something with Your Hands

Effort level: Low to medium ●●○○○

The Eight of Pentacles is a very tactile, kinesthetic card. I've seen versions of it depicting all kinds of handicrafts and trades. Although the idea of practice and honing a craft certainly applies to a broader spectrum of skills, a quick way to tap into Eight of Pentacles energy is to do something with your hands. On the simplest level, this could be playing with some kind of fidget toy, or paying special attention to the textures of the objects and surfaces you touch throughout the day. In several of my jobs with theaters, I've been responsible for folding programs or stuffing envelopes to mail to patrons, and I've always found the act of folding paper oddly soothing—even just folding something in half over and over.

If you'd like to do something a bit more elaborate, there's any number of ways to occupy your hands. Get some string and try to learn a few forms of cat's cradle. Do origami. Knit or crochet. If you don't consider yourself a crafty sort, put on some music and grab something to use as an impromptu drum or tambourine, even if it's a pan from the kitchen. Your only limits here are the amount of time and energy you must spend on this activity—*how* you get your hands moving in tandem with your brain is entirely up to you.

Practice Something You've Let Fall by the Wayside

Effort level: Medium to high ●●●●○

Think of a skill or a hobby that you haven't picked up for quite some time. Maybe you played piano when you were in school, or maybe you took tap dancing classes a few years ago, or maybe you used to speed read books in your spare time. Then carve out a little time in the next few days to practice that activity again. Don't do this with the idea that it's like riding a bike and you'll be able to pick it right back up with the same level of aptitude. You're going to be rusty, in all likelihood. Don't let yourself fall into the trap of comparing yourself to the you of the past and mourning how much ground you've lost. This hobby, skill, or activity hasn't been a part of your regular routine for quite some time, and there's nothing inherently wrong with that—you shouldn't feel guilty for letting go of the practice if it wasn't serving you at the time.

That's not the point. The point isn't even necessarily to rekindle your interest in this activity (although if you end up remembering how much you loved tap dancing and decide to make it a more regular activity again, by all means). The purpose here is simply to participate in an activity that you once practiced and honed, to enjoy it for its own sake, and even to enjoy the rustiness and uncertainty of it. Stumble through the moments when your fingers or feet lose their place and embrace the nostalgia of the parts you still remember well.

Nine of Pentacles

Nearing the end of the journey of the Pentacles, the Nine is a love letter to independence and self-sufficiency. Our hard work and careful management of our resources has brought us to a position where we can truly take care of ourselves. We have a firm grasp on our resources, our responsibilities, and our self-care, and we are capable of balancing those with grace and confidence. I also associate this card with well-maintained boundaries—being able to say no even when it's uncomfortable and prioritizing yourself even when you're inclined to put others first.

When this card appears in a daily reading, you should take a moment to be proud of your independence. Even if you're in a situation that doesn't *feel* particularly independent (perhaps you're relying on a loved one for emotional or financial support, for example), the Nine of Pentacles assures you that you're learning more about your own needs and requirements, and you are becoming more adept at meeting those needs. When you recognize that you need help and ask for it, that is itself a kind of independence.

 ## Affirmations

I AM self-sufficient.
I CAN satisfy my own needs.
I WILL enjoy my independence.

 ## Reflections

How can I celebrate my independence?
We all need some combination of solitude and social time. What ratio we prefer varies from person to person, of course, but as important as it is to spend special time with your loved ones, it's equally important to spend quality time with yourself. And when

you accomplish something on your own, you should celebrate it just as you would celebrate the accomplishment of a friend or family member. So how might you embrace and nurture that spark of independence? When you manage a stressful situation largely on your own, do you take the time to acknowledge how hard it was and how well you stepped up to the plate? If not, how might you remind yourself to do so next time?

What does self-sufficiency mean to me?

Just as nobody can be completely dependent on the assistance of others, nobody can be entirely self-made. Nothing is black or white. So what would a healthy, ideal self-sufficiency look like for you? Would it be a scenario in which you always had the means to meet your own needs without help from others? Or would it include those people in your inner sanctum who you could trust to give you a hand? What role models do you look up to as positive examples of healthy self-sufficiency? Or, alternatively, do you know anyone who models a type of self-sufficiency that you feel is unhealthy or that just wouldn't work for you?

Who could I share my successes and failures with?

Independence is a worthy goal to strive for. But it can easily lean too far into complete solitude or an unwillingness to invite anyone into your most intense triumphs and tragedies. As I mentioned in the intro for the card, I believe that part of self-sufficiency is knowing your own limits and recognizing when it's time to call on your squad. Who are the people who you immediately text with good news or bad news? Who would you be comfortable seeing your darkest or brightest moments? If you don't have many people in this category, who *might* be good candidates? If nobody comes to mind, consider what you might need to do to find those kinds of people.

 **Actions**

Schedule Some Me Time

Effort level: Low to medium ●●○○○

If tarot cards were all characters, I think the Nine of Pentacles and the Hermit would be friends. They both carry an energy of solitude, but a solitude that has been chosen, not imposed. Both cards tell you that you can be your own best friend if you spend time cultivating a relationship with yourself. The primary difference is that the Hermit carries a mysticism that the Nine of Pentacles counters with practicality. While the Hermit would tell you to drift through your alone time on the waves of your own thoughts, the Nine of Pentacles tells you to roll up your sleeves and put your alone time to good use.

Even if it's only ten minutes toward the end of the day, block off a bit of time to be on your own. You can use this time however you choose—maybe you'd just like to go for a quick walk after work, or spend your lunch break in your car reading a favorite book. If you've got a little more time to play with, you can choose a more involved activity. Cook or bake something for yourself, or watch a movie, or take a long bath. The *what* isn't as important as the conscious, intentional scheduling of some time for you and you alone, and sticking to that schedule as much as possible (e.g., not letting loved ones encroach or life's little demands upstage your alone time).

Make Your Bathroom a Welcoming Space

Effort level: Medium to high ●●●●○

Few places are more private than a bathroom, right? Not just because it's the place where we take care of bodily functions and clean ourselves, but also because it's where we put ourselves together at the beginning of the day. Therefore, I think it's one of the most important places to make inviting and relaxing for yourself. I'm not just talking about keeping it clean—I mean taking the trouble to put little touches into your bathroom that make it uniquely *your* space.

There are, of course, as many ways to accomplish this as there are bathrooms and people who use them. A super simple way that I like to enhance my bathroom is by doodling and writing on the mirror in dry erase markers. They wash off the reflective surface easily, and it's a quick way to give myself little self-care reminders (like "take your meds!") or add inspirational quotations that I'll see first thing in the morning and right before bed. Post-it notes could accomplish the same thing.

If you'd like to go a bit more elaborate, take a long look at your bathroom space and consider what might make it feel more inviting. Maybe you want to get a fluffy bathmat so your bare feet don't have to touch the cold tiles in the morning. Maybe a colorful shower curtain would bring some vibrancy to the space. Maybe you just want to rearrange a few of your drawers so all your beauty products are better organized. Don't try to tackle an enormous home repair/makeover project here—you don't have to strip the bathroom from top to bottom and start from scratch. Just choose one or two actions that you can take today that will improve your daily getting-ready routines.

Ten of Pentacles

Some cards touch on very similar territory, which is unsurprising when you think about it—life isn't neatly divided up into 78 perfectly sectioned-off categories. But it can make it challenging to distinguish between certain cards when you're a developing practitioner of tarot. For me, the Ten of Cups and the Ten of Pentacles were two of the most difficult cards to tell apart. Both have to do with family, home, and abundance. Here's how I eventually came to understand the difference. Cups are the suit of relationships and emotions, so the Ten of Cups is all about the people who symbolize home for you in a spiritual and emotional sense. The Pentacles are a more practical suit, and so the Ten of Pentacles represents the home you make for yourself and your family. It has more to do with long-term stability that you can provide for your people.

When this card appears in a daily reading, you have created (or are in the process of creating) a steady, lasting foundation to build your home on. There are parts of your world that are constant enough to rely upon, and standing upon those constants you are able to see a long, prosperous future ahead. And unlike the solitary Nine of Pentacles, this is an abundance and security that is made to be shared. Your abundance will not be diminished by inviting others into its light; indeed, that abundance will grow and multiply when your loved ones take part in it.

Affirmations

I AM surrounded by abundance.
I CAN share my success.
I WILL not grow complacent.

 *Reflections*

What does stability look like?

The idea of stability or security reminds me of the adage "one man's trash is another man's treasure." Someone in a state of constant moving and shifting may feel that they are in a position of perfect stability, while someone else who's living in an identical situation may feel completely off-kilter. It's a sense of comfort and trust which, of course, comes more from within than without. Your idea of stability might feel like complete chaos to your neighbor. What do you need to feel stable and secure? What elements of your life feel off-balance or unstable at the moment? What elements feel more centered? What might you need to do to align those off-balance elements?

What are my long-term hopes for my family?

As always, I caveat "family" to mean your chosen family, not just your blood family. When you imagine the future, what are your highest hopes for yourself and the people you surround yourself with? Perhaps this includes the folks you currently live with, but it may also include significant others who you aren't currently cohabitating with, dear friends who you connect with on a regular basis, etc. What kind of future would you want for them? What ideas come to mind? Try not to let societal bias get in your head too much as you answer this question. Perhaps your ideal future family includes partners who dwell in separate spaces, for instance, or cohabitating with a beloved friend. This is your imagined future, not anyone else's.

What do I hope my legacy will be?

The Ten of Pentacles is usually depicted with a few generations of a family gathered together. The card feels as though it's putting you in the headspace of the older characters in the image, the ones reflecting on the life they've built for their family and wondering what memories they'll leave behind. Even if you're in your youth, I'm willing to bet you've thought about this question. What would you want to leave behind? What mark do you hope to make on the world around you? Do you have grandiose dreams of changing the world or creating something immortal? Or are your aspirations quieter, like leaving happy memories with your descendants?

 *Actions*

Do Something for Your Household

Effort level: Low to medium ●●○○○

In the independent Nine of Pentacles, one of the suggested activities was to improve your bathroom space. Now with the more family-focused Ten of Pentacles, I invite you to take that same energy and apply it to your household in general. You don't need to undertake an enormous renovation project to improve your home in little ways. Look at the shared spaces in your house—the living room, dining room, kitchen, family room, entryway, etc. What small tasks could you do to make things easier, more comfortable, more inviting, or more all-around homey for you and your family?

Here's a few ideas to get you thinking. Is the family coat closet in the front hallway overstuffed? Spend a half hour reorganizing it or weeding out your unworn items to make more space. Do wall outlets in the living room get tangled up with cords and plugs when everyone's home? Dig out a power strip and set up a dedicated charging station for everyone's devices. You can make a difference with something as simple as finding a few colorful magnets to put on your fridge to make your loved ones smile when they're making their morning coffee. Get creative, and get as involved as you want to (and have time for). And although this likely goes without saying, make sure you're respectful of your cohabitants' possessions. It might be easy in the momentum of cleaning out the coat closet to assume your spouse doesn't want to keep that old holey raincoat and throw it away, but unless you have preexisting standing permission to do so, you should always, *always* check before you move or discard someone else's belongings.

Host

Effort level: Medium to high ●●●●○

Inviting people into your home is a quintessential Ten of Pentacles activity. It's a statement that not only are you proud enough of your home to open it up, but you also have the time and energy to plan an evening of food or fun. As always, this doesn't have to be wildly elaborate to be effective. You might invite a few close friends over for a casual afternoon of board games, for example, or ask a partner to share morning coffee with you. Or if you'd like to invest more time and energy, you can, of course, cook a lavish meal or spend hours decorating for a special occasion. More important than *what* you choose to do with your hosting is *who* you choose to invite. This is not a time to bend to social obligations. If your in-laws make you anxious, don't invite them. If you're more comfortable in one-on-one hangouts than larger groups, invite one friend over rather than an entire cast of characters. If you're choosing to open your home, your safe haven, you should be selective about who to ask inside. Hosting is always a bit stressful, but you should be stressing about getting the bread out of the oven on time or making sure there's a comfortable chair for everyone, *not* stressing over whether you'll get in yet another argument with your father-in-law.

THE COURT OF PENTACLES

The members of the court of Pentacles are, in a phrase, down-to-earth. Although I've chosen different characters to represent each of them, I'd be remiss if I didn't say that this court as a whole reminds me of the motto of the Ents in Tolkien's *Lord of the Rings* trilogy: "Let's not be hasty." Unlike the emotional court of Cups or the impulsive court of Wands, the court of Pentacles plays the long game. They know that all good things come to those who wait, and since this is the suit of material abundance and physical comfort, they are prepared to wait and work patiently for the things they desire.

Some words to describe the court of Pentacles: *reliable, stable, patient, painstaking, methodical, prepared, detail-oriented, cautious, prudent, practical, loyal, generous, resourceful, down-to-earth, honest, sensible, deliberate, diligent, steadfast, disciplined.*

If you've drawn a card from the court of Pentacles in your daily reading and you'd like to visit someplace to invoke their personalities, here are a few suggestions:

- Someplace with trees and natural foliage, such as a park or a forest, to invoke the Pentacles' earth energy
- An old neighborhood full of houses with individual personalities, to invoke home and community
- A furniture store, to invoke homemaking and material abundance
- A history museum, to invoke time, legacy, and objects
- Your favorite space in your own home, to invoke stability and comfort

Page of Pentacles

If you want to get a feel for the Page of Pentacles, look no further than the patron saint of the Sunday funnies, Charlie Brown. He's something of a hapless everyman who frequently encounters bad luck, teasing and mockery, and anxiety. As *Peanuts* creator Charles Schulz said, "Charlie Brown must be the one who suffers, because he's a caricature of the average person. Most of us are much more acquainted with losing than winning." And yet he's persistent. He continues to care about his loved ones, even when they're teasing him or outright tormenting him (looking at you, Lucy). He sticks with activities like kite-flying and baseball even when he's struggling with them. There's a line in the opening number of the musical adaptation *You're a Good Man, Charlie Brown* which perfectly captures Charlie Brown's Page-of-Pentacles tenacity: "All I need is one more try, gotta get that kite to fly, and I'm not the kind of guy who gives up easily."

The Page of Pentacles is someone who prepares and endures. Where their fellow pages might leap headlong into something and leave it behind just as quickly, this Page runs through it four or five times in their head before starting, and they'll power through even when they're tempted to give up. They're steadfast and loyal friends and family members. If they have a fault, it's that they can get too caught up in the planning of something to actually *initiate* it. Partner this organized Page up with someone from the action-oriented court of Wands, and there will be no stopping them.

 **Affirmations**

I AM a planner.
I CAN devise the perfect strategy.
I WILL focus on the details.

 *Reflections*

Who in my life reminds me of the Page of Pentacles?
What aspects of the Page of Pentacles do I see in myself?
What aspects of the Page of Pentacles would I like to cultivate in myself?

 *Actions*

Make a List

Effort level: Low to medium ⬤⬤◯◯◯

Even though I'm more of a spontaneous, go-with-the-flow sort of person by nature, I have come to really appreciate a good list. Whether it's a to-do list, a shopping list, or a list of inspiring words, a list gathers otherwise-disparate thoughts and organizes them in a centralized location. And it's an easy way to tap into the energy of the Page of Pentacles—you're taking an overarching theme or goal (such as "things to get done this weekend" or "pros and cons of moving to a bigger apartment") and then zeroing in on the individual details that make up that larger idea.

If you have a major project or goal currently underway, you can use this prompt to sit down and list out all the steps or smaller milestones that you need to accomplish to finish the project. You can even use this as an opportunity to consider the practical details of a more day-to-day event or task, such as listing all the items you'll need to pack for an upcoming day trip, or creating a reading list of books you'd like to finish by the end of the year.

Alternatively, create a list out of a more abstract concept. I love creating lists of reasons why I love and appreciate people in my life (and as a bonus, these lists make great just-because gifts). Make a list of everything you love about your chosen profession, and revisit it anytime you have an especially bad day at work and need a reminder. Put together a list of your favorite quotations on a particular subject, such as love or spirituality or determination.

As a final option, you could choose to *begin* a list with the intention of adding to it as you go. For example, I have a list in my phone where I save especially touching or kind things that my loved ones have said to me. It's not the kind of list that I could sit down and put together all in one session. Rather, it's an ongoing list that I build as I have new things to add. You might start a list of gift ideas for upcoming holidays or birthdays, and then anytime a loved one mentions something they'd like or an area of interest, you can add it to the list. That way you don't have to come up with tons of new ideas when the gift-giving occasion gets close. Or you might begin a list of your favorite restaurants and coffee shops when you've moved to a new city, which you can add to as you try new places.

Organize Something in Your House

Effort level: Medium to high ●●●●○

The Pentacles are the suit that governs home and hearth, after all, and the Page of Pentacles thrives on organization and structure. What better way to channel that energy than to organize something in your own living space? As with all of these activity prompts, the size and scope of the task you take on is entirely up to you. It could be as small as choosing one shelf in your pantry to empty out, clean, and reorganize. Or it might be as large as tackling an entire room and rearranging the furniture and all the pictures on the walls.

You might notice a similarity between this activity and one that was suggested for the Empress (clean your space). That's not an accident. I often think of the suit of Pentacles as the day-to-day synthesis of the Empress and the Emperor: warm and nourishing, yet orderly and structured. The Empress would want your home to be a welcoming and relaxing space, while the Emperor would want it to be functional and organized. So as you consider what part of your house you'd like to work in for this activity, try to keep both of these ideals in mind. What can you change, reorganize, or adjust in your home to improve both its functionality and its comfort level?

Knight of Pentacles

The knights of the tarot are movers and doers, but what motivates them and how they move differs from suit to suit. The Knight of Pentacles might seem slower than their fellow knights, but take a closer look: this Knight is the tortoise racing the hare, proceeding with methodical but tireless steps until they reach the finish line. If J.R.R. Tolkien had created a tarot deck based on his classic fantasy epic, I can't imagine anyone but Samwise Gamgee as the Knight of Pentacles. Even though Sam is partial to the comforts of home and hearth, he steadfastly journeys alongside his beloved Frodo through three books of peril and heartbreak. Never once does he seem interested in the glory or the heroics of the quest, and never once does he even consider turning back: "I made a promise, Mr. Frodo. A promise. *Don't you leave him, Samwise Gamgee.* And I don't mean to."

Where the Page of Pentacles can get too stuck in planning to act, the Knight of Pentacles acts and acts and *acts*. They're the ones doing the regular little maintenance and upkeep tasks that no one else would think of (until something fell apart on them). Think of Sam reminding Frodo to drink and eat, even when he's so overwhelmed by the influence of the ring that he can't taste his food anymore. We often take these dedicated knights for granted, but without them the world would cease to function. Sometimes, though, we must be willing to cut our losses and leave a project behind, and that's where this Knight can struggle. They hate leaving things unfinished or giving up on anything, even when it's the best option.

Affirmations

I AM a hard worker.
I CAN accomplish anything I set my mind to.
I WILL progress at my own pace.

 *Reflections*

Who in my life reminds me of the Knight of Pentacles?
What aspects of the Knight of Pentacles do I see in myself?
What aspects of the Knight of Pentacles would I like to cultivate in myself?

 *Actions*

Gather Resources

Effort level: Low to medium ●●○○○

A theme we've returned to throughout the suit of Pentacles is that resources are more than just dollars. Resources might mean how much time you have to spend on each of your responsibilities and how much you have left over afterwards. Your resources might include how much physical energy you have on any given day, or how much food you've got in your fridge, or how much time you and your partners can spend together. The trickiest part of this activity is identifying what resources you need the most right now. Here's a few examples to get you thinking.

Reading is a huge component of my mental and emotional health, but when I'm in the middle of a pain flareup or an anxious day, I often have to talk myself into picking up a book. (Even though I inevitably feel a bit better after reading.) It's a lot easier to convince myself to read if I don't have to go through the process of deciding what book to open. So for me, books are an important resource—having a few books chosen and ready to go helps me manage better during poor physical or mental health days. I might take this activity as a reminder to buy a book from my wish list or to check out an e-Book or two from the library.

What if the resource you want to gather is more intangible? For instance, maybe you're someone who needs lots of alone time. Consider how you might incorporate a little more solitude into your day. Could you get up a bit earlier before the other residents of your house are awake? Could you ask your partner to spend fifteen minutes with the kids in the evenings while you meditate or read or just sit in silence? You don't have to look for huge swaths of time in crowded days—instead, search for small, actionable ways that you could get a regular dose of alone time.

Set Your Own Pace

Effort level: Medium to high ⬤⬤⬤⬤◯

We all do it. We look at our friends, our college acquaintances, our rivals, just about *anybody*, and we say to ourselves, "Look at how much they've done with themselves, and look at *me*." It's easy to do, after all—when it comes to others, we only see the celebratory posts on Facebook and the work promotions, not any of the struggles or setbacks that lie beneath the surface. Meanwhile, we're intimately aware of every wart and blemish of our own journeys. How could we *not* feel inadequate when we read that Claire from junior high has started their own business while we're still struggling to make ends meet in a thankless, passionless day job?

But the Knight of Pentacles reminds us that we set the pace for ourselves, not by looking at our fellow wanderers. As tempting as it is to look around and wonder why everyone seems so far ahead of us, we'll get a lot farther by staying focused on *our* path. Revisit the story of the tortoise and the hare—the tortoise wasn't concerned with the hare's speed relative to his own. He wasn't concerned about winning the race. He just kept up his slow and steady pace, knowing that if he stuck with it, he'd reach the finish line in his own time.

Perhaps this isn't an *activity* in the same way as many of the activities in this book. There's no particular task to complete or exercise to do. It's more of a mindset that you can work to actively incorporate into your daily life. If you recognize any patterns or habits that prime you to compare yourself to someone (those monthly phone calls with a friend who boasts about their accomplishments and never asks about yours, for example), see if you can let them go or at least reduce their frequency. Otherwise, simply work to catch yourself when you start beating yourself up for not achieving as much as someone else. And perhaps consider a mantra or an affirmation when you do catch yourself in the act. "I WILL progress at my own pace" from above is a good all-purpose one, but if it doesn't resonate, come up with your own!

Queen of Pentacles

The Queen of Pentacles is equal parts glamorous and practical, with an eye for both style and comfort. Princess Tiana of Disney's *The Princess and the Frog* is a perfect example of this balance. She's a tirelessly hard worker, and she knows just what to do to accomplish her goals. Just look at one of her first songs in the film, "Almost There," where she proclaims, "This old town can slow you down, people taking the easy way. But I know exactly where I'm going—I'm getting closer and closer every day!" But over the course of the movie, she also learns how important it is to embrace the company of people you love. All the Queens of the tarot are community builders in one way or another. Tiana builds her community by starting her own restaurant in memory of her father. The food she cooks is her expression of love and family, and while she opens her heart to Prince Naveen, she doesn't stop being the independent, fierce businesswoman she always was.

The Queen of Pentacles is someone who knows precisely where their corner of the world is. They inhabit that corner with an easy elegance that belies how much work they've done to get there. They know when to provide support to their loved ones, but they aren't likely to do the work for you. They're in their element when they're able to roll up their sleeves, work hard, and see the fruits of their labor. If they find themself in a time of scarcity, though, they may draw inward and grow cynical as they struggle to keep their little corner of the world thriving.

 Affirmations

I AM a provider.
I CAN nourish my community.
I WILL be of service to myself and those who need it.

 *Reflections*

Who in my life reminds me of the Queen of Pentacles?
What aspects of the Queen of Pentacles do I see in myself?
What aspects of the Queen of Pentacles would I like to cultivate in myself?

 *Actions*

Community Reading

Effort level: Low to medium ⬤⬤○○○

If you feel confident enough in your regular tarot readings for yourself, the Queen of Pentacles may be inviting you to expand the scope of your reading to include members of your family or community. This can be as simple as pulling a card or two, the same way you would pull a card for yourself, but interpreting it for your family as a whole. If you'd like to go more in depth, you can pull a card for each individual person. (As always, interpret "family" in whatever way feels the most right for you.) This will give you more detailed information about where each person may be at the moment emotionally, spiritually, etc.

Now, unless one or more of your loved ones are also tarot practitioners (or at least open to hearing about it), I don't recommend that you grab your sibling and unload about how you pulled the Nine of Swords for them and how worried you are. Rather, use this reading as a way to check in on your own relationship with your family members. If you draw a card that reads more negative than positive, for instance, consider spending some extra time with the person in question, or doing something special for them just because. Use the insights you gain from this reading to suggest ways to connect with your loved ones.

Family Night

Effort level: Medium to high ●●●●○

In the Ten of Pentacles, one suggested activity was hosting. A family night has a lot in common with hosting, but it feels more informal and personal. Hosting implies planning and preparation. A family night can be as simple as gathering on the couch to watch a favorite movie. The key element isn't the activity itself, but the people you choose to share it with. For me, for example, the perfect family night would include not just my spouse, but my mom and brother and my best friends. Gathering all of us under one roof might involve a good deal of planning, since my spouse and I currently live many states away from everyone else. If you already live in the same space as your nearest and dearest, it makes the family night that much easier.

Whether you're gathering members of several households together or just coordinating a few live-in family members' schedules, I encourage you to keep the activities themselves simple and flexible. When you're in the company of your closest loved ones, things tend to flow naturally and easily. Watching a movie may turn into an hour-long debate about the characters' motivations, which may turn into a spontaneous trip to the ice cream shop down the street. You don't have to leave things completely open-ended, but even if you make very specific plans, be open to new directions that may arise in the moment. At least in my experience, these moments of shared spontaneity can be some of the most memorable.

King of Pentacles

The Wonderful Wizard of Oz is a character we all grew up with, whether you watched the classic film or read the amazing book, or both. And although the Wizard turns out not to have the kind of magic that Dorothy and her companions are initially looking for, he is still a powerful and insightful man. Call him a fraud for using illusions to shore up his power, but at the end of the day, the Wizard understands how to use material things to reinforce abstract ideas like power. He doesn't ask the heroes to bring him back the Wicked Witch's head, after all—he asks for her broom, the symbol of her magic. And he understands right away that the Scarecrow, the Tin Man, and the Cowardly Lion are already brilliant, compassionate, and courageous; they just need something tangible to hold onto, to prove to themselves that they have the virtues they've sought from the beginning. That is Pentacles power at its best: not materialistic or greedy, but well-versed in the energy and meaning we bestow upon the objects in our lives.

Out of the four kings of the tarot, the King of Pentacles is the most classic example of a traditional king. They have the experience and the hard-won wisdom to oversee vast kingdoms, projects, or families with a just hand. It's second nature for them to look at the big picture and understand how one decision impacts everything in their domain. But they can zoom in and direct their focus at the individual pieces of a puzzle just as naturally. (I didn't want to use too many Disney characters as references, but if you want another example of a classic King of Pentacles, look at Mufasa from *The Lion King*.) In a more negative aspect, however, this King can become *too* concerned with the interconnectedness of their world, and this may find them hung up on the letter of the law rather than the spirit. They may enforce a rule that no longer makes sense or refuse to allow an exception even under special circumstances.

 Affirmations

I AM a leader.
I CAN keep an eye to the bigger picture.
I WILL manage my charges with discipline and care.

 Reflections

Who in my life reminds me of the King of Pentacles?
What aspects of the King of Pentacles do I see in myself?
What aspects of the King of Pentacles would I like to cultivate in myself?

 Actions

Tidy Up Your Devices

Effort level: Low to medium ●●○○○

Is your desktop a mess of old documents, folders that no longer make sense, and games you haven't played in years? Is your inbox filling up with old emails you haven't had time to sort through? Do you have to scroll through seven pages of apps on your phone to find the one you're looking for? Take a few minutes today, pick one of your devices, and do some tidying up. It may not seem like a King of Pentacles sort of activity, but remember that the Pentacles are the suit of home and material resources, and our technology houses a great deal of our lives, our work, and our connections. Your phone and your computer are your home bases, and if they're disorganized and cluttered, the King of Pentacles would argue that you are, too.

If you're already a pretty organized person, this may not be a massive undertaking. But if you tend to put this sort of thing off and looking at your overloaded inbox or desktop gives you agita, break it down into something that's manageable for today. You might set a timer for thirty minutes and only work on organization/tidying up for that length of time. Or you might choose something specific, like one folder of old documents to sort through, or one page of apps to reorganize on your phone, and tackle that much and no more. The King of Pentacles would tell you that there's no sense in all-or-nothing thinking; even clearing up a small patch of space on your desktop is progress.

Ancestors/Descendants Letter

Effort level: Medium to high ⬤⬤⬤⬤◯

Even though the Cups are the suit of relationships, the Pentacles deal with many of the nuts and bolts of managing a family. And the court of Pentacles in particular care about lineage—not the lineage of nobility and exclusivity, but the lineage of knowing who you come from and who will come after. When the King of Pentacles appears in your reading, it may be a good time to write a letter to one or more of these past and future members of your family.

If you don't know much about specific people in your family tree or aren't comfortable with writing to any of them, you can choose to address your letter to a general bloodline ("Dear Smiths of the past," or "To my ancestors from Germany"). But you can also narrow in as much as you'd like—if there's a great-great-grandparent who you've heard stories about, by all means write to them. And you can absolutely interpret "ancestors" in ways other than blood relations. If you're adopted, for example, you might want to write to your adopted family rather than your family of origin. Or you might prefer to write to ancestors by virtue, such as historic figures who share an identity or calling with you.

The same goes for descendants. If you have children or grandchildren, you could address the descendant part of your letter to them specifically. Or you could paint with a broad brush and address your letter "Dear future members of our family." If you never want children of your own but you have a sibling or a chosen family member who has or wants to have children, you could write to those future children, too.

The meat of this exercise is writing *both* letters (which is why, incidentally, this is the medium-to-high level activity, effort-wise). What will you say to the people who came before you, and how will it differ from what you write to those who will come after? If there are particular questions you'd like to ask your ancestors, are they questions that you can answer for your descendants? If there's wisdom you're sharing with your descendants, what curiosity does it inspire about your ancestors?

CONCLUSION

Tarot has been a rock for me. I started my tarot practice shortly after losing my incredible dad to cancer. As I mentioned in the introduction, I thought tarot might help me meditate and reflect on myself with a bit more clarity. When I say that it changed the course of my life, it's no exaggeration. I truly feel that practicing tarot has made me a more mindful, more compassionate, and more forgiving person. And yes, a more spiritual person, too—but that element of it could fall away altogether. I'd still draw a card for myself every morning and keep it in mind as I approached the new day.

Do I expect—or even want—every person who picks up a deck to have this same experience? No, not necessarily. But I *do* believe that tarot has the potential to bring anyone into a closer relationship with themselves. It turns self-reflection into a practice of storytelling and interpretation, and that's a language that I find missing in a great deal of current mindfulness/meditation literature. I would love to see tarot more wholeheartedly embraced in mainstream culture the way that mindfulness has been embraced. I hope that even beyond the affirmations, reflection questions, and activities I suggested, you're able to develop your own relationship with the characters and themes in your deck. I hope that you come up with new activities and affirmations of your own as you befriend your cards. And if you take nothing else away from this book, I hope you've learned that tarot can be more than a fortune-teller's McGuffin in your favorite Halloween movie. Tarot can be a dynamic, practical tool. The more you invest in your practice, the more you engage with your card intentionally, the more you'll get out of it. May you return to it again and again with the curiosity of the Fool, the wisdom of the World, and everything in between.

FURTHER READING

Tarot Books and Guides

Cynova, Melissa. *Kitchen Table Tarot*. Llewellyn Publications, 2017.

McCloud, Cedar, published under the name Heimpel, Noel Arthur. *The Numinous Tarot Guidebook*. Self published, 2018.

Moore, Barbara and Fell, Aly. *The Steampunk Tarot*. Llewellyn Publications, 2012.

Moore, Barbara and Smith, Eugene. *Wonderland in Tarot*. Llewellyn Publications, 2018.

Wands

Gilbert, Elizabeth. *Big Magic: Creative Living Beyond Fear*. Riverhead Books, 2015.

Gill, Nikita. *Fierce Fairytales, Poems and Stories to Stir Your Soul*. Hachette Books, 2018.

Cups

Brach, Tara. *Radical Acceptance: Embracing your Life with the Heart of a Buddha,* Reprint edition. Bantam, 2004.

Sieghart, William. *The Poetry Remedy: Prescriptions for the Heart, Mind, and Soul.* Viking, 2019.

Ter Kuile, Casper. *The Power of Ritual.* Harper One, 2020.

Swords

Brown, Brené. *Rising Strong,* Reprint edition. Random House, 2017.

___. *Rising Strong as a Spiritual Practice.* Sounds True, 2017. Audiobook.

Owens, Rod. *Love and Rage.* North Atlantic Books, 2020.

Parker, Priya. *The Art of Gathering: How we Meet and Why it Matters,* Reprint edition. Riverhead Books, 2020.

Pentacles

Miller, Rachel Wilkerson. *The Art of Showing Up.* The Experiment Publishing, 2020.

Taylor, Sonya Renee. *The Body is Not an Apology: the Power of Radical Self-Love.* Berrett-Koehler Publishers, 2018.

WORKS CITED

Alcott, Louisa May. *Little Women,* Illustrated edition. New York: Amulet Books, 2019.

Austen, Jane. *Pride and Prejudice*. Overland Park, KS: Digireads.com Publishing, 2018.

Bancroft, Tony, and Barry Cook, dirs. *Mulan*. Walt Disney Productions, 1998.

Baum, L. Frank. *The Wonderful Wizard of Oz (Illustrated First Edition): 100th Anniversary OZ Collection*. Orinda, CA: SeaWolf Press, 2019.

Brown, Brené. *Rising Strong as a Spiritual Practice*. Louisville, CO: Sounds True, 2017. Audiobook.

Chapman, Gary. *The 5 Love Languages: The Secret to Love that Lasts,* Reprint edition. Woodmere, NY: Northfield Publishing, 2015.

Clements, Ron, and John Musker, dirs. *The Princess and the Frog*. Walt Disney Productions, 2009. Cynova, Melissa. *Kitchen Table Tarot*. Woodbury, MN: Llewellyn Publications, 2017.

De Saint-Exupéry, Antoine. *The Little Prince,* 75th anniversary edition. Boston: Houghton Mifflin Harcourt Publishing Company, 2018.

Dickstein, Mindi and Jason Howland. "Astonishing." *Little Women - The Musical.* Sh-K-Boom Records, 2005, track 12, *Spotify.*

DiMartino, Michael Dante and Bryan Konietzko, creators. Avatar: the Last Airbender. Nickelodeon Animation Studios, 2005.

Fleming, Victor, dir. *The Wizard of Oz.* Metro-Goldwyn-Mayer, 1939

Gesner, Clark. "Opening/You're a Good Man, Charlie Brown." *You're a Good Man, Charlie Brown (New Broadway Cast Recording),* BMG Entertainment, 1999, track 1, *Spotify.*

Greno, Nathan, and Bryan Howard, dirs. *Tangled.* Walt Disney Productions, 2010.

Henry, O. *The Gift of the Magi,* Illustrated ed. Illustrator P.j. Lynch. Somerville, MA: Candlewick, 2008.

Jackson, Peter, dir. *The Hobbit: An Unexpected Journey.* Directed by Peter Jackson. Metro-Goldwyn-Mayer Pictures, 2012.

___. *The Lord of the Rings: The Fellowship of the Ring.* Metro-Goldwyn-Mayer Pictures, 2001.

___. *The Lord of the Rings: The Two Towers.* Metro-Goldwyn-Mayer Pictures, 2002.

McCloud, Cedar, published under the name Noal Arthur Heimpel. *The Numinous Tarot Guidebook.* Self published, 2018.

Milne, A.A. *The Complete Tales of Winnie the Pooh.* New York: Dutton Children's Books, 2016.

Miranda, Lin-Manuel. *Hamilton (Original Broadway Cast Recording).* Hamilton Uptown, LLC under exclusive license to Atlantic Recording Corporation, 2015. *Spotify.*

Moore, Barbara, and Aly Fell. *The Steampunk Tarot.* Llewellyn Publications, 2012.

Moore, Barbara, and Eugene Smith. *Wonderland in Tarot.* Woodbury, MN: Llewellyn Publications, 2018.

Osbourne, Mark, dir. *The Little Prince.* Orange Studio, LPPTV, et al., 2015.

Schulz, Charles. *The Complete Peanuts 1959-1962 Box Set*, Illustrated edition. Seattle: Fantagraphics, 2006.

Stevenson, Robert, dir. *Mary Poppins*. Walt Disney Productions, 1964.

Stuart, Mel, dir. *Willy Wonka & the Chocolate Factory*. Wolper Pictures, 1971.

Sugar, Rebecca, creator. Steven Universe. Cartoon Network Studios, 2013.

Ter Kuile, Casper. *The Power of Ritual*. New York: Harper One, 2020.

Tolkien, J.R.R. *The Fellowship Of The Ring*, Topeka, KS: Turtleback School & Library Binding Edition. Ballantine, 1986.

Travers, P.L., *Mary Poppins*. HMH Books for Young Readers, 2006.

To Write to the Author

If you wish to contact the author or would like more information about this book, please write to the author in care of Llewellyn Worldwide Ltd. and we will forward your request. Both the author and publisher appreciate hearing from you and learning of your enjoyment of this book and how it has helped you. Llewellyn Worldwide Ltd. cannot guarantee that every letter written to the author can be answered, but all will be forwarded. Please write to:

Ru-Lee Story
℅ Llewellyn Worldwide
2143 Wooddale Drive
Woodbury, MN 55125-2989
Please enclose a self-addressed stamped envelope for reply,
or $1.00 to cover costs. If outside the U.S.A., enclose
an international postal reply coupon.

Many of Llewellyn's authors have websites with additional information and resources. For more information, please visit our website at http://www.llewellyn.com.